GROUP MEMORY

A Guide to
College and Student
Survival in the 1980s

ALSTON CHASE

An Atlantic Monthly Press Book

Little, Brown and Company   Boston / Toronto

FIRST EDITION

A portion of this book has appeared in *The Atlantic.*

LIBRARY OF CONGRESS CATALOGING IN PUBLICATION DATA
Chase, Alston.
   Group memory.
   "An Atlantic Monthly Press book."
   Bibliography: p.
   Includes index.
    1. Universities and colleges — United States.
 I. Title.
LA227.3.C465   378.73   80–15866
  ISBN 0–316–13817–7

ATLANTIC-LITTLE, BROWN BOOKS

ARE PUBLISHED BY

LITTLE, BROWN AND COMPANY

IN ASSOCIATION WITH

THE ATLANTIC MONTHLY PRESS

BP

Designed by Susan Windheim
*Published simultaneously in Canada
by Little, Brown & Company (Canada) Limited*

PRINTED IN THE UNITED STATES OF AMERICA

To the Memory of My Father

PREFACE

America spends as much on education as do all the other nations in the world combined.[1] There are over three thousand colleges and universities in this country.[2] Given these facts, it is natural to think that our educational system would be characterized by diversity. With so much money spent on such a large number of institutions, the variety of these institutions, and hence the options open to the high school senior choosing a college, must be considerable. Right?

Wrong. Unfortunately, despite the money and numbers, the differences between America's colleges and universities are not as outstanding as their similarities. That this is so is demonstrated by the existence of many studies, such as those conducted by the Carnegie Council on Policy Studies in Higher Education during the last decade, many of which make sweeping, critical, and largely accurate generalizations about the academy. It is also demonstrated by this book, which is devoted to explaining how this sameness came about, why it persists, and what students and colleges can do about it.

Few educators today, of course, believe there can be *any* true generalizations about the system of higher education. Most of them are scholars who treat any generalization with the same suspicion doctors have for home remedies. They are trained to note differences, not similarities, between things. They live close to campus and fail, often, to distinguish the forest from the trees, the college from the individuals who comprise it at a given moment in time. Finally, so much hype about each college's "uniqueness" is poured into the pages of college catalogues nowadays that many are taken in by their own propaganda.

But perspective makes all the difference. If someone were to come from Mars, say, he could scarcely tell the difference between Harvard and the University of Minnesota. If he were to come from a place nearly as exotic as, say, Montana, he might, although being able to make the cruder distinctions, still note affinities between institutions that passed unobserved by the local inhabitants. If, further, this visitor had been brought up in this educational system, had taught in it, and played every role in it, if he had read its history, but then had left it for this exotic place and, after years, returned, immersing himself in it again, this bland topography might take on another dimension. Not only would the similarities seem greater to him than to others, but he would, unlike the Martian, understand them as well. If, further, this visitor were also a parent whose children were studying at these institutions, he might also feel a certain passion, a sense of urgency, about what these schools were teaching and what they were not.

This book is written from these perspectives. I was a product of this system. As an "army brat" I attended fourteen primary and secondary schools, mostly in this country but in others as well. My ninth grade, for instance, was spent at Clover Park Junior High in Tacoma, Washington, and with the Calvert School Correspondence Course in

Copenhagen. Tenth grade was spent at Ordrup Gymnasium in Copenhagen. Eleventh with the American Dependents' School in Heidelberg. Senior year at Carmel (California) High School. I received B.A. degrees from Harvard and Oxford and graduate degrees from Princeton. I studied language at the University of Vienna and the University of Grenoble and taught philosophy at Princeton, Ohio State, and Macalester. I served on every conceivable academic committee; spent eight years as an advisor to undergraduates at Macalester and six screening applicants for the Harvard College Office of Admissions.

Three years ago I left all that, giving up my tenure with a sense of sadness for the state of education in America. My wife, Diana, and I left for Montana to concentrate our energies on an environmental program we had founded four years previously for teenagers. It was at that time of our life, sharing with these young people their hopes and aspirations, and seeing our children go off to college, that our concern for higher education took on a new dimension.

I have tried to write this book so that it combines these perspectives, these dimensions: the insights of an educator, the concerns of a parent, and the feelings of the student. I have done so by uniting, quite literally, two points of view. For this book, besides being expository and advisory, also contains a short roman à clef as prologue. This is the story of Noah Robinson, his wife, Kate, and their three sons.

Although all characters Noah meets are fictional, all his interviews, save two, are verbatim interviews I conducted while visiting colleges and universities during the writing of this book. The two exceptions are Noah's visit with the Princeton University Admissions Office and his talk with Professor Icarus. I did not visit the Princeton Admissions Office, but I did correspond with them, and this sequence is taken from that correspondence. The interview with Professor Icarus was made up out of whole cloth, a montage of

conversations I had throughout my trips. In fact, I was totally unsuccessful in my attempts to interview a Harvard
philosopher. Here Noah's and my experience coincided. We
were both stood up by a former colleague; but I, unlike
him, was unable to reschedule my appointment. Inciden-
tally, I found professors everywhere harder to make appointments with than anyone else. College presidents are
easiest to see. The lower on the ladder, it seems, the more
elusive.

Although all the characters and institutions (Farnsworth,
Micawber, and Bison) that populate the opening scenes of
each chapter of Part I are fictional, the events that they
depict are, unfortunately, very real. Almost all of them, in
fact, are based on firsthand experience.

Noah, Kate, Sam, James, and Seth Robinson are not real.
They differ in many important ways from me, my wife and
my three sons. The differences between me and Noah are
significant. He is less willing to judge others than I. He is
more forgiving and has greater self-doubt. He is more generous. In fact, he is a better person. As he is more nostalgic
than I, his memory is worse. He has already forgotten, as I
have not, those dark days in the sixties, when we were
pariahs for keeping the faith, when we were denounced at
faculty meetings for thinking about the past and worrying
about the future. Many of those who did the drumming
then are riding at the forefront of "reform" now. I am inclined to suspect them of hypocrisy, whereas he takes them
at their word: that they simply changed their minds. If in
changing step they happened to keep in tempo with the
times, then so much the luckier for them.

Lying behind these differences between Noah and myself
is a more fundamental one: that he is a Platonist and I an
Aristotelian. He believes that no one ever knowingly does
evil; that to know the good is to do it. I believe there is such
a thing as weakness of the will; that some people, some-

times, knowingly do evil. This is a point about which we have had many heated arguments, seated in my study around a wood heater, drinking Top Ramen soup, sipping sherry, and watching the snow deepen outside on the mountains. Despite our differences, however, I respect his point of view and therefore include it in this book.

There is, finally, one point on which Noah and I agree (although he is not always consistent about it): that whether this country is better or worse off than it was, whether education is better or worse now than it was, does not depend on whether we or anyone else *thinks* it has improved or declined. It either has or hasn't.

One final point. I visited dozens of colleges all over the country before writing this book, and I was in contact by phone and letter with many more. You might be surprised, therefore, at the frequency with which "elitist" institutions — such as Harvard and Yale — are used as examples. This is both intentional and inevitable. It is intentional for the same reason that what is a scandal in high society is simply sordid elsewhere: when Harvard does something wrong, it shocks; when a less visible institution does the same thing, people shrug it off; and if conditions are disgraceful at Yale, they are disgraceful everywhere.

The frequent mention of the richer institutions is inevitable because only they have the money and the willingness to know the worst, which is necessary to keep records of those trends — such as faculty-student contact, effectiveness of distribution requirements, the giving of examinations, the changing conditions of student life — which often show the college in an unfavorable light. So it was often that only they had the data for which I was looking; and it is to their credit that they not only had it, but parted with it too.

I must confess there is another reason why I have cited more examples from these more selective institutions. I have no desire, in writing this book, of embarrassing anyone or hurting any institution. Many colleges are struggling for their survival now, and I would not like it on my conscience that my criticism, even though true, was another nail in their coffin. On the other hand, the elite institutions are doing better now than they ever were. They're tough, or so it seems, and there is little effect (probably for better or for worse) that my criticism could have on them.

Although I alone am responsible for the shortcomings of this book, whatever parts of value it contains could not have been written without the help of many people, all of whom share my concern for the future of higher education. This book, in fact, could never have been written, certainly not, as it was, on a Montana mountaintop, without the informed help of those, working with or within the academy, who sent me material, arranged visits, or kept me informed about developments in their particular arena. In this connection, I would like to thank, for being my eyes and ears, Paul J. Aslanian, Vice-President for Financial Affairs at Macalester College; Donald H. Burnett; Ernest Bartell, Director for the Fund for the Improvement of Post-Secondary Education; Robert L. Bunting, Professor of Economics at Macalester College; Steven M. Cahn, Program Officer of the Exxon Education Foundation; David Cameron, Professor of Biology at Montana State University; David P. Campbell, Vice-President of the Center for Creative Leadership in Greensboro, North Carolina; J. Martin Carovano, President of Hamilton College; Joel Colton, Director for Humanities, the Rockefeller Foundation; Jill Ker Conway, President of Smith College; William D. Dana, Jr.; John Fox, Dean of Harvard College; John Gambs, Professor of Economics, *emeritus,* Hamilton College; Patricia A. Graham, Director of the National Institute of Education; Richard A. Falk, Professor of International Law at Princeton University; Eldon Harvey, Jr., Associate Director, Office of Development, Connecticut College; Timothy Hubbard,

Professor of Journalism, Syracuse University; Alberta Huber, President of St. Catherine's College; Carl Kaysen, Director of the Sloan Commission on Government and Higher Education; Phyllis Keller, Associate Dean of the Faculty of Arts and Sciences, Harvard University; Elizabeth Kennan, President of Mount Holyoke College; Henry Koffler, Vice-President for Academic Affairs, the University of Minnesota; Winton Manning, Senior Vice-President of the Educational Testing Service; Henry C. Moses, Dean of Freshmen, Harvard College; Walter Rosenblith, Provost, Massachusetts Institute of Technology; Hans Rosenhaupt, President, the Woodrow Wilson National Fellowship Foundation; Karl C. Sandberg, Professor of French Literature, Macalester College; Adele S. Simmons, President of Hampshire College; Horace D. Taft, former Dean of Yale College; Richard D. Weigle, former President of St. John's Colleges of Annapolis and Santa Fe; and Stephen Williams, Professor of Anthropology, Harvard University. In addition, I would like to thank the many dozens of people whom I interviewed or who supplied me with information and whom space does not permit me to mention here.

I am particularly grateful for the repeated help I received from David Riesman, who put me in touch with so many others who in turn were so helpful. He was my central source, the one to whom I turned when stumped in my efforts to turn up some critical bit of information.

My editor, Robert Manning, and his colleagues at the *Atlantic* deserve special thanks. They nurtured me from afar, encouraging my best efforts with tolerant and thoughtful criticism.

How can I thank my family? Perhaps, instead, I should apologize for all the trouble I have caused them. They lived with the writing of this book, for better or worse. My sons, David, Lawrance, and Sidney, and their many friends supplied much valuable material and offered continual encouragement to me. In addition, David recently graduated from college and, now a young editor, read the manuscript and improved it in numerous ways.

My wife, Diana, naturally, falls into a special category. It was she who gave me the courage to take the risks necessary to write this book and it was she who urged me to write it. It was she who insulated me from the many details — some petty, some not — of our lives during the past year so that I could concentrate on the task at hand. She has been, always, my insightful alter ego, who listened to me with infinite patience while I thought out loud; and she commented with incision at every stage of the gestation of the manuscript.

Millegan, Montana
September 1, 1979

CONTENTS

II. The Survival of the Student

The behavior of introduced bighorn sheep populations resembles those of goats and ibex. . . . Introduced sheep remained limited in distribution and colonized no new habitat in addition to that about the release area. . . . It appears that sheep transmit home range knowledge from generation to generation. . . .

It is evident that any factor causing juveniles to lose contact with adults would lead to wandering and dispersal of juveniles, and would decrease their chances of survival. Thus a violent separation of ewe and lamb in which the lamb is chased off could well lead to aimless wandering of the disturbed lamb and to its untimely death. . . . It appears that social inheritance of home ranges is adaptive to the individual sheep, but dispersal is not.

— Valerius Geist

The social structure of a wolf pack is all-important. . . . What evidence we have of the wolf's ability to teach its young to hunt . . . suggests that social structure plays a strong role. . . . Wolf pups raised without a pack structure adapt very poorly to life in the wild.

— Barry Holstun Lopez

The Buffalo herds have gone; they have succumbed to the rifles of the hunters. The Antelope droves are nearly gone; Hound and lead were too much for them. The Blacktail bands have dwindled before axe and fence. The ancient dwellers of the Badlands have faded like snow under the new conditions, but the Coyotes are no more in fear of extinction. Their morning and evening song still sounds from the level buttes, as it did long years ago when every plain was a teeming land of game.

— Ernest Thompson Seton

However characteristic pack-units may have been of *Canis latrans* [the coyote] under aboriginal conditions, the animal became increasingly solitary after man broke into 'Nature's social union.'

— J. FRANK DOBIE

Sound humanism does not begin with oneself, but puts the world before life, life before man, and respect for others above self-interest.

— CLAUDE LÉVI-STRAUSS

GROUP MEMORY

PROLOGUE: GROUP MEMORY
A Story

Survival studies have shown that those who adapt successfully in a stress situation share some common attributes which set them apart from those who don't. A survivor possesses determination, a positive degree of stubbornness, well-defined values, self-direction, and a belief in the goodness of mankind. He is also cooperative. He does not feel that man's basic nature is to promote only self-interest.

— LARRY DEAN OLSEN

Although it was noon, the sun was cool and distant on the horizon. The snow lay hard and high at the edge of the ridge where Noah paused to catch his breath. Except for his little cabin one thousand feet below, pluming white mist from the nostrils of its chimney, there was no sign of life. A rim of mountains formed a vast and empty amphitheater, its bleachers dark with pine and its open playing field shimmering silver in the sun.

He was looking for Buster and Charlie, hoping to find them on the high ground where the wind kept the grass clear. But they were not there. So Noah felt his nose with the back of his mitt, to see if there was still feeling in it, and then trudged off, on his bearpaws, toward the lip of the river canyon. He might find them there, but he hoped he wouldn't.

He came to the canyon abruptly, an orange-and-rust limestone face whose receding chin disappeared below him. Far below lay the river, frozen and white. The snow, always in shadows, was deep; for he could see none of the boulders that, in summer, decorated the shore like pearls on a necklace. With glasses he saw tracks, or rather, two convoluting trenches in the snow. At the center were Butch and Charlie, floundering through soft powder.

"Poor bastards," thought Noah. "They'll die." He turned for home.

He was sitting on the porch unlacing his Sherpa bindings when Kate came to the door, a broad frown on her face. She was in her uniform, Marine fatigues and a turtleneck, and carrying a little dog, whom she tossed gently onto a snowbank.

"Honestly," she said, "Finian has potty dyslexia. He thinks the house is for pooping and the snow must be kept clean at all costs. Trying to housebreak a dog in Montana in January is like teaching a fish to walk."

"Some do. Catfish in Florida."

"All right, smarty. But I've been worried about you. The radio says another storm is on the way. More than a skiff this time. Did you find the two rams?"

"Yup. They were at the river."

"Oh, no. The last males. So pretty too. I guess that's the end of the herd." She opened the door for Finian, who flew into the house, then added, "Poor fellows, they've got to learn sometime."

"Too late for Buster and Charlie."

"No, I mean the dogs."

"Well, Fish and Game has got to learn too. This is more evidence that it's easier to wipe out a population of sheep than it is to reintroduce one. It was worth a try, but they had no chance in a winter like this when they didn't know where to go. No group memory of the territory.[1] Once the memory is gone, it is gone for good."

"Well, at least it can go into your book, can't it? I mean group memory. That should be proof that animals can't survive unless knowledge how to has been passed down."

Noah winced. He wished she hadn't mentioned the book. "I guess," he said. "But can we learn from sheep? Have to think about it."

The book wasn't going well. It was supposed to be about survival, but the truth was that, although they ran a summer survival school together, he didn't know what survival was. He knew what it wasn't. It wasn't learning special skills his school taught, such as building a snow cave or eating arrowroot. He remembered a friend, a doctor, who had taken the Outward Bound winter survival course in Minnesota and a year later had run out of gas on the Baja. He knew how to avoid hypothermia and keep his clothes in his sleeping bag at night to keep them from freezing, but he did not know how to distill the radiator coolant of his car to get drinking water. He would have died if prospectors in a helicopter hadn't spotted him.

Noah also knew survival wasn't learning how to live solo, as Outward Bound teaches. Rather it had something to do with making a group work. The spectacular cases of annihilation, such as the fate of the Donner Party during the winter of 1846–1847, always began with a social breakdown. Even out here, where Kate and he lived, they depended on others. It was just that the community covered a wider area. The nearest neighbor was ten miles away, but there had been times when they needed each other.

No, he thought, the things that Kate and I, NOLS and Outward Bound teach are fun, but they are not survival. It is romantic to believe we are still Robinson Crusoes struggling in a protean wilderness. Yet wilderness is gone and only a few energetic, middle-class people need to know how to set up a Gerry tent in the wind. For most, knowing how to drink the juice from cactus may be fun, but it is no more useful than knowing how to find flat spots on ball bearings.

So the chemistry of survival remained, to Noah, elusive. He only knew it was some knowledge imparted and some traits of character instilled. But like the process chemists call emergent, the results cannot be predicted. What this knowledge is and traits are he could not say, even though, as teacher and parent, he had sometimes, inadvertently it seems, served as catalyst for such a process.

Yet had he not survived? No, it was too early to say. All he had done was trade the security of tenure as a college philosopher for a six-figure debt and this place, a cabin in cattle country without phone or electricity. He had gone into the mountains, not so much to escape reality as to gain a better view of it. It was a gut step, some of his friends thought a death wish. Yet somehow, after passing the midpoint in life, inviting risk had restored him. It was a way to grow again, but it was terrifying too. For if he didn't write the book, he wouldn't survive; and he couldn't write it until he knew what survival was.

It was getting dark. Noah began to pump the gas lamps while Kate sliced some cheese.

"That storm," she said, "will close the road for another week or so. For sure. I wish we could phone the boys. I hate being so out of touch with them. Especially after Christmas."

"It bothers me too, Kate. But maybe we're just suffering from the empty nest syndrome. Goodness knows we've added enough pets since they left. Anyway, growing up and leaving home is a rite of passage."

"But three at once? They're too close in age. And with all that business going on at college. You know, the things we discussed at Christmas."

Discussed was Kate's euphemism for *argued,* although, to

tell the truth, the more serious differences never surfaced during their visit. Instead they smoldered, like a peat bog fire, barely heating the surface; a sense of justified grievance on the part of the children and a sense of moral queasiness, of necessary advice ungiven, on theirs. The tension grew, incubated in the heat and closeness of the isolated mountain cabin, as each of them searched, like strangers on a train, for neutral topics of conversation.

It was hard. James, the oldest boy, at Harvard, had announced that the next term he was moving off campus to live with his girl, Nancy. Sam, a junior at Princeton, was practically living with his girl friend at Bison. Once the straightest of arrows, he now sported an earring and talked about the virtues of pot. Seth, the youngest, a sophomore at Farnsworth, about to go to Paris on spring term abroad, already had a haunted look and talked darkly about conspiracies hatched by one generation on another.

"Honestly," Kate was saying as she began beating eggs furiously with a fork, "you work so hard to protect your children from the bad influences of this society and then, to give them a good education, you throw them to the wolves. Now I don't know if we've been too protective or not protective enough."

"Well, there are things I wish I had said," Noah replied. There always were; but he usually remained silent, fearing too much nagging would drive the boys away for good. What could he do? Stop paying their term bills if they didn't behave? What would that accomplish? Perhaps their education at this point was more important to him and Kate than it was to them. Besides, when could he be sure he was right and when was he hypocritical or acting out of a sense of nostalgia, wanting them to live the life he had enjoyed?

He remembered his affair with Lucy his junior year. They hadn't been angels and only fear of pregnancy, not the dormitory rules, made them cautious. The "parietal rules" taught them to dress quickly and ensured that he got to know Bob, his roommate, whom he completely ignored when Lucy was in the rooms. Poor Bob, how he hated Lucy! Noah and she would be lying in bed, naked, in the room he shared with Bob, when they would hear the outer door slam. They would plunge into their clothes just in time as Bob would come into the room, eyes narrowed, with nose in the air, sniffing like a bird dog. It was the odor of Lucy's perfume that offended him, for that would linger after she left.

Kate splashed eggs into the frying pan. "I'm trying something new tonight," she said; "limburger omelet. Got to use up the old cheese before the mice get it. You know, I wish you had given them more advice."

"The mice?"

"No, the boys."

"Wouldn't have done any good. They won't listen. They are all looking for John now, and I can't compete with a dead man."

"Let's not start that again. They never knew John. You are the only father they ever had."

Everyone has a point where the quick is exposed. This was Noah's. He was their adoptive father. Their biological father had been killed when the children were infants. Noah had married Kate soon after. Now the children had discovered John. It was in him, not Noah, that they now saw themselves. Since he had no children of his own, the boys represented his complete investment, his nest egg, his link with immortality. Unable to give them genes, he tried to give them love and knowledge. But now he was feeling the fragility of love and entertaining doubts about his wisdom.

It was Finian's potty dyslexia that broke into his thoughts.

"He's a bad boy," Noah said.

"James?"

"No, Finian. He just pissed on the rug."

"Oh, no! Why didn't you stop him? Quick, throw him out. I'll get the sponge. Damn, he's leaving his scent everywhere."

She rushed to the spot with a sponge, rubbing frantically. "Let's get down to basics," she said.

"You are."

"Not about this, about the boys. All the stories we've heard from Cousin Beth and Linda's friend Anne sound just awful."

"We've got to be philosophical about it, Kate. It's sink or swim. The survival of the fittest. Let's hope we've taught them how to survive and they have the character to do it." He felt strange, for this was a reversal of roles. It was usually he who fretted and she who tried to be fatalistic.

Thunderfoot, the Abyssinian, jumped into Kate's lap as she sat on the couch. Immediately Burr, the Siamese, landed on top of him. They began growling like Waring blenders running at different speeds. Fur began to fly.

"I've got it," she said, pushing the entangled cats to the floor. "Your book is about survival, right? And we're concerned about the survival of our children, right? Why not write a book about *their* survival?"

"Interesting, but what would I write about? If I knew how to help the boys, maybe I'd know how to write a better book about survival, and vice versa. But right now I don't know how to do either."

"But you don't see what I'm getting at. What are colleges anyway but survival factories? At least they should be. They teach skills that help people cope economically; they help the economy and research. They encourage the development of character and values that are the stuff of life; they store knowledge and pass it from one generation to the next, and, like your friend Socrates, they midwife the birth of new ideas. What is that if not the business of survival? Survival of the next generation, of the culture, the country and, at least indirectly, the *species*. If anyone should know about survival, they should."

Finally Noah caught on. "I see," he mused. "We know what group memory of the mountain sheep is. It is the information necessary for survival which is passed on from one generation to another. But we don't know what *our* group memory is. If anyone should know, the colleges and universities should. If I were to visit them, interviewing everyone connected with them — students, faculty, trustees, administration, foundation and government people — perhaps I'd learn what our group memory is, could understand our boys better, and could get on with my book."

"And then perhaps you'd have some helpful advice to give the boys. Besides, you could visit them."

"Just a minute. You're going with me. I'm not leaving you in the wilderness alone."

"No, too expensive. Besides, it would be good for you to see the children alone — less overpowering, if you know what I mean. I've got to get going on my book about horses, so I'll stay with the cats and dogs in town and do some work on it."

So it was decided. Right after the next blizzard, Noah Robinson and his wife herded Mumtazi, the wildcat, Burr, the Siamese, Thunderfoot, the Abyssinian, Finian and Ifrit, the terriers, and Basil and Una, the mastiffs, onto their sled behind the snow machine and began the journey off the mountain to town. Noah had begun his search for an idea.

It was that kind of day. Snow had closed Washington's National Airport. Metroliners to New York were canceled because, it seemed, ice breaks the connection which makes their electric motors run. Regular trains, powered by diesel, were still going, but were over four hours late. So Noah took the bus to Princeton. The bus, however, broke a windshield wiper and now was sitting on the interstate, somewhere in Maryland. Noah and his fellow travelers were waiting, in the bus, to be rescued, either by a mechanic with a new blade or by another bus. They were not sure which.

Noah slumped in his seat and tried to think of something else. His mind was whirling with the events of the past two days. Having started his trip at what he had hoped would be the source — the font of knowledge — he had discovered instead a sink.

The federal government spends ten billion on higher education each year and, as they pay the piper, they must call the tune. If anyone knows what is essential to education, what should be taught in the eighties, it must be Uncle Sam. But Noah had been disappointed.

He began with a visit to Dr. Dan Gloss, Director of the Foundation for Appropriate Education. This federal organization, which described itself in its brochure as "risk-taking and innovative," had just begun a program of inviting proposals directed to establishing a "new consensus for liberal learning" by the design of curricula that "served the needs of all the constituencies of higher education." Dr. Gloss was, at this moment, trying to put together a White House Conference on the liberal arts.

Noah found his office in a building across the street from the Air and Space Museum. A convoy of tractors was passing as he arrived. It was colorful to watch, yet sad to see the farmers trying so hard to be noticed. "Tilting at windmills," thought Noah. The buildings they passed looked so permanent, and the farmers, well, so old-fashioned, with their hand-painted signs about food and family.

Dr. Gloss was a warm, intelligent man with a large smile and nervous hands. He bedazzled Noah with his command of the new lexicon of bureaucratic buzzwords. He explained that he had recently attended a conference sponsored by the Stoneyboy Foundation and had found it unhelpful. It was, he felt, an unrepresentative group and its suggestion of returning to the old curriculum, well, inappropriate. "There are a great variety of clients of today's postsecondary education which were not represented at the Stoneyboy Conference," he said. He was, in fact, organizing a series of meetings that would have representatives from these "traditionally bypassed constituencies." He did not like the term *liberal education*, finding it too elitist, preferring the more neutral *liberal learning* instead. The White House Conference, he hoped, might effectively define a core of desirable liberal-learning outcomes. To this end his agency was funding projects on such topics as appropriate technology, problem solving, women's services, adult development, neighborhood studies, and health care.

Although finding it difficult to question Dr. Gloss's good motives, Noah wondered if these many constituencies — some of which are interest groups created out of whole cloth by government grants and depending on these grants for existence — might not be less concerned than Gloss in reaching a consensus. Besides, he was employing a quaint methodology, trying to find the essence of learning by a process of elimination. If the government funded every conceivable project, then, over time, it would find what worked and what didn't. A truly empirical approach, somewhat like trying to construct a core out of peelings. Or worse, like peeling an onion. When all the skins were removed, nothing would be left.

In any case, Noah needed an answer more quickly than Dr. Gloss could provide one, so he hurried to the office of Dr. Froide Sang, a true VIP in the HEW empire. She was friendly but businesslike, seating him on a couch with his back to a clock. She sat opposite him so she could keep her eye on him and the time simultaneously. He asked if the federal government was increasing its control of higher education.

"If they're going to take government money, then they're going to have to accept public control of its use," she said.

"The trouble with the academy," she went on, staring at the clock above Noah's shoulder, "is that they want federal money but no responsibility for it. Yet they are lousy lobbyists. The education bill is coming before Congress shortly and all the profit-making research organizations are down my neck, but I haven't heard from one — not one — college or university. The truth is," she continued as she looked at her watch redundantly, "higher education does not lobby well because they cannot agree on what forms of aid they want. The only kind of federal aid they can all agree they want is financial aid to students. That's why such aid constitutes about 80 percent of federal aid to education."

By the time he signed out of the building with the security guard, Noah was reeling. The government, it was clear from Dr. Sang, was determined to bring the academy to heel. But then, judging from Dr. Gloss's remarks, it wasn't clear the government was sure what orders to give. It was clear that the academy knew it needed federal money, but it was not clear they knew what they needed the money for. Perhaps Dr. Cassandra would be able to explain all this.

Dr. Cassandra, a brilliant scholar and administrator with an impressive track record in both academe and government, was perhaps the leading authority on the relations between the two. When Noah visited him, he was at his desk working on the very subject, surrounded by untidy stacks of bound material from the U.S. Government Printing Office. He looked very much like Perfesser Fishhawk in the comic strip "Shoe."

"The trouble with relations between the academy and the government," he said as he swiveled around on his chair and put a slim leg on the desk, "is that no one in Washington is worrying about colleges and universities as institutions. Instead, there are a large number of agencies which have their own programs, mandates and policies, each good in itself, but together they often conflict and pose special problems for academic institutions. Academic communities, you know, are like medieval guilds, used to running themselves. Thus, what we have is a mess. The various student aid programs, for instance, which are the major form of U.S. aid, are a shambles, a no-man's-land between the Social Security Administration, the Veterans' Administration, and HEW. And Congress, for political reasons, has just killed another opportunity to straighten it out."

"Aha," thought Noah, "Dr. Cassandra is clarifying things for me. The situation is no longer as confusing when one recognizes that it is simply a mess."

"Then the government is increasing its control while at the same time doing it incoherently?" Noah asked.

"Exactly."

"Can colleges escape control? What about Brigham Young University, which has refused aid so it could stay independent?"

"A few colleges which are in good financial shape and have a homogeneous student body can do it. But for the majority it is just a pipe dream."

"Then are you optimistic that the quality of government control can be improved? Can academe and the feds work out a modus vivendi?"

He leaned forward conspiratorily. "I'm working on that now," he said in a half-whisper. "That's what I'm paid to do. Therefore, officially, I must be optimistic. But between you and me, privately, I am pessimistic."

"Are the differences between private and public colleges disappearing?"

"What differences?" he rejoined. Then he began to puff on his unlit pipe, adding, "Permanence. That's what private

institutions have or should. They should outlive govern-
ments."

"When," thought Noah, "will they get this bus back on
the road?" The windows were covered by steam and someone
had turned on a radio. Next to him, a girl-woman somewhere between twelve and thirty was wiping the window
to see her reflection. She was chewing gum. Her chin,
hinged like a puppet's, worked with the regularity of a
metronome.

It was getting dark, and Noah was impatient. He had
scheduled a full day in Princeton tomorrow. Some alum had
charged that students there didn't work as hard as they once
did. The University had responded in the *Alumni Weekly*
by reporting the responses of two administrators, one student, and five faculty members. They all said the same
thing. Students didn't work less, they said. They just
learned different things from what they once did.

If so many distinguished people say so, thought Noah, it
must be true. He was anxious to find what these things
were. Then, too, he was looking forward to his visit with the
Pedagogical Sorting Service. Since they were the college entrance examiners for the country, they must know what is
important to know.

He was seeing Sam tomorrow too. That would be fun. He
would take him to a fancy restaurant. A brief sally into
gracious living for the eleventh-hour gentleman scholar. He
wondered if he would find his favorite dish: sautéed mushrooms on toast. And what would they talk about? Why was
it so hard to talk with Sam? Most people are like bats, finding themselves by radar; Sam was an automated starship,
guided by a gyroscope. His insights came from apperception, not from perception. But then, thought Noah, I am
that way too. We are both monads.

That's it, thought Noah. We're monads. Gottfried von

Leibniz, the seventeenth-century German philosopher, thought all things — and we — were made of them.

Monads responded, not to each other, but in accordance with the programming of their own internal computers. It was God, the master programmer, who synchronized these computers to establish order in the universe. This was what Leibniz called the Principle of Preestablished Harmony, which produced "the best of all possible worlds." He was proud of this discovery. More proud than he was of the calculus. It proved that we needed God.

Dr. Gloss, thought Noah, sees us as monads and himself as the master synchronizer. He wondered if all government did. Does it see us, not as a community of citizens, drawn together in a cooperative association by common needs and interests, but as monads, each with unique needs and properties, who require a superagency to harmonize us? If so, it would provide an interesting rationale for government. We would not need each other, only the bureaucrat. And if people like Dr. Gloss perceive us this way, it would explain why they emphasize the differences between people and not the similarities, and why their programs, like Dr. Gloss's, discourage the discovery of affinities. As long as people need their own special programs, they need him.

The classical political theorists, like John Locke, believed that political association was based on an implied contract between members of a society. They saw they had a common need for security, a central arbiter for disputes and an enforcer of contracts. So they made a deal, giving up authority to make and enforce law in return for these benefits. It was a symmetrical relation. Obligation to authority was created in return for certain benefits. But now, it seemed to Noah at least, the state no longer talked about obligation or common interests. Now the relationship between government and people was an asymmetrical one. The government was simply a benevolent agency supplying individual needs.

In this new relationship the government's authority does not appear to rest on implied contract. In fact, like Atlas holding the world, it does not appear to rest on anything at all, for no support is needed. As long as government and the people are both getting richer, needs can be satisfied at no one's expense and government need not invoke authority to ask anything of anyone. But what happens, Noah wondered, if we become poorer? Then, to give to one the state must take from another. This would seem to require invoking authority. For otherwise how would it persuade anyone to give something up voluntarily? But where would this authority rest, now that the state bases its legitimacy not on the citizen's obligation but on satisfaction of the citizens' needs? Perhaps then this new relationship, although providing a convenient rationale for bureaucratic growth, will in fact undermine political authority. This may already be happening, Noah thought. We are reaching our limits to growth and now, all of a sudden, there are taxpayer revolts, court tests of affirmative action, the emergence of a "new right," and a call for a constitutional convention.

And how does all this affect education? wondered Noah. The eighteenth-century Scottish philosopher, David Hume, had noted that laws are necessary only for the regulation of transactions involving scarce goods. We do not, yet, have laws rationing fresh air. Where water is plentiful, there are few laws regarding it; but where, as in Montana, water is scarce, it becomes the subject of a vast network of laws. The 1960s were a period of plenty, and a period of plenty on campus. So it was not surprising that college "laws"—distribution requirements and parietal rules — were considered unnecessary. There was enough money for everyone to have everything. But now, with the educational world poorer, there might be more incentive to reintroduce rules. For rules governing the curriculum and student life are like any other law governing the distribution of a good. They limit choice and thus consumption. When a college cannot afford to teach everything or let students live any way they want, they must reintroduce rules that in a sensible way close off options. But how are they going to do this if the concepts of law, authority, and obligation are no longer understood?

The bus door opened with a hiss, and the lights went on. A uniformed man stepped inside.

"Our apologies for the delay," he said. "You will be transferring here to the bus behind you."

Noah picked his briefcase off the rack and stepped out into the snow.

Noah had just taken a bit of his sautéed mushrooms on toast when Sam served an ace.

"Father, I've decided not to return to college next fall."

Noah stared across the tablecloth at Sam, his tongue wrapped around a mushroom, as Sam warily dipped his fork into his crab Louis. "Masticate," thought Noah. "Thoroughly. Stall." For Noah was in a state of shock. He didn't know what to say. He didn't want Sam to quit, but he wasn't sure why, nor did he know how to stop him. His mind raced through various responses. He could try dismay: "Think what you're throwing away." But did Sam care? And what *was* he throwing away? He could try emotional blackmail: "Mama will be heartbroken." But that would be a dirty trick. He could try indifference: "Whatever you want. It's your choice." But that would make him a liar, for Sam's future did matter to him and Kate, and Sam knew it.

So he said, sipping wine and trying to look calm, "Oh, really? Why?"

"Because I'm not getting out of it what I should."

The ball was back in Noah's court. Was Sam asking him what he should get out of college? Especially after today, he didn't know.

Today had, in fact, been another wild-goose chase. He had arrived by taxi at the Pedgogical Sorting Service a little before noon for a luncheon date with Dr. Quantum, one of its division chiefs. PSS lies just off an interstate highway on spacious, carefully landscaped grounds. Its low buildings look like any corporate center and could be mistaken for the national headquarters of Interstate Pipe and Gas Transmission Corporation not far away. "Look at them geese," said the driver, pointing to the pond. "This place is famous for its geese. They stay here all winter."

Noah found the entrance door locked. There was a little sign which said, "Ring the bell," which he did. There was a buzzing sound, and the door opened. Inside, he gave his name to a girl at the desk and she, after checking with someone on the phone, gave him a little plastic card to put on his lapel. Swarming through the halls were dozens of people with vacant smiles on their faces and all wearing plastic cards.

"Who are they?" Noah asked the girl.

"Test score graders. They read the English essays."

"Why is there such high security here?" The place reminded him of the National Security Agency, the super-secret decoding outfit at which he had worked when in the army years before. "Are they afraid," he added, "that some kids will break in and steal exams?"

"I don't know. In fact, I've always wondered. But there's more security here every day."

"How long have you worked here?"

"Nine years."

Wondering why she had been afraid to ask, he followed her as she took him to Dr. Quantum's office.

Dr. Quantum was, Noah discovered, a psychologist by training. So were several other staff members he met. They all wore three-piece tweed suits despite the over-warm central heating. They had a way of looking Noah straight, long, and *meaningfully* in the eye. Noah wondered what it meant.

Dr. Quantum took him to another building for lunch. Dr. Bushy, Quantum's assistant, followed behind at a respectful distance. Noah noticed that Bushy only spoke when spoken to, which was each time after Noah asked Dr. Quantum a question. "Why don't you answer that one, Bushy?" Quantum would say. And Bushy would. Noah wondered if all this was part of PSS protocol.

Over avocado salad, Noah broached his question. Not wanting to expose his idea of group memory, which he was afraid these men would think hopelessly romantic and (worse) unquantifiable, he tried to couch his question in a jargon he thought they would understand.

"What do the Scholastic Aptitude Tests try to measure?" he asked.

"You tell him, Bushy," said Quantum.

"They are meant to predict one thing," Bushy drawled with the care of a scholar; "namely, how well the examinee will perform in college."

Strikeout. Realizing that PSS didn't know what group memory is, Noah went, right after lunch, to the Princeton Admissions Office. "Our deliberations are intended to accomplish two things," he was told; "first, to select a diverse student body, and second, to choose only those students who will do well in college."

Wondering whether these goals were possibly contradictory, Noah asked them whether doing well in college led to doing well later in life. They couldn't tell him. "Answering that," they confessed, "would require making a value judgment. We cannot make a value judgment."

"What do *you* think you should get out of college?" Noah asked Sam, lobbing the ball across the table.

"I don't know," said Sam, "but whatever it is, I am not getting it. It's like est: everyone says you're supposed to get 'it' — an education — but no one will say what 'it' is. What do you think 'it' is? What did they tell you on campus today?"

Oops, overhead smash. Sam wasn't fooling around. He realized that a good offense is the best defense.

"I didn't find it either," Noah admitted, putting a backhand into the net. Love-fifteen.

Actually it had been worse than that. He came to Princeton to ask about Donald H. Burnett's article. Burnett, a graduate of Princeton's class of 1952, had personally conducted a study comparing the workload of students in the class of 1952 with the class of 1977. He discovered that, despite the fact that twenty-five years had added many hundreds of members to the Princeton faculty, they spent less time with students and assigned less written work.

"When you go to Princeton," an ex-Princeton administrator had told Noah, "don't be surprised if they have the wagons drawn in a circle. When they sense criticism coming from an outsider, they clam up."

Perhaps that was the wrong metaphor. Noah felt more like a visitor to Mao's China. Some were afraid to talk; others were spouting the party line. One professor Noah phoned replied that he had "nothing important to say on general education." He referred Noah to his department chairman. "Those things are his business," he said. Elsewhere he found everyone telling him the same thing, as though some Intourist guide had been running ahead, handing out prepared scripts. "Burnett is wrong," they said. "Students today are given more freedom because they come to college better prepared. They are more sophisticated at analysis and ready to specialize earlier."

Why, wondered Noah, if students entering college today are better prepared than their predecessors, did Dr. Quantum lament the serious decline in SAT scores? And what, he asked, are they specializing *for*? What is Princeton trying to teach? "Students," he was told, "are different from what they were. They are serious and know what they want. They have definite goals: the professions, scholarship. Princeton's job is to help them reach these goals."

"If you don't want to go to college," Noah asked Sam, "what do you want to do?" He was now serving, trying an American Twist. Perhaps, he thought, Sam has something special in mind. Working in a Yukon oil field, perhaps, or sailing around the world in a dinghy. Something like that might be a good way to spend a year. Help him grow.

"I'm moving in with Sally at New Haven as she starts Yale Law. She's house-sitting for a faculty member next year."

A volley right at Noah. Not knowing whether to take it with a forehand or a backhand, he let it hit him right in the gut. *Apparently not all students know what they want. Perhaps they are just made to feel they should know.*

The Olde disease, thought Noah. Bob, his college roommate, had it, and now he wondered if Sam did too. A mutated strain, perhaps.

Bob was a proper Bostonian, but tried to live it down. He wanted to rebel, but didn't know how. He went to Groton and hated it, but stayed. In college his father insisted he wear Brooks Brothers suits. Bob did, but expressed his defiance by refusing to button the middle of the three buttons. He buttoned the bottom one instead. A subtle gesture, this infuriated his father. He also rebelled by majoring in fine arts and by launching himself on a career of painting rather than by tracking to law school. But he could not bring himself to paint very *big* pictures. All his work was miniature, no larger than four square inches, which he painted with squinting eyes and a tiny brush.

Penny Olde was a member of the All American Gang. That's what Noah and Bob called it. They were preppies who loved being preppy. They were wholesome and beautiful and athletic, if not very bright. They were the ones who played softball on the Radcliffe Quad: girls and boys in crewnecks, chinos, and dirty tennis shoes. They seemed to have no care in the world.

That's what drove Bob crazy. Penny seemed so happy. She showed no self-doubts, no reflections, no vulnerabilities. To Bob, who was one mass of self-doubts and who exposed them to everyone, she seemed to have no insides. But he couldn't believe she wasn't pretending. This was her fascination for him. This was the "Olde disease," as Bob's friends called it. There must, Bob thought, somewhere deep inside Penny, be a beautiful sensitive soul that had been smothered by preppiness and that it was Bob's mission in life to uncover. Bob could never believe the truth: that she would marry another preppy after graduation, who would, after law school, work for Sullivan and Cromwell; that they would live in Far Hills, ski in Vail, and summer in Maine. And their children would go to Groton.

Perhaps, thought Noah, Sam has the Olde disease. He is full of self-doubts and wants to revolt, but doesn't know how. And the superachiever Sally, who knows just what she wants, holds, in her way, the same attraction for Sam that Penny did for Bob. People don't change, thought Noah; only institutions do.

The butter had congealed on the asparagus, and the waitress took it away, only the butt ends eaten. An incorrigible puritan, Noah had saved the pleasurable things, the tips, until last, and then somehow missed them. Sam asked the waitress to show them cigars, "A treat on me," he said.

Through the smoke and brandy, Noah gave his parental speech despite himself, knowing that the game was over and that he was merely banging the ball against the wall. "I don't object to your and Sally's living together," he lied. "And I don't object to your leaving college with a clear purpose in mind," he added somewhat truthfully. "But to leave and go to New Haven, of all places, when you don't have a job, is asking for trouble. Sally will be preoccupied with her studies and too busy for you. You will vegetate and your self-esteem will decline."

"What's wrong with being a househusband?"

Noah coughed. One of them didn't understand what life was about, but he wasn't sure which.

The next day, before leaving Princeton, Noah paid a visit to his old tennis partner, Professor Vicarious. Professor Vicarious was an expert on revolutions and had just returned from one. He was always going to, or coming from, some country in the throes of upheaval. Noah found him at the door of his cellar office. He was trying to force it open. The door wasn't locked, but the room was so full of books that, when one of the piles toppled as Vicarious had slammed the door behind him, the door, which opened inward, had become barricaded. Now it would not budge.

Standing outside the blocked office, Noah explained what he was after, how PSS and the Admissions Office had said their job was to predict college success, but that the college had said its job was to ensure success in graduate school. Each stage in the process was simply a preparation for the next one. "Doesn't Princeton have an educational philosophy?" he asked.

"There's definitely an establishment at Princeton," Vicarious answered as he kicked at the door. "And they have a party line. The faculty that don't agree with it, as I don't, tend to go underground, to stick to their work. The line is that Princeton didn't go bananas in the sixties, didn't change its curriculum, as many colleges did, so now it doesn't need to change back, to reform, as every other college is apparently pretending to do. For Princeton that means it can stop thinking about educational philosophy and get on with its business."

"What's its business?"

"Harvard's business is training people to be bureaucrats, apparently. But here it is training the cohort."

"What's a cohort?"

"Their own replacements."

"I guess, then, I won't find what I'm looking for here."

"I'm afraid not. Why not try Harvard? They're fussing with this now. Or better yet, why not an experimental college like Hampshire? They're obsessed with these questions."

"They're both on my itinerary," said Noah, whose mind was turning back to Sam and Sally. Bison was near Hampshire. Perhaps be would look Sally up. Noah liked Sally. She always remembered his birthday.

It was cold, gray, and windy when Kate arrived at the Great Falls airport. The temperature was twenty below and swirls of snow swept by the hangar while she waited for Biggy Viande. She had misgivings about the whole idea, but felt she didn't have any choice. She had to get back to the ranch to put out more hay for the horses and she couldn't get within twenty miles of it by road. A forty-mile round trip was too hazardous for one person alone on a snow machine. So when Biggy offered to take her in his helicopter and wait while she fed the horses, she felt she had to accept.

What bothered her was that Biggy was a professional coyote hunter and she loved coyotes. She would be going along on a hunting trip. Biggy and the copilot would fly the craft while a hired gunman shot their prey from the sky with a shotgun loaded with buckshot. They had made over two hundred kills already this winter. At $120 a pelt, Biggy was doing well.

At the Robinson ranch, coyotes were treated as friendly neighbors. A trusting relationship had developed between them over the years, and the coyotes would often come and play with their dogs. In fact, Kate and Noah had raised two, turning them loose when they grew up. She remembered Little Orphan Annie, the last one, who used to sleep under their porch and go for walks with them. Noah taught her to hunt by catching live gophers and giving them to her. She and Una, the mastiff, had been good friends and would play together. Then one day she disappeared. The Robinsons hoped she had gone wild.

Now Kate was praying that Biggy would be skunked on this trip. She did not want to see the chase, the shooting, the packing of the carcass on the pontoons, or the skinning. She was terrified one of the coyotes might be Annie.

Biggy and his crew arrived and began towing the helicopter out of the hangar. Biggy *was* big. He had a hearty laugh, cherubic face, and skinny legs. His belly was too large for his belt, so his trousers hung below his hips. Kate wondered how he could walk. The crotch of his trousers seemed to be around his knees.

There were four seats in the craft, two in front and two in back. Kate took a rear seat next to the gunman. Everything was light and fragile, like a transparent eggshell.

"Put these on, so you can hear," Biggy said to her.

He handed her huge earphones that made her and the others look like Mickey Mouse. Because of the noise, they could talk to each other only over the intercom.

"Got the ammo?" Biggy asked the gunman.

He nodded and held up a box of shells. The gun pressed against Kate, and she tensed. The gunman, noticing, laughed and pointed at the open, empty chamber.

As they took off a cloud of dusty snow enveloped them. Kate closed her eyes. She began to think of Seth. He was in Paris now, and she had received a letter from him that morning. It was an odd, disturbing letter. Something was going on in Paris with Seth that she did not understand. He wrote in a mystical, dreamy way of how he could control others with his mind, of how all life was now clear. The letter was full of nonsequiturs. He concluded by writing, "P.S., I love you. But don't tell Father."

Kate thought of Seth as an infant, all red, mad, and silent, a silent baby, of how, at eighteen months, away on a weekend, she had been exposed to chickenpox and had had to be separated — quarantined — from him for three weeks. A vulnerable age for him to have been abandoned. She had often wondered what damage that had done to him. He never cried; nothing ever came out. Was all that coming out now?

It was time for Kate, once again, to practice her fatalism.

It was her way of coping. Although not religious in the churchy sense, she saw the value in the Christian idea of sacrifice. That is how she differed from Noah; about life, about death, and about the children. She tried to expect less from life than he. Whereas he raged at the world's stupidity and evil and worked for change, she tried to accept imperfection as the natural course of things. One of her favorite sayings was from the Gospel according to Saint John, "In the world ye shall have tribulation: but be of good cheer; I have overcome the world."

Noah expected certain things from the boys, wanted them to do admirable or outstanding things so that he could admire them. She just wanted their happiness. Whereas he wanted them to be his companions and felt hurt and lonely by their desire for independence, she struggled mightily to accept their departure. Another remark she often made was "We enter the world alone and we leave it alone."

If Noah had a human perspective on life, she assumed a geologic one. He worried about the coming Dark Age; she waited for the next Renaissance. "Why suppose knowledge and civilization are like a perennial plant?" she would ask. "Perhaps it is like that flower which blooms only every hundred years. The fact that things are going downhill now doesn't mean that in a hundred years or so they won't be better." Another of her favorite expressions was "We never know enough to be pessimistic."

If Noah fretted about continuity, Kate was consoled by eternity. "It is important, not that things last," she would say, "but that they have existed." Man, she noted, has lived only a few million years at most and will probably live only a few million more, if that. In time even Mozart will be forgotten. But what matters is not that his music achieve immortality, but that he wrote it. Even a day's gift of life is priceless; immortality is unimportant. She liked to say, "Vanity of vanities; all is vanity."

Noah was paid to philosophize, but Kate was the philosopher.

The helicopter was skimming the hills now. They were moving fast, and each time they came over a hill Kate would gasp as the void of the next valley fell below them with a sudden rush. They were somewhere over the river canyon. Biggy was taking the chopper up and down each of the feeder coulees and smaller canyons that drained into the big one. He would bank at an angle so the gunman could get a good view into the sparse timber that dotted the steep terrain.

Kate wondered if they weren't getting too close to the ground. The motor coughed.

"Too damned cold," Kate heard the copilot say over the intercom. "The cocks — " — he looked back at Kate — "motor won't warm up."

"Look," said Biggy; "take a gander at those mothers."

Kate tensed. "They see a coyote," she thought.

But no. Two bull elk were floundering through deep snow. They did not know which way to turn as the helicopter circled them.

"Shit, wouldn't you like to get them between your sights?" asked the copilot.

"Lots in this country," said Biggy, "too many. The bastards are eating all the grass."

They continued weaving up and down the deep, slender, snow-covered valleys. Frost was appearing on the glass canopy of the cockpit.

"Can't you make the heater work?" asked the copilot.

"It's working. Just too damned cold," replied Biggy.

Suddenly the craft went into a steep turn. "There! There's a coyote. Let's get the sonofabitch."

He was there all right, running across the hillside. He had seen them and was running for his life. Twice, as he ran, he looked back. He was heading for a bushy draw at the end of the field and Biggy was racing to cut him off.

"Get ready," Biggy said to the gunman. The gunman was ready. Kate saw him slam the chamber shut.

She was feeling queasy. The atmosphere seemed to Kate thick with blood lust. She was rooting desperately for the coyote, but afraid to say so. She just wanted to get out. They were very close to the ground now, closing fast. She thought about jumping.

Suddenly, there was silence.

"What the hell?" asked Biggy.

"Fucking engine's quit," said the copilot.

They were going down fast. Kate just had time to think, "Oh dear, poor Noah. He'll be lost without me."

Noah was already lost in Emerson Hall at Harvard. It had been rebuilt since he had been an undergraduate majoring in philosophy there. He was trying to find his way out after a disappointing visit with Professor Icarus. Professor Icarus had been a fellow graduate student of Noah's but had stuck to his work rather than fretting about the *meaning* of it all. Thus he was now in the big time.

It had taken Noah three weeks to get his appointment. Icarus did not answer the phone, ever, nor did he return calls. When Noah had arrived three days previously, he discovered that no one above assistant professor bothered to post office hours. A few had little cards on their doors, which read, "By appointment only." The junior professors, those without tenure and more eager to please, did have regular hours, but these averaged about one and a half hours a week. This was Harvard, after all, the land of the inaccessible professor. Noah had made his appointment with Icarus through the Philosophy Department secretary. The original appointment had been for the previous day. But when Noah arrived he found a note on Icarus's office door. There had been, it seems, a bad rain that day (which Noah, who had made his way there with a borrowed umbrella and no overshoes, knew about). Professor Icarus had stayed home to tend a flooded cellar.

When they finally met, the conversation was brilliant, but elusive. Group memory remained undefined.

"I teach philosophy," Icarus had said, "and I'm damned good at it."

"But what of students who don't take philosophy courses? What should they know?"

"Search me. How can you say. Remember Plato's *Meno*?" He pulled a book off the shelf and read,

" 'Can you tell me, Socrates — is virtue anything that can be taught? Or does it come by practice? Or is it neither teaching nor practice that gives it to a man but natural aptitude or something else?'[2] That was the question," Icarus went on, shutting the book, "that Plato tried to answer. Are you asking the same thing?"

"That's part of what I'm asking, I guess."

"Well, you should remember how it ends. Plato concluded that virtue cannot be taught because, if it were teachable, the virtuous men of Athens would have been able to teach it to their sons, and they were unable to do this. Listen." He picked up the book again and read, " 'There is

Pericles, that great and wise man. He brought up two sons, Paralus and Xanthippus, and had them taught riding, music, athletics, and all the other skilled pursuits till they were as good as any in Athens. Did he then not want to make them good men? Yes, he wanted that, no doubt, but I am afraid it is something that cannot be done by teaching.' "[3]

"So you see," Icarus had continued, "Plato had to conclude that virtue cannot be taught, but must be a gift of the Gods. 'Divine dispensation,' he called it. I agree with Plato. Virtue cannot be taught. You are expecting too much of educators."

"But surely," Noah had replied, "there must be more to what you do than teach students what Wittgenstein means by the word *game*. There must be more to what Kate and I have done as parents than to have potty trained the boys. It's this more I'm after. Besides, you omitted that Plato also says in the *Meno,* if I remember correctly, 'When people are so confused about a subject' — he means the subject of virtue, of course — 'can you say that they are in a true sense teachers?' "[4]

Noah found the back stairs and began to descend them. He had not found group memory, but perhaps, he thought, he was closer to an answer. Colleges trained specialists. This did not help the student, for someday their specialty would not be needed and they would no longer be needed either. But perhaps this kind of specialized training helped society? At least colleges thought it did.

He began to think about wolves and coyotes. Colleges train wolves, but parents train coyotes. Wolves are social animals. They live in packs that exhibit a considerable division of labor. Because of this social sophistication, they are formidable, but also vulnerable. For wolves cannot live without the pack, and the pack itself is brittle; if it loses a few key members, the rest will die. By contrast, the coyote is a solitary animal. It does and can live alone. This makes it so adaptable that it can survive where the wolf cannot.

"Our society," thought Noah, "is like a pack of wolves: sophisticated but brittle, where the loss of a few key people can incapacitate it. A little disturbance at one place reverberates through the entire system. A strike of truckers means people go hungry. There is a change of government in Iran, and a few weeks later there are long lines at filling stations in California.

"The colleges are serving this society. They are providing the specialists which a society based upon the division of labor needs to operate. But they may be making society more vulnerable by doing so, and they are definitely making the individual less secure." As a parent, Noah thought, he wanted his children to be trained as coyotes, not wolves. He wanted them to survive, even if society changed.

He found himself facing Lamont Library, the scene, for him, of many all-nighters. It was raining hard. "Better hurry," he thought. He had a date to meet James at Mather House and take him to lunch.

"So this is where you lived," Noah said to James as he arrived at Mather House. James was there to pick up his things before moving into an apartment with Nancy. The apartment was twelve miles away — in Waltham — and James planned to commute. Mather is one of the newer Harvard Houses, built, unlike the earlier ones, like a high-rise, with a barren courtyard in place of a quad. The view from James's window could have been Cleveland.

The suite looked gray and neglected and made Noah want to wash his hands. James had shared this space with five others.

"How did you find five compatible people to room with?" Noah asked James, remembering how hard it had been for him to find two roommates.

"I didn't. The computer did."

Noah still didn't like James's housekeeping with Nancy, but now he sympathized. He thought how different all this was from his earlier life at Harvard, where he had a suite of rooms with a fireplace and view of the Charles River, where he and Bob had punch parties after football games and argued for hours about Keynes, Freud, and modern art. He wondered now what all that had to do with education.

"Let's go for a walk," Noah asked James as they left Mather House. He wanted to talk with James but wasn't sure what about. The trouble was that he wanted to be James's pal and parent both. When James was younger and they went on hikes together, that was easy. But now James seemed to be forcing him to choose. He couldn't be both. Making it even more difficult was that James was so self-assured. He always had been. Even as a young boy his passionless objectivity had made Noah and Kate feel like impulsive children.

"I just got a letter from Seth in Paris," James said, breaking the silence as they walked down a narrow street filled with randomly dressed men and women. "It was an odd letter, spaced out. He says he can think of nothing but John. His letter was full of words like *reality* and *cosmic*. He seemed very fearful, but I don't know of what. I think he is into drugs. One thing funny, though. He said he was looking for the cosmic pussy. Trying to be Henry Miller, I guess. Anyway I wrote him back warning him that the cosmic pussy led to the cosmic womb."

"We are trying not to worry about him," Noah replied, "for what can we do? But, my God, it's hard. He's too young to be in Paris on his own. He's only just turned eighteen. We should never have let him skip seventh grade."

They stopped to look in a bookstore window. A young man or woman — Noah couldn't tell which — in a three-piece tweed suit glared at him through the glass.

"How are you finding school now?" Noah asked, trying not to think about Seth.

"If it weren't for my magazine work, I'd be bored to death. Students here are so *affected*. You're expected to be politically radical and never to admit working. Everyone has a persona a foot thick."

"Dirty necks," said Noah. "That's what we called them. They were around in my day too." He thought about James's persona. James would succeed, no doubt of that. He had the Midas touch and he could handle people. But it had been a long time since Noah felt he knew what was going on in his head.

"How have your interviews gone?" James asked.

"Harvard was interesting, but Western Massachusetts was a disappointment," said Noah, suddenly conscious of the cracks in the pavement. "I learned from a sociologist here that the separation of sexes is not unnatural, as many believe, and I learned from an anthropologist at the Peabody Museum that rapid social change is dangerous to societies."

"Reminds me of a sociological law I learned: 'Most social change occurs during periods of transition.' What about Western Mass.?"

They arrived at the door of a tiny restaurant crowded with plants. It reminded Noah of a terrarium.

"The President of Bison tried to convert me to the existentialist theory of education. That education is whatever one *wills* it to be."

"What about Hampshire?"

"Dr. Vicarious was right. They are obsessed with the meaning of education. *Holism* is the favorite word at Hampshire College, but like any hole, they find that the more they put into it the less there is." Noah smiled apologetically at his own pun.

"What do you mean?"

"The dean of students told me that the fact his office

exists is a sign that they've been unable to meld the students' intellectual and social lives. They tried to establish more overlap by holding classes in the dorms, but both students and faculty objected to it, so they quit."

"Have they tried asking students to bring their bunks to the classrooms yet?"

After lunch James and Noah walked toward the Charles. It was one of those prematurely warm spring days that found people unprepared. Everyone looked pale and overdressed.

"What do you feel Mama and I have taught you?" Noah asked. "Professor Icarus and I were talking about this yesterday."

"To love," James said without hesitation. "What did Grandpa and Grandma teach you?"

"Funny, I never thought of being taught to love. It was something I was given, like food. I always believed the way to repay my parents' love was by giving an equal amount to my children. No, I think I learned something else. Grandpa, you know, was an army officer who was passed over for promotion without knowing the reason why. He had to live half his life with that stigma. His nickname, though, was Happy. He taught me that what kind of person you are does not depend on what happens to you. And Grandma, with all her energy and willpower, taught me that a person can do anything he wants if he is willing to work at it."

"But these philosophies are kind of anachronistic now, aren't they? I mean when the country was young, when they and perhaps you were young, an individual could make a difference. But the world I'm coming into is one where the jelly has set. Our generation cannot make a new world for ourselves; we must fit into an existing one."

"You may be right. But I refuse to believe it. It is mainly a matter of willingness to accept risk, I think. Your generation thinks it has too much to lose to take risks, when in fact it hasn't anything at all to lose. When I gave up tenure and moved to Montana, Mama and I were telling ourselves, 'The worst that can happen is that we will lose everything.' We meant it and accepted it. Grandpa taught me that losing isn't everything, as long as one is happy with oneself, one's mind. Knowing that gives you a great sense of freedom."

"But at the same time you seem to think things are getting worse."

"I can never tell when things are getting worse and when I'm getting nostalgic. It's also difficult to tell when things are getting hard for me and when they're getting hard for everyone."

"I don't understand."

"Everyone in this society believes in upward mobility, but no one believes in downward mobility. But if some go up, others go down. I am the third, and you may be the fourth, generation of a downwardly mobile family. We're WASPs; we're males. We're the negative side of affirmative action. My grandfather and father were someone's poor relatives. As we are now. And my standard of living isn't what my parents' was. So we're worse off in a material sense, but many, perhaps most, people are not. Maybe the country is better off, and only we are worse off."

"But, Father, as I learned in a course on welfare economics, one cannot say whether a country has become better or worse off by keeping score of who wins and who loses. There are too many intangibles, like the 'quality of life,' which is hard to measure economically, and the wellbeing of later generations. That is what worries me. Perhaps we are living off the fat and leaving only bones for our children. We are running out of energy. The whole country is going to experience a decline in its standard of living."

"Do fewer electric hairdryers mean a decline in a standard of living? Wealth is a stimulant, and we are living in a nation jazzed out of its mind. Perhaps poverty will slow us down so that we can take notice of the little, good things of life again. Like this beautiful day. Perhaps poverty might help education. Someone once said, 'Education is an ornament in prosperity and a refuge in adversity.'"

"Only a Stoic like you, Father, could make a depression seem like a cultural revolution."

They found themselves back at Mather House. The building superintendent was waiting for them. "Ah, Mr. Robinson," he said to James, "I've been looking everywhere for you. The Great Falls, Montana, sheriff's office wants you to call them. Your mother has been in a helicopter crash. They think she's dead."

Kate wasn't dead. In fact, she was living quite well. At the moment Noah and James received the dreadful news Kate was breaking bread with Cal Isle. Having no teeth, Cal had no truck with anything which required chewing. But if it had starch in it, he could cook it: griddlecakes with chokecherry syrup, boiled, baked, and fried potatoes, biscuits and butter, turnips. Tonight, they were eating Cal's favorite: sourdough biscuits with huckleberry sauce. Kate thought it tasted darn good, too.

They were in Cal's cabin. Ten feet square and made of logs, it was warm as toast. Kate was sitting on the bunk while Cal stoked the fire. He was a trapper of uncertain age and origin who had spent winters along the river tending his trapline since anyone could remember. Some say he had once been a rustler, even spent time in prison. Others say he had an Indian wife he kept in town and never saw, that he had hoarded a fortune in furs and stored it in caves along the river. But to Kate he seemed too harmless to play such roles. He was a slip of a man who had long since lost whatever aggressiveness he may once have had. Now he had a beard that wouldn't grow and solid white hair, once crew-cut, that grew too much and now stood, as if electrified, three inches straight up from his scalp. Kate and Noah had met him the previous spring when he arrived at their cabin "to find out what time of the year it is."

How did Kate get to the cabin? Like many cases of survival it was luck, combined with a will to live and the right instincts.

Biggy was able to get the motor going again, enough to cushion their fall. The helicopter came to rest on the top of a tall pine.

"Get the sonofabitch out of here," the copilot said.

Kate decided to bail out. She opened the door.

"Where the hell are you going? It's thirty below, and we're forty feet off the ground."

Kate paid no attention. She slid onto a limb. That moment the helicopter began to fall. Biggy gunned it and it took off, blowing snow in Kate's face as she straddled the branch.

The helicopter rose uncertainly and aimed across the canyon. But it didn't climb. Kate watched in horror as it plowed straight into the side of the other wall. There was a terrific explosion.

Adrenalin really flowing now, Kate shinnied along the branch upside down, and down the trunk like an opossum. She landed in deep snow and, she knew, in deep trouble. She had remembered to bring her mittens and was wearing her survival gear, but the snow-covered terrain was nearly impassable, and the cold would kill her within a day if she didn't find shelter and a fire.

She began to shake uncontrollably. "Hypothermia," she thought. "Keep moving. Go down. Always go down. To the river. Follow the river out."

Twenty feet above the valley floor she reached some packed snow, hard and smooth as ice. She slipped and glissaded down, landing in a heap at the bottom.

She was next to a cabin. It had a sod roof covered with an

additional foot of snow. No one seemed around. Nor were there any footprints. The door had no lock. Inside was a woodstove made from a fifty-gallon drum. Kate found some wood and started a fire. Then, like Goldilocks, she lay down to sleep.

A noise outside wakened her. The squeak, squeak of footsteps in the snow. A gun barrel poked through a crack in the door. Then it opened. Standing there at the entrance was a tiny, ancient man in rubber hip boots and what seemed a half-dozen pair of army fatigues.

"Cal, it's me, Kate Robinson," she said.

Cal had a way of prefacing his remarks by inhaling with an "Oooo" sound and exhaling with an "Eeee" sound.

"Ooooeeee," he said. "Mrs. Robinson, thought you were them rascally Benson boys messing around in my cabin again. They're always up to no good and bring that, what you call, marywana with them. It makes the place *stink*." He pursed his lips.

Kate enjoyed Cal's company, but she had now been there a day and already had high cabin fever. She knew Noah and the boys were worrying about her. She was still worried about Seth in Paris.

"Cal, I've got to get out of here. Noah will think I'm dead."

"Ooooeeee, cain't go now. Snowin' and blowin' too hard. Where's Mr. Robinson?"

"He's east, on a trip, looking for material for a book he's writing."

"What about?"

"Survival."

"What's that?"

"What you're doing, I guess."

"Ooooeeee," he grinned. "I ain't survivin'. I'm *livin'*."

"I guess survival is what I just did, then."

"You didn't *do* anythin'. You were lucky."

"But I was smart enough to get off the chopper."

"And dumb enough to git on it. I don't know much about that fancy survival stuff, but I know it ain't fun. *Livin'* is fun. Where's Mr. Robinson gone to find this survival, anyway?"

"To schools."

"Oooooeeee. He won't find nothin' there. You don't learn to live by studyin' livin'. You learn by livin'. He oughta stay with me. I'd show him."

The snow stopped and the sun began to burn a hole in the gray canopy of clouds above the cabin.

"It's clearin'," Cal said. "Tonight I'll build ya a set of snowshoes out of quakers. Then tomorrow we'll head up Mud Gulch and over Castle Hill."

It was one of those treacherous late-winter days. The sky, when clear, was bruise blue. But thick, snow-laden clouds would suddenly envelop the surrounding mountains and rush into the valley, each cloud a storm center, fierce with wind and blindingly white. Just as suddenly they would lift, leaving a new layer of snow sparkling in the sun.

Noah and Sam were on the first snow machine. James followed. The machines were laboring, their sterns sinking deep into the fresh powder and their bows jutting into the air like speedboats, raising a spray that coated their riders like batter.

They were looking for Kate, but without much hope. After learning the news in Boston, James and Noah had rendezvoused with Sam in New York for the flight to Great Falls. They were unable to reach Seth in Paris. He had apparently moved, leaving no forwarding address. The authorities at Farnsworth College did not know how to reach him.

The sheriff gave them little reason to hope. The helicopter had ended up in the river. Its wreckage was found a hundred yards downstream from where, they surmised, it landed. All bodies but Kate's were found. There was no way anyone could have walked out from the site. Probably, they thought, her body had been swept downstream.

The three had stayed, waiting for a storm to pass, for three miserable days in the small apartment Kate had rented while Noah was east. The first day, still numb, no one wanted to talk. The only subject on anyone's mind was taboo. Finally, James broke the silence.

"Father, where, I mean if Mama's dead and she's found, where will we bury her?"

"I don't know, James," Noah replied. "Where do you bury someone who has lived in New York, California, Ohio, and Montana, whose father is buried in Massachusetts and mother in Arizona? Where is home?"

"We are all we've got," Sam said. "Home is where we are."

They fell silent again, but now all thinking and feeling the same things. They were feeling as the Pilgrim families probably did that first winter of 1620–1621: very close, very aware of their vulnerabilities, of the fragility of life; very conscious of their need and love for one another and very far from home.

This time Sam broke the silence. "Father," he said, "you and Mama had been worrying about us, hadn't you?"

"Yes, Sam, we had."

"But why? Aren't we doing well? Is it Sally and Nancy?"

"Nothing so specific. We worry about the world you're entering, about the future. We worry you might be making mistakes with your lives that would cost you happiness later. We worry about what we taught you and we second-guess ourselves a lot."

"But what did you raise us for?" asked James, tensely. "I mean, what do you expect from us?"

"We could never decide, James. Sometimes we only

wanted your happiness. Other times we wanted you to be brave, moral, productive, to amount to something. Those aren't all compatible. It's hard to be a consistent parent."

"But," said James, "we are human beings, not puppets. Parents take too much blame and too much credit for what their children do. Besides, if you raised us conscientiously, why don't you trust us, trust that we don't make drastic mistakes? Please forgive me for saying so, but is it that you don't trust yourself?"

"Where, today," replied Noah, "can we find any source of self-confidence? Once upon a time, parents sacrificed for their children, and society made them feel they were investing in the future. Today they are made to feel like salmon. They swim against the stream, paying mortgages, attending Cub Scout meetings, chauffeuring their children to hockey practice, paying tuition bills; but as soon as their children can swim on their own — even before that time — society expects the parents to die, to disappear. Present mores expect, demand, that children leave home and reject their parents' values. But there is nothing universal about that rite of passage. It is bad, too, because it punishes the good parent. It makes him feel he wasted his time. Too many are saying, 'Why make sacrifices for my children if they are going to reject everything I think is important anyway?' Perhaps you've noticed our country is beginning to turn against or ignore young people. Now that the baby boom is passing, the young are a minority. The age of majority is being raised, retirement delayed, talk of the draft is starting again, juvenile delinquents are being punished as adults, children are being shunted, increasingly, to day care centers, parents are less willing to sacrifice for their children's education, colleges and schools are ignoring student wellbeing. I think all this is partially an expression of resentment many adults feel toward their children. It is frustration, anger, a feeling of impotency. You're right. There is a decline of trust in this country, and it is insidious, because it makes us believe things are even worse than they are. But Mama and I trust you, for God's sake. Our future is in your hands. Most parents trust their children. What they don't trust are the institutions of this society and what they might be doing to all of us. But how is it possible to criticize these institutions and what they are doing to our children without seeming to criticize the children themselves?"

Now, several days later, they were approaching Castle Hill, and it was nearly dark. They were heading for their cabin, still five miles away, to use as a base in their search. But they were behind schedule. They had lost many valuable hours of daylight getting stuck, repeatedly, in the deep snow. It had taken them all day to make the nineteen miles from Hound Creek.

As they reached the top of the hill a blizzard hit them, just as though someone had thrown a switch. The wind blew straight at their backs, sending a suffocating barrage of snow past them. The beams of their lights were reflected back at them. They could see nothing. With the crystals racing past his ears, Noah had the eerie feeling he was moving backward. He stopped.

He knew he had to be careful. Castle Hill had vertical drop-offs on two sides. Once past this hill, they'd be all right. From there on a fence followed the road; they could follow it. But what could guide them over the hill? It was as seamless and white as the top of a refrigerator.

James approached him. "Don't get more than a few feet ahead of us," he shouted over the din of the motors and wind, "I can't see you past that. We could get separated, permanently."

"I can't see a thing," Noah replied. "We've gone too far to turn back, though, and if we did, the snow would be in our faces. Perhaps we should dig in and wait this out."

"What is that?" James asked, pointing past Noah's right

foot. There was a dirty streak in the snow. It was a tire rut, made by Noah's truck in December. The wind had uncovered it. James had found the route finder.

James took the lead, following the black streak, steering the machine so that the rut was just to the right of his right foot.

It was still snowing hard as they approached the cabin. There was a light on. As they drew up to the large drift by the front porch, the door opened. Kate stepped out.

"Is Seth with you?" she asked.

Anna was crying, and, as Noah remembered, Kate was too. At least she was red-faced as she tugged on his sleeve and whispered in his ear, "Darn, I wish the boys were here."

The translator's voice could be heard through the drizzle. "The Western World has lost its courage, both as a whole and separately . . . political and intellectual bureaucrats show depression, passivity, and perplexity in their actions . . . the constant desire to have still more things and still a better life, and the struggle to attain them imprints many Western faces with worry and even depression . . . a society which is based on the letter of the law and never reaches any higher is taking a very small advantage of the high level of human possibilities."[5]

No, the boys weren't there, and Noah was sorry too. James, typically, was too busy to attend his own college graduation. He was working for the 50th Reunion Committee, from whom he had obtained these great seats, front row, center, where they were surrounded by the wives of the class of '23. Sam and Seth were having tea, somewhere on Brattle Street, with their Aunt Betsy. They were smoking too, no doubt (and why did that bother Noah?). He hoped they were holding onto Seth. He was in no state to be on his own. At the awarding of degrees at the Loeb Drama Center he had had to be steered, literally: he would go where pointed, but nowhere else.

It was raining on and off, and the umbrellas in the crowd went up and down like a genuflecting congregation of monks. This was James's graduation from Harvard. They were listening to the commencement speaker, Alexander Solzhenitsyn. He stood in front of them, a large, Lincoln-esque figure, with full beard and a bold chest, reading in Russian. His voice boomed at them and then, under the control of an unseen audio engineer, became a murmur in the mist as the translator's voice emerged from another microphone, to fill the air with different cadences.

They were aware, as they listened, that not many were liking what they heard. Occasionally there were hisses. As it ended, a plump lady dressed in a wilted floral outfit turned to Anna, Noah's sister-in-law, and said, "I didn't like it," then walked off. Much later, they were to learn that the speech, which received much national attention, had pleased no one. The press was furious that they were accused of "hastiness and superficiality." Civil libertarians did not like Solzhenitsyn's reference to "destructive and irresponsible freedom," and to our overreliance on law. Many were offended by his hint that leaving Vietnam was a sign of national weakness.[6] Others noted that Solzhenitsyn was just making an unoriginal plea for old-time religion.

Noah and Kate heard these things in his speech that day, and they did not agree with them entirely, either. Yet, at the same time, he moved them. To Anna, who had emigrated from Poland to this country as a young girl, his words seemed to strike resonances in her past, of her girlhood memories, of what she had hoped America was, of what these hopes had meant to her, and of how different it all had been from her hopes. To Kate, it cut to the bone of her eclectic religiosity, of her mystical, fatalistic temperament. Noah was affected because it was the first time in twenty years he had heard, out loud, what Kate and he had been whispering to each other: talk of character and courage, sacrifice, and the possibilities of the human spirit. But the previous week had prepared all of them for this speech. It had made them receptive. They were listening to what they had wanted to give their children.

For Seth had arrived from Paris. Kate and Noah had met him at Boston's South Station. They hardly recognized him. He was gaunt and looked at them with a fearful, vacant stare. His sandy hair, short and boyish a few months earlier, was now long and stringy. He looked terrified and talked about having psychic powers. What had happened?

They never discovered. All they knew was that he returned to Farnsworth a week before his brother's graduation to take a summer job and was found by his employers to be in no condition to work. Noah got a frantic call from an aunt who lived near Farnsworth that he needed help. She put him on the train to Boston. Noah spent the rest of the week on the phone or at the hospital, arranging conferences with doctors and trying to help Seth put his life back together.

All this was going on as Noah and Kate attended tea parties, met James's tutors, listened to Solzhenitsyn. How strange this graduation seemed to Noah! He remembered his own at Oxford: the dances, the fist-sized strawberries and whipped cream, lying with his date on the grass in the gardens of New College, watching the sun rise on the Cherwell. He remembered his graduation from Harvard: driving madly around in his old Mercedes, of picking up a girl whose father was attending his twenty-fifth reunion, of crashing some parties with her. All that gaiety, spontaneity, romance, where was it? Was he just hopelessly nostalgic; were his children living in a world that was less fun, or did they not know how to have fun? Were Seth's troubles, which seemed so typical, such a pedestrian tragedy, caused because he, and perhaps his generation, did not know how to play?

James seemed old too soon: so serious, so narrowly specialized, so realistic. Seth was lost, still on his trip. And where was Sam headed? What was happening to him at Princeton? Were Noah's and Kate's worries simply signs that they could not accept their children's growing up, that they now had beards and sometimes contradicted their parents? Would Noah and Kate be irresponsible parents if they interfered in their children's lives, or irresponsible if they did not? Was the boys' growth natural, or was it a sign of bad health? What were the colleges doing to them? Was college making them strangers to their parents, or had Noah and Kate never really known them?

Noah still did not know what survival, what group memory was. Survival of the individual seemed to be luck, the way he had survived the blizzard and Kate the crash. There seemed to be nothing — nothing he could patent — that one generation could pass to another to help each individual survive.

But what about group survival? Was the survival of the society, the *species*, something that, like the survival of mountain sheep, could be taught and passed on? Is there a special instinct or insight, a sense of community, an awareness of a common fate, a knack for living with each other and with our surroundings, that we need to know? If so, who could teach it? Apparently not he and Kate, and surely, he discovered, not the universities. For James had not yet learned the good life, Seth could not cope, and Sam seemed cut adrift. What was this elusive idea and why was no one teaching it? Surely it was vital.

The voice of Solzhenitsyn's interpreter sifted through the drizzle. "If the world has not come to an end, it has approached a major turn in history, equal in importance to the turn from the Middle Ages to the Renaissance. It will exact from us a spiritual upsurge: we shall have to rise to a new height of vision, to a new level of life, where our physical nature will not be cursed as in the Middle Ages, but, even more important, our spiritual being will not be trampled upon as in the modern era.

"This ascension will be similar to climbing up to the next anthropologic stage. No one on earth has any other way left but — upward."[7]

The speech was over. Kate, Anna, and Noah got up to leave. They had to find the boys.

1
INTRODUCTION
Surviving the 1980s

And when the thousand years are expired, Satan shall be loosed out of his prison, And shall go out to deceive the nations which are in the four quarters of the earth. . . .

— The Revelation of Saint John the Divine

"Some say the world will end in fire, Some say in ice."

— ROBERT FROST

This book, like Noah's, is about survival, and it tries to answer the questions with which Noah's story ends. What do colleges teach, and what effects do their teachings have on us and our society? Why are our colleges and universities now in such trouble and what can be done about it? What can the student and family do?

The experiences of the Robinson family are not unusual. During his trip Noah discovered, unwittingly, the tip of an iceberg. For, far from knowing what group memory is, or from having a sense of mission, our colleges and universities today literally do not know what they are doing. As a consequence, they have quite unconsciously adopted an educational philosophy by default, one that not only fails to serve students and society, but that also harms the institutions themselves.

This failure raises larger questions. If our system of education pursues the wrong goals or, worse, is without purpose, where are we, as a civilization, headed? Must we, as individuals, simply acquiesce to what we may think is inevitable? What can we do?

We are now entering a new decade, one that many greet with anxiety. This fall the college class of 1984 will matriculate. The novel *1984*, by George Orwell, was written about a country where love was forbidden, history rewritten, and thought suppressed.[1] It was about a society without humanity and a time without hope. The class of 1984, in all probability, will not face easy times ahead. It is emerging into a society still struggling to accept the idea of limit, whose individuals will be absorbed with questions of personal survival. When it graduates, will it have found a college education a source of strength and hope?

Periodically, throughout Western history, societies have become preoccupied with thoughts of impending doom. We are, apparently, entering another such period. New concerns about the threat of thermonuclear war, power plant meltdowns, eco-disasters — the greenhouse effect, depleting ozone, melting icecaps, a new ice age, acid rains, overpopulation — and declining energy resources, combine, with historical doubts about the viability of Western society, its economy, politics, and leadership, to fill popular literature with talk about the "coming crunch," Spenglerian scenarios, decline, decay, and Armageddon. The same forces have also led to the emergence of a new specialist, the futurist, who makes his living predicting what will happen to us.

Yet in the past the predictions of seers have not fared well. The dates, like 1984, set for doom have come and gone and life has continued as before. It is unlikely that today's futurist, for all his extrapolations, will fare any better than did the soothsayers, chiliasts, millennarians, historicists, and Marxists who, in their time, told similar tales of grim expectation.

In all likelihood, therefore, the class of 1984 will find that, indeed, life will go on after it graduates, and that there is still reason to hope. But, unless our institutions of higher education change soon, and unless students and their families take care to avoid the dangers that face them, these hopes may be disappointed.

The student of the eighties will be entering a society in the process of revising some of the fundamental premises on which it rests, and this revision will present as many opportunities as obstacles. The challenge will be to find these opportunities, for they will be different from what they were. Life is like that: just when we learn how to play the game, someone changes the rules.

That will be the challenge for 1980's freshmen and their successors. The rules for surviving and for enjoying life in the eighties are changing faster than anyone could imagine. How will this class and ones following avoid the problems Noah and his family faced, and how will this class learn what it needs to realize its opportunities? This book provides some answers.

America's colleges and universities are in trouble. During the last decade over one hundred and thirteen private colleges and universities closed their doors for good, thirty-nine merged with others, and fifteen were taken over by the public.[2] More are likely to follow. According to a 1978 study, conducted by the U.S. Comptroller General, of small, private liberal arts colleges over 79 percent of those colleges studied see themselves in some financial trouble, and 25 percent see themselves in substantial financial trouble.[3] Moreover, state institutions have been losing students,[4] and, although it is more difficult to close a community college than an air base, many of these have gone under, and others will follow. Even elite colleges, although not in immediate danger of extinction, are facing serious problems and have found it impossible to avoid unbalanced budgets altogether.[5]

What are the causes of these troubles? Conventional wisdom — itself largely the product of the education industry — has it that they are all of external origin, lying beyond campus control. Usually cited are inflation, declining college-age population, and government interference.[6] Yet these factors, although significant, are not the root causes. The more fundamental problems are self-inflicted: they lie within academe. As we shall see, the pervasive influence of a new academic ideology with a new social, political, and educational philosophy has created inefficient and self-destructive policies that in turn make the colleges increasingly vulnerable to any downward turn in the national economy.

In any case it is the students who suffer the consequences of this decline. Although most colleges won't disappear, they will change, often in unfortunate ways, as they try to cope during the hard times ahead.

In two ways they are changing already. First, as their resources shrink, so does the quality of the education they offer. This deterioration affects not only the curriculum, recently called a "disaster area" by the Carnegie Foundation,[7] but also the whole fabric of student life as well. Dormitories are deteriorating, libraries are crowded, and the increasingly isolated undergraduates, the "lumpen students," as Harvard's Dean Henry Rosovsky calls them, largely neglected by the colleges under the guise of student rights, live in a gray world of loneliness, anarchy, and what one Harvard dean calls "creeping squalor." Second, admissions departments and development offices, pressed to raise revenues, are working harder than ever to sell the college and maintain the illusion of sustained quality. They have become sophisticated image makers, resorting to effective

PR techniques to produce a halo effect for their colleges. As a 1979 Carnegie Foundation report notes, this has gone, at many institutions, beyond legitimate promotion to "hucksterism," where many have resorted to "inflated and misleading advertising . . . in search of students."[8]

By now everyone knows that the generation of students following the boom babies will have to try harder if they want to survive economically. One out of every four college graduates will be working during the 1980s at a job that does not require a B.A. degree.[9]

Students, knowing this, are more serious than ever. According to a 1974 National Assessment Survey, 44 percent of American seventeen-year-olds desired a professional career at a time when only 20 to 25 percent of existing jobs were professional or managerial.[10] With two people for every space, competition and survival have become bywords. "Everyone comes to Harvard a winner, but many leave as losers," says the Harvard sociologist David Riesman. This is becoming more true at other campuses as well.

Yet despite this nearly universal concern about one's personal future, present trends make it increasingly difficult to get a good education. Admissions soft sell and the rapid rate of change in academe make it hard to pick a college based on reliable information. Like marriage, it is easy to make a wrong choice and not discover the mistake until after the ceremony. Like divorce, transferring after freshman year, once hardly heard of, is now endemic. Nearly 20 percent of the undergraduates in small liberal arts colleges transfer each year, and over 50 percent of all college students experience an interruption (trial separation?) during their undergraduate careers.[11]

Despite these dangers, however, it is possible to get a good education and have a happy college life. What it takes is making the right decision in choice of college, course of studies, living and extracurricular activities. These decisions require more planning and thought than they once did. No longer, for instance, can one feel safe about choosing a college on the basis of suggestions by a high school advisor (whose information may have been supplied by a college admissions officer or may be hopelessly out of date), *Barron's Profiles,*[12] and a conducted visit to the campus. Now it also requires peering behind the ivy or painted cinder block, knowing what questions to ask, and how to read between the lines of a college catalogue.

This book is intended to help in making these decisions. It will explore what is happening and will happen to academe and why. It will assess the apparently bleak fate of our colleges and universities and will suggest what must be done for them to survive. It will serve as a guide for those choosing a college; for undergraduates planning their curricula, private lives, and careers; for alumni who want to see their alma maters in perspective; and for parents of college-age students who are looking for useful advice about choosing a college, admissions, finances, advising their children, and coping with the difficult and ambiguous rite of passage that occurs during this period of their family's life.

In short, the book is a kind of ombudsman's report, which attempts to answer one question: How is it possible to get a good education in America in the 1980s?

I

THE SURVIVAL OF THE COLLEGE

Higher Education in An Age of Limits

2

COLLEGES AND STUDENTS IN CRISIS
The Funny-Money Sheepskin

The extreme plasticity of human social behavior is both a great strength and a real danger. If each family worked out rules of behavior on its own, the result would be an intolerable amount of tradition drift and growing chaos. To counteract selfish behavior and the 'dissolving power' of high intelligence, each society must codify itself. Within broad limits virtually any set of conventions works better than none at all.

— EDWARD O. WILSON

"Twenty-two, twenty-three, twenty-four." Sally hesitated with her arms straight against the carpet.

"Twenty-five." She stood up. Her freckled face was dripping wet. She was wearing a Princeton sweatsuit and Adidas shoes, without socks. Sam, the owner of the sweatsuit, was lying on the mattress, reading Baudelaire's *Fleurs du Mal*. Rotorooter, a large Thurber dog with floppy jowls, was orbiting around Sally, sucking in microscopic breadcrumbs, like a whale seining plankton. The small room was crammed with objects, each in itself designed to enhance life, but as a group somehow managing to subtract from it. It was a clear case of the whole being less than the sum of its parts. A hi-fi set, under a pile of dirty clothes and now mercifully silent, took up one end; at the other was a small refrigerator next to a table, which held a hotplate and a stack of unwashed dishes. There was no sink or closet. In the middle, against one wall, was Sam and the mattress, and against the other wall two small desks, a wardrobe, and a bookshelf. Sally and the dog took up most of the available floor space, except for a few empty milk cartons and Oreo Sandwich wrappers.

All these things faced each other askew, for the walls in the room were not parallel. In fact, none of the walls in any room on campus were parallel. This building was called Pineapple, for it was shaped like a slice out of a Dole's can. It was built on the round, each room a truncated wedge facing a large central circular room—the hole in the pineapple — which the planners called the community room but which was actually a no-man's-land where things were stored and students met in passing. The room had Astroturf over a cement base and at present held a few bicycles, trunks, and bed frames. In the middle was a pool table missing a leg. Outside Sally's door was a double-decker bunk with the top mattress missing. The bottom bunk was made. That was Lynda's bunk. Lynda was Sally's roommate.

The architecture of Bison College was an intentional rejection of the neo-Georgian and pseudo-Gothic of Farnsworth, her better-established brother college down the road. It was "hi-tech": the structural girders remained exposed, rust red to the air; and the red, orange, and yellow plumbing and heating pipes ran outside the buildings, making this South Siberia, Massachusetts, campus look from a distance like some untidy Miocene battlefield, strewn with the petrified remains of disemboweled mastodons.

"Sam, I'm going running in a minute," Sally said. "Don't sit there like a lump on a log. Will you please go to the library and save me a seat? I'll meet you there at five."

Sally was a person who knew what she wanted and got it. She wanted Sam, and she got him. She wanted to be Phi

Beta Kappa, and she was. She wanted Sam to stay with her during his midsemester break, and he did. She wanted to be admitted to Yale Law School, and she would be. Now she wanted Sam to leave. He had overstayed his welcome, and she was beginning to get dirty looks from her dormmates, especially when she and Sam ate in the cafeteria. And Lynda, whom Sally could usually handle, was complaining. Today she had given another ultimatum. She might soon actually speak to the dean. Sally had to be careful.

"Bastard!" It was Lynda's voice.

As Sam put his book down he was hit smack on the lips of his "Kiss" tee shirt by an L. L. Bean's rubber moccasin. Following the moccasin came Lynda, holding the other one in her hand.

"We've just been made illegitimate," she went on; "Bison's finally done it. They're folding. 'Consolidating with Farnsworth,' they call it." For a change she didn't notice Sam.

"Belly up?" asked Sally. "We should have known. After all, they promised not to raise tuition next year."

"Very funny. You can afford to laugh. The law schools will be fighting over you. I'm still looking for a job, and what help is a diploma from an extinct institution? It's like being a bastard. After four years, what will we get? A counterfeit, funny-money sheepskin." She began trying to extricate the remains of her moccasin from Rotorooter's mouth.

Sally, doing deep knee bends, tried to comfort her. "Don't worry, Bison is — was — an accredited institution. So our transcripts have to be good. Who knows, they may become more valuable with age."

"Like Confederate money?"

"Well, at least like a buffalo nickel."

Sam, Sally, and Lynda are real. Although Bison is a composite, it is based on fact. In consolidating with Farnsworth, it is doing just what Pembroke did with Brown, Kirkland with Hamilton, and (de facto if not de jure) Radcliffe with Harvard. Next year Farnsworth will be coed, just as Yale, Princeton, Dartmouth, and Hamilton are now. According to the National Center for Education Statistics, the number of men's colleges has dropped by 49 percent and women's colleges by 54 percent, since the mid-sixties.[4]

And poor Lynda! She will, as Sally says, get her degree and it will be bona fide. Yet it won't be worth much because she didn't learn much; and she didn't learn much not because Bison didn't offer some good courses, but because she didn't take them. Bison and her more prestigious sibling, Farnsworth (like Wesleyan University, Smith, Hamilton, and many others) had no general education program, no distribution requirements, no language requirements, no required English essay writing course, and no mandatory mathematics course. All one had to do to graduate was take thirty-two courses and satisfy the requirements of the major. In addition, Bison, which advertises itself in the catalogue as "A College with a tradition of innovation," tried to copy Hampshire and Kirkland colleges by offering experimental, interdisciplinary majors which did not require formal classes, examinations, or papers. Unfortunately, the students became the guinea pigs in the experiment, and "interdisciplinary" quickly became "nondisciplinary." An English professor was conducting a seminar in "nonverbal communication," a political scientist taught the novel, and a French professor gave a course on "the omelet."

Lynda took the experimental major because it sounded good. The truth is that Lynda was unprepared for the academic liberty available at Bison. Whereas Sally, the daughter of a New York corporate lawyer and a graduate of Andover, was savvy to many of the possible traps in an over-optioned curriculum, Lynda, daughter of a Rochester,

Minnesota, physician and graduate of a conservative Catholic boarding school, was not.

Thus she will be in for a surprise when she tries to impress prospective employers with her transcript. All her work was done on a "pass/fail" basis and, even though she was a good student and all her work was of the highest quality, it went on record as a "pass" and so would appear to anyone who read it as an indication of average work. The written evaluations the instructors gave were useless to her. Aware of the federal law providing students access to all evaluations and afraid of libel suits, her teachers simply praised everyone indiscriminately. Again, despite her efforts, her transcript would look average.

So Lynda, whose parents spent $30,000 sending her to college, may not have a funny-money diploma, but she does have a funny-money transcript.

Sally, of course, avoided these problems. She knew from freshman year that she wanted to go to law school and she knew what courses and grades she needed to get there. She majored in political science. Although she learned much about that subject, she learned little or nothing about economics, literature, foreign languages, art, mathematics, or science.

Sam, Lynda, and Sally typify the aspirations and problems of college students today. Sam had entered Princeton with high hopes. He had grown up in a small Montana town, where he had gone to the local high school. But, being a reader in a community where *Grit* magazine is considered high culture, he was always a loner. His parents, transplanted Easterners, encouraged his bookishness, talking often and glowingly about the kind of college life they remembered. When he complained about the inanity of his peers' conversations, his father would say, "Wait till you go to college. Then you'll have good bull sessions." When he was teased for wearing his father's old tweed jacket to school instead of the plastic tricolor letter jacket he had won in track, his mother told him, "Just wait till you go to college. Life there is civilized. Then you can dress like a grownup without sticking out like a sore thumb." When his parents complained about what he was and was not learning at school, they consoled themselves with the thought that at college he would make up for his miseducation received in high school.

Sam had been, in short, square; and his high hopes had been the product of his parents' nostalgia. So when he finally arrived at Princeton his hopes were quickly dashed. The students dressed like his high school classmates; conversations, although different, were equally boring, and learning didn't turn out to be as exciting as his parents said it would. Expecting to find bull sessions about existentialism, God, Marxism, and free will, he found instead classmates consumed with competition for professional school. In his freshman year he was put into a tiny room in the basement of the annex of the recently acquired Princeton Inn, surrounded by cinder block walls and the omnipresent pipes and living with an equally disillusioned roommate who played his stereo system at 120 decibels. Finding his classmates boring, he did not join a club. He moved into a single and ate from a hotplate. In four years he made no college friends but spent every spare moment at Bison with Sally. His only other interest was comparative literature, the early French surrealist poets, to be precise. They seemed, in their searching and self-absorption, to be soul mates. He did not know, of course, where such study would lead him, and that was a worry. His four years at Princeton, beginning in the great flush of triumph for having been admitted, was ending a bummer. He was learning to expect less from life.

"Modern dorm life," says Alice Johnson, dean of Connecticut College, "probably hurts the conservative student the most. She does not approve of premarital sex and is not comfortable living in physically close proximity to members of the opposite sex. At the same time she is too inhibited to complain when the actions of her roommate or others bothers her. Instead she suffers in silence and often leaves without telling us why." Lynda, from a strict Midwestern family, is that kind of woman. Her dormitory, like most in the country, is self-governing, which means it is governed by peer pressure. This, as any English public school boy can tell you, is the most cruel form of government there is. In this system Gresham's Law operates and bad drives out good. Behavior sinks to the lowest common denominator, and the absence of proctors leaves no one to whom the oppressed student can turn.

Lynda's mind was blown when her more sophisticated roommate asked Sam to move in with her. "We don't mind if you watch," Sally said. Lynda, however, did mind and moved the double-decker bunk into the community room. This is a common problem. "We have a warehouse full of double-decker bunks which students won't use because they want privacy to entertain members of the opposite sex," says John Fox, dean of Harvard College.

In this environment, only Sally has thrived. She knew just what she wanted to get from college, and she was comfortable with the new postparietal-rule morality. She was also happy that Bison let her do what her parents wouldn't. Yet she, too, made few friends other than Sam; so college to her was not a special experience, but merely a stepping-stone toward her chosen career.

Lynda and Sam represent college casualties, the victims of a system that works only for a few. For many reasons which we shall learn, responsibility for both the curricular and extracurricular parts of students' lives has been virtually abandoned by most colleges and universities, while economic factors conspire to lower their standard of living. Because most colleges have gone coed, for instance, few bother to sponsor social events, like mixers, where students can meet. The administration has abandoned in loco parentis and in many cases leaves running the dorms to students; this gives students rights but no responsibilities (since the dorms belong to the college) and virtually guarantees chaos. Because dorms are crowded and there is little control of noise, crowded libraries have become a national phenomenon. At Yale, according to former Dean Horace Taft, students must get to the library by six P.M. if they expect to find seats for evening study. "In the good old days," says Princeton's Provost Rudenstine, "proctors could worry about enforcing parietal rules and breaking up noisy parties. Now they are too busy fighting real crime." Money problems encourage colleges to defer maintenance, causing premature decay in the students' living environment. "The river houses, although still the most popular, are in terrible shape," says Stephen Williams, professor of anthropology at Harvard and former chairman of their Student Life Task Force; "wood is chipped, paint is falling off, and the rooms look seedy. And the new dorms look as though they have been designed by a submarine commander." The transition from single-sex to coed living has also produced casualties, as we shall see. According to many Harvard officials, the Harvard-Radcliffe consolidation was a "disaster."

In these conditions it is no wonder that many students are lonely and alienated. "I think we should be as concerned about the quality of student life as we are about the curriculum," says Dean Henry Rosovsky of Harvard. "The students who become involved, whether it be with the *Crimson*, Dramatic Club, or Young Republicans — it doesn't matter what, so long as they do *something* — are the ones who will have a good college experience. The ones I'm worried about are the ones who do not become involved. They are the lumpenproletariat of the student body, and their experience will not be good."

With the exception of a few voices such as those above, however, few college officials want even to talk about the problems of student life, much less do anything about them. This is ironic today, when talk about curricular reform has become fashionable again. But the decline in undergraduate living standards, the formless curriculum, and the current financial crisis are all part of the same problem. They are all indices that liberal arts education no longer pursues the goals it once did. In place of its ancient purposes it now teaches consumption. But by making the student a consumer, it is making him a victim as well.

For many centuries the liberal arts have been guided by three simple ideas. These are unity, continuity, and value. The various scholarly disciplines, severally and as a body, have been in the business of applying and promoting these ideas. Let us consider them in detail.

First, unity. This is one of the oldest and the most universal of ideas. It is nothing more than the supposition that while the universe appears to be composed of many apparently unconnected objects behaving in a haphazard way, these objects are actually related to each other systematically, or are appearances only — misleading manifestations of an undivided universe. This idea is the centerpiece of most major philosophies from Parmenides' poem "The Way of Truth," in fifth-century, B.C., Athens to Rudolf Carnap and the Unity of Science movement in twentieth-century America, and it is a persistent theme in Eastern thought. It is a presupposition in the aesthetic theories of Plato, Kant, and Schopenhauer, the histories of Burkhardt, Gibbon, and Tolstoy, and the works of Chaucer, Milton, Dante, Cervantes, and Melville. It is also the foundation of all modern science. It lies behind all these because it is, at bottom, nothing more than the belief pursued so successfully by Einstein, that truth is simple.

This idea also has a corollary which applies to man. It is that underlying the diversity of human beings is a unity. Aristotle called this an essence, Christians call it soul, and Freud called it ego; but whatever the name, the use implied that human needs do not differ greatly and that the similarities between people are more fundamental than the differences.

Higher education has been built upon this idea of unity. The word *university* expresses it, for it means both "universe or totality" and "community or individual corporation."[2] For centuries academe perceived itself as a community of scholars, united by their common attempt to make the universe intelligible and to teach what they learned. Classical education and liberal education were derived from this idea, for they were designed to encourage the student to integrate widely disparate areas of knowledge by the study of a central residue of inherited insight to which everything else could be related.

So this idea of unity is an integral part of the liberal arts. It lies behind the scientist's search for general theory and not merely disconnected descriptions; the philosopher's pursuit of truth, not opinions; the historian's study of history, not events; the writer's portrayal of the human condition, not private foibles; and the painter's or sculptor's attempts to create art, not decoration.

Second, continuity. The philosopher Immanuel Kant observed that to be aware of change required persisting through time — indeed, having a memory.[3] For to be aware of change is to be aware that the present is not in all respects like the past. If I have no memory, I have no way of knowing anything has changed. In short, if I, including my memory, changed every instant, I could not be aware of change.

If change becomes too rapid, then awareness of it is impossible.

This is true of societies. If change becomes too rapid, the society loses the ability to make rational judgments about the desirability of the changes taking place. Indeed, it will have no social memory and will be unable to learn from the past.

This role, of preserving perspective, has always belonged to academe. To perform it, the universities had to persist — last through time — and had to change more slowly than the society itself. Oxford University began before the signing of the Magna Carta and has persisted through the reign of forty monarchs. Harvard University has endured four forms of government on this continent.[4] At Oxford, the Laudian Code, written in 1636 and covering every detail of University life, was not superseded until 1864, and Greats — the study of classics and the oldest course of study — is still the most prestigious.[5] In this country, twelfth-century caps and gowns are still worn to commencement exercises; and the liberal arts, whose roots go back to the thirteenth-century curriculum, divided into the quadrivium (arithmetic, geometry, astronomy, and music) and the trivium (logic, grammar, and rhetoric), are themselves a commitment to continuity, for they are based on the supposition that knowledge from and of the past is useful to the present.[6]

Third, values. Every act, whether by an individual or society, is directed to some end. The rules that prescribe these acts, or are presupposed by them, express the values by which we live. The academy has, and has always had, three roles with respect to these values: first, to demonstrate by example the intrinsic and extrinsic value of knowledge; second, to help the student to discover, through rational inquiry, moral and aesthetic truth; and third, to encourage both individuals and society to reflect critically on their values, and if necessary to reject or revise them. This value-laden mission found its historic expression, not only in the very existence of educational institutions (thereby showing the value we place upon education), but also in the sectarian commitments of most of our colleges; in the willingness, on the part of most faculties, to say what was important to learn and what was not; and in the acknowledgment by most colleges, until recently, of their responsibility not only to produce good scholars but to develop good character as well.

This idea of value, moreover, has a specific direction. This direction is determined by the preceding ideas of unity and continuity. As the idea of unity suggests that the similarities between people are greater than the differences, and the idea of continuity suggests that the similarities between generations are greater than the differences, then the search for moral and aesthetic truth must be a search for *universal* truth. If we are all essentially the same, then we must all be subject to essentially the same rules. The liberal arts therefore eschew relativism, for relativism is nothing more than the supposition that, as people are different, the same rules do not apply to everyone. Although it may be impossible to achieve a consensus on values, this should not deflect scholarship from pursuing the goal of universality. Such a goal, in fact, may never be achieved; but it is, always, as Kant would say, "set us as a task."

These three ideas, then, not only traditionally lie at the heart of the liberal arts, but they have also always performed an important social function. They constitute the glue that holds a community together: unity, in the recognition of common needs; continuity, as awareness of sharing a common past and future; and value, as commitment to a common set of goals. Together these conspire to produce the sense of mutual trust and acceptance of personal sacrifice to a common good that is the essence of community.

It is in this way that the liberal arts have a special role to play in our society. They are, or should be, a unifying force, for the three ideas to which they are uniquely dedicated are also the ideas which can preserve a sense of community.

All one needs do, however, is visit almost any campus in America to see that the liberal arts are no longer a unifying force. For the three ideas we have discussed are being subverted by current academic policies. In these policies centrifugal forces have replaced centripetal ones as the cohesion of the community has been eroded.

On campus today in place of unity there is disunity. Here the destructive force is the policy of options. Never before have so many been offered, both within the curriculum and for student living. The prevailing paucity of general education and distribution requirements increases the range of choice, while simultaneously courses are added, more often at the periphery of the liberal arts than at the core, and often stressing the differences between people rather than their affinities. Smith College, for instance, with 2,800 undergraduates, has over one hundred courses in English literature from which to choose; the Harvard History Department has nearly two hundred offerings; Yale has recently added a major in film studies, and the Wesleyan *Classics* Department now offers a course in American culture.[7] And there is scarcely a department in this country that does not display offerings specially designed for blacks and women.

Compounding the confusion created by these overgrown and haphazardly constructed curricula, students are permitted or encouraged to make frequent decisions regarding grading options, dropping or adding courses, special programs, and getting extensions or incompletes. At Yale, where there are 59 major programs and 5,200 undergraduates, there were in 1978–1979 over 50,000 course changes![8]

Within the area of student life, decisions must be made to live on campus or off, whether to opt for the ten-meal-a-week plan, the twenty-meal-a-week plan, or to eat off a hotplate; and, if the options are available (as they are at some universities), whether to live in a coed or single-sex dorm, drinking or nondrinking dorm, noisy or loud dorm, or one with liberal or strict visiting privileges. If the dorms are self-governing, decisions must be made for the legislation of rules about quiet, smoking, drinking, visitors, and sex.

Second, rapid change has disrupted the continuity of academe. It is not an accident that the name of the major professional journal of higher education is *Change* magazine, for change, not continuity, is the name of the game today. Within the last ten years, for instance, the typical liberal arts college made many, if not all, of the following changes: it first abolished general education and distribution requirements and more recently reinstated some of them. It experimented with special programs, such as African studies, environmental studies, business and social welfare internships, urban studies, physical therapy, business administration, courses on television and radio, continuing education, and women's studies; then it phased some out. It dropped its church affiliation. It introduced preprofessional programs such as nursing and law. It abolished parietal rules, and it changed its method of governance.

Change is, in fact, becoming so rapid that many institutions are losing their sense of continuity. The average tenure of a college president is not much longer than the average tenure of a college student, and the annual rate of turnover among deans of faculty and deans of students at liberal arts colleges is nearly 20 percent.[9] In this state of rootlessness there are few in power who can say what the institution was like six years ago. There is no institutional memory. Few in the administration will have to live with the consequences of the latest innovation. It is ironic, too, that universities, whose libraries store knowledge, typically cannot tell you, for instance, what curriculum they employed in, say, 1965. The president may just happen to have an old college announcement around, but he may not. The students themselves do not know what the college was like before they came and have no basis of comparison with which to judge their present circumstances. Faculty, too, until recently, was highly mobile, so only a few older faculty members may remember the way things used to be. In these circumstances one might think that the group most likely to have knowledge of the school's history would be the custodians. And this would be true if it were not for the fact that most custodians have been replaced by students on work-study.

Third, values. Rules that prescribe actions, as we have seen, express values. Yet the increase of options has meant the decrease of rules. There are fewer rules governing the curriculum and student life, and in many cases distribution requirements and parietal rules have been abolished altogether. Yet these rules performed an important function. *They defined the community.* Distribution requirements and general education courses not only ensured that students would at least attempt to integrate disparate areas of knowledge; they were also the institution's way of saying, "This is what we think is important to know. Studying this is what is distinctive about our community, and its pursuit is the interest which we share." Likewise, parietal rules defined the community good. They said, in effect, "This is the kind of behavior that we value and that is consistent with the general good." Both kinds of rules reinforced the view of the universality of human needs and served to protect the individual. Distribution requirements and the absence of options protected people from wasting their time at college by taking unnecessary or unhelpful courses, and parietal rules protected students who were uncomfortable with the prevailing norms of their peer groups by limiting those activities, such as cohabitation between sexes, visiting, noise, and smoking, where one person's actions might impinge on another's wellbeing.

The absence of these rules has atomized the community because there is no longer any common knowledge or sense of common good. The emphasis has shifted to the differences, rather than the similarities, between people and to individual preference rather than universal value. Students, whose studies have often narrowed in the pursuit of special projects, find they have nothing to talk with each other about. "The difficulty in teaching today," says one member of the Smith College faculty, "is that we can no longer presume any common knowledge among the students. We cannot, for instance, assume all students are familiar with the Bible and know who was swallowed by a whale. It makes it difficult to get a point across. Communication breaks down."

The great sociologist Emile Durkheim called the absence of rules the state of anomie, meaning literally "without law."[10] In his classic study of suicide he said this state led to loneliness, a growing sense of anonymity, and a loss of a sense of identity. In extreme cases it led to suicide. Anomie characterizes student life today, and it is therefore unsurprising that there are signs of increasing isolation and alienation among undergraduates. The suicide rate for the college-age group is at an all-time high and many college mental health services report that anxiety and depression are far more prevalent than they were ten years ago.[11]

Why, when they are so destructive, do colleges and universities persist in offering so many options? A full answer must come later, but one reason is *finances*. As the U.S. Comptroller General's study notes, many colleges try to solve their short-term financial problems with "the addition of occupational programs to satisfy a wider variety of student interests and needs."[12] As they try to survive economically, they see themselves less as educational institutions and more as businesses; and the worse off they are, the more options they are tempted to add.

Offering options is, after all, a market ploy, borrowed from Detroit. The more options offered, the greater, theoretically, the size of the potential market. Ironically, however, this strategy, although perhaps working for automakers, does not make money for academe, and for two reasons.

First, in increasing its options, a college loses its distinctiveness. When it ceases to be for women only, or drops its unique classics program or affiliation with the Presbyterian Church, the college is abandoning a guaranteed, if limited, market; and when every other college does the same thing, all become more alike. No longer possessing a limited monopoly of a distinctive product, each college is approaching a perfectly competitive situation with every other. As any economist knows, in a perfectly competitive situation profits drop to zero, and only the most efficient — that is, the bigger — will survive. Schools such as Vassar or Macalester, having lost much of their distinctiveness, suddenly find themselves competing with Harvard, Princeton, the University of Minnesota, or the State University of New York. Students ask themselves, "Why should I go to Vassar when I can go for less money to SUNY? Why should I go to Macalester when I can go for just a bit more money to Harvard?" So, as recent enrollment figures indicate, the rich get richer and the poor get poorer. Harvard and Princeton are receiving more applications than ever, while applications to the lesser colleges are dropping.

Note that an important principle is operating here. It is:

the more options, the less real choice. At college, allowing students the option of deciding how their dorm is run leads to all dorms being run the same way. Allowing students to take any course they want leads to great overcrowding in the most popular ones, making the experience of finding the course closed all too frequent. At Harvard, nearly 50 percent of enrollment was in courses which had fifty or more students, even though courses of this size represented only a little over 11 percent of the courses offered.[13] For a student who can find no congenial dormitory or cannot get the course he wants, these options, like an automatic transmission on many GM cars, turn out to be "mandatory."

The second reason why the system of options does not alleviate economic problems is that it costs more to administer. A system where each student's undergraduate career must be plotted separately requires much administrative and faculty time. Where there are fewer rules for the curriculum, there must be more advisors and more people to train the advisors. When students exercise choices concerning on-campus or off-campus living and eating, someone must run the system or the computer that supervises this. When students have latitude in dropping or adding courses, getting grades changed or receiving incompletes, the registrar's office must be bigger. This extra expense is especially evident in the area of student life, typically the responsibility of the dean of students. Although twenty years ago many colleges did not even have such a position in the administration, it is now often the largest office on campus.

The fact that the proliferation of options has exacerbated, rather than alleviated, colleges' financial problems, is touching off a downward spiral. For as the options subtract from their revenue and add to their cost, they are finding themselves in worse shape than before. As this occurs, many, as the Comptroller General's report shows, respond by adding even more options, thus not only deepening their money problems, but also increasing the agony of anomie as well.

Given this, it might seem surprising that academe does not try to break the vicious circle and, instead of equating bigger with better and options with income, try to put together a smaller, cheaper, better product. Why not produce Volkswagens rather than Cadillacs? If each college were to offer fewer, but more distinctive and better defined, programs, and through sensible social engineering were to reestablish a sense of community to campus, both college and student would be better off.

Money troubles are not the root cause of the current deterioration on campus. Although the proliferation of options may be aggravated by a shortage of money, or by excessive spending, they actually began when and because colleges had *too much money*. Even the money problems have an ideological, not economic, origin. Colleges have capitulated to a new ideology; one that has created, on campus, an atmosphere hostile to learning and living. Moreover, this ideology is still pervasive, the problems it causes still persist, even though its destructive effects are becoming obvious. Breaking the vicious circle, therefore, requires more than economic acumen; it also requires nothing less than that academe be born again, and rediscover the concepts of unity, continuity and value on which its raison d'être rests.

The new ideology, which we shall explore in the succeeding chapters, is a philosophy of governance, a form of relativism and a particular approach to scholarly research. One of its many implications is that the campus is and ought to be a microcosm of the nation. Rather than perceiving itself as having an active role in shaping a future society, the college today sees itself as having a passive role, of copying society. If our government works by the principle of balance between countervailing interest groups, so should campus government; if ours is a consumer society whose economy rests on choice, so should the curriculum, and if our society has been swept off its feet by a new morality, this new morality should be the ethic of academe as well.

This perception has initiated the era of options. The college has become the supermarket and the student the consumer. This has been particularly disastrous for private colleges, for they are quickly reaching the point where they differ from public institutions only in the greater size of their tuition. As they lose students to the state and as their costs increase, they depend further on the government for financial help. So by inviting public control they further lose whatever was unique about them. In this way the new ideology, which perceives no difference between college and country, becomes a self-fulfilling prophecy: believing this, in the end, makes it so.

Only a few in academe would concur with this diagnosis. The majority, like a prominent family infected with a social disease, are reluctant to admit its existence or cannot see its ill effects. So the conventional interpretation of these events absolves academe for most responsibility for what has happened. According to this conventional view, the three problems of deficit budgets, formless curriculum, and deteriorating student life are largely unconnected and are the results of factors lying beyond campus control.

The financial problems, according to this view, are due to a decline in student age populations, increases in costs, particularly energy and salaries, increasingly expensive government regulations, greater competition for the private colleges from the subsidized public ones, and, for public institutions, growing resistance from taxpayers for further levies.[14] The school solution to these problems is more money, especially more federal and state money, through increased federal loan programs, more federally sponsored student aid, larger per capita subsidies, more research money and the forgiveness of debts already incurred. Secondarily the solution is more efficient bookkeeping, more aggressive student recruiting, and more effective fund raising.[15]

The conventional wisdom on the curriculum is that the emasculation of the liberal arts was a casualty of the sixties, the result of the cataclysmic impact of the civil rights movement and the war in Vietnam. But these are past, and academe, now licking its wounds, will soon heal. Sensible academic programs are on their way back, as can be seen by the beginnings of reform at Harvard, Yale, Amherst, the University of California at Berkeley, and Syracuse, among others. At the same time, according to this view, any simple attempt to restore the old standards should be avoided for two reasons. First, it would be retrogressive and elitist, for it would have the effect of denying access to higher education to those people who only recently gained access to it. Second, there has been such an explosion of knowledge in the scholarly world that the sheer volume of it precludes finding a particular set of topics sufficiently more important than the rest to be required, and precludes expecting students to integrate such widely disparate and complex subjects.[16] Thus, although structure must be reintroduced to the curriculum, it must be a different kind of structure from what existed in the past.

When questioned about the decline in the quality of student life, most college administrators will either deny its existence or declare that it is due to factors lying beyond campus control: the lack of money makes crowding inevitable and upkeep of dorms difficult, while the squalor of dorm life is simply a reflection of a new national morality. Yet in fact most colleges perceive their responsibilities in this area differently from the way they once did. They see the question of responsibility to be a choice between a system of deans of students catering to individual student needs and the old business of in loco parentis with its Old Testament parietal rules. They have opted for the former system. Their reasons for this choice are first, parietal rules were hypocritical, unenforceable, and vastly unpopular; second, students are now legally adults and, being fully entitled to all rights prescribed by law, can no longer be treated paternalistically. Colleges' hands are tied, and therefore they must limit their educational responsibilities to curricular questions and leave students' private lives alone.

To paraphrase Dr. Johnson, and as we shall see, these three theses are both apposite and true. Unfortunately, the parts that are apposite are not true and the parts that are true are not apposite.

3

GOVERNMENT
The Green Eminence

The impatient reader of history may be disposed to count the two centuries of order between 27 B.C. and A.D. 180 as among the wasted opportunities of mankind. It was an age of spending rather than creation.

— H.G. WELLS

We have seen how under the Roman Republic economic and social order was destroyed by the too great fluidity of property that money brought about. Money became abstract, and lost touch with the real values it was supposed to represent. Individuals and communities got preposterously into debt.

— H.G. WELLS

They sat, forty of them, all college deans and presidents, wearing their pinstripes and tweeds, their cordovans and wing tips, their narrow Brooks Brothers ties and button-downs, around a huge square polished walnut table, listening as Dean Menninger read his report on the latest curriculum reform at Farnsworth. Behind him, on the wall, hung the portrait of the foundation's founder, Jerome J. Stoneyboy himself. It was difficult, in this intimate setting, not to feel the proximity of power. Indeed, was it not the original Stoneyboy who amassed billions and then, passing on to his descendants along with their trust funds a legacy of guilt and noblesse oblige, created a vast machine to give the money away? Was there a major university in the country that was not shaped in some significant way by his benefi-cence? And was his family not the most influential in the United States, counting among its members several gov-ernors and senators, and serving as patron to two whole generations of distinguished public servants?

The meeting was another in a series sponsored by the Stoneyboy Foundation on higher education. It was entitled "Liberal Education: Phoenix or Dodo?" The morning ses-sion was devoted to Professor Holloway's very clinical ac-count of academe's ills. There had been general concur-rence on the basic point that things were not good, and then the assemblage had adjourned for a luncheon of smoked salmon, cold asparagus, Gruyère cheese, and California wine. Now revived, they were listening to Dean Menninger tell very wittily and with a slight German accent how he managed to get his well-publicized "Dead Center" curricu-lum proposal through a reluctant and sometimes hostile faculty. The basic idea for this proposal was that there is a body of basic skills and "methods of inquiry" that every person called educated should know and that lies at the dead center of all scholarly research. Getting this by a fac-ulty divided into powerful and warring departments, even with the many compromises which were necessary for pas-sage, was indeed a political tour de force, but it failed to impress Dean Menninger's fellow participants.

"What's wrong with the old general education program?" asked the president of a small liberal arts college famous for its Great Persons program, who added, "I think one should simply go back to what we knew worked."

"But it didn't work," said the president of a newly estab-lished experimental college. "That's what's wrong with the Dead Center proposal. It's just like the old one. Why as-sume there is just one way to give a liberal education? Why not try something truly innovative, which really recognizes individual needs?"

"The trouble with your reform, Menninger," added the dean of a large state university, "is that you politicized decision making too much. And in the process of compromise, you threw the baby out with the bathwater. Your new curriculum isn't even as tough as the old one." /

"Whatever curriculum you have there," said another with equal finality, "won't make any difference until you have broken the power of the faculty and made them teach instead of selfishly pursuing their personal research interests. You are just proving that a good undergraduate education is impossible to achieve at a major research university."

Clearly, they were all having fun. But no one was saying what was on everyone's mind. It was that this conference *didn't make any difference.* Here was a gathering of the chief officers of the thirty-five most important colleges and universities in the country, sponsored by one of the most powerful foundations, and everyone knew that nothing would come of it. For the ambience of influence, once based on fact, was now, like the portrait, merely part of the decor, a reminder of what had long since disappeared.

The foundation, of course, was under no illusion about its influence. It held the conference because, as one of its officers said, "It seemed like a good idea to get people together to talk about things." But it knew that the invitees, despite their impressive titles, had, or thought they had, little power to effect real reform at their home institutions even if they had come away with a new idea. And the foundation itself knew that for all its prestige it no longer had the carrot or stick necessary to coax meaningful reforms.

The direction that higher education takes in the future is unlikely to be determined, as it was in the past, by wealthy foundations or by powerful college presidents. The movers and shakers will no longer have names like Ford, Rockefeller, Harkness, Lowell, Eliot, or Hutchins. They won't have individual names at all. Instead they will be public agencies, largely federal ones, whose regulations control events on campus by a system of rewards and punishments based on the promise of money and the threat of its withdrawal, and they will be campus-based surrogates and protégés of these agencies who, often owing their presence not to the institution but to the government, effectively limit the area of discretion open to campus administrators. The transformation is a double one: it represents not only a shift of power from New York to Washington, but also on campus, from individuals to interest groups. Through this twofold devolution of institutional power, the college is being transformed to its very roots. What is happening is not just that reform is becoming more difficult and that colleges are losing their independence, but also that the distinction between public and private has all but disappeared; and with this a whole host of valuable social services, once performed by the academy, is gone as well.

In an earlier era, foundations and private individuals, through intelligent philanthropy, were able to have considerable influence on the nature of education. By making one well-placed gift to realize a creative idea at an influential university, they were able to create paradigms to be copied elsewhere. This ripple effect could start and end trends. With Edward Harkness's gift to Harvard, for example, President Lowell was able to build the highly successful house system. Yale soon followed, and by today this idea has been adopted by other colleges as far away as Santa Cruz, California.[1]

Today, however, there are so many colleges needing so much money that the relatively small amount that foundations can give is not big enough to make a difference. In 1911, according to Alden Dunham of the Carnegie Foundation, the Carnegie Foundation's giving represented 6 percent of the entire amount spent in the country that year on higher education; today their giving is .0004 percent of all spending on higher education. The combined operating budget of America's colleges and universities is over forty billion; yet the combined *assets* of the private foundations are only twenty-two billion. So if the foundations were to give away their entire wealth tomorrow, they would supply the needs of higher education for only six months. As it is, since there are many other pressing social needs that can lay a legitimate claim on philanthropic giving, only 30 percent of all foundation grants in fact go to higher education, and one-half of these go to only sixty-five colleges and universities! Finally, the foundations' ability to help the academy has been hurt by recent tax reforms, which make giving to charity more expensive and which, through excise taxes and payout requirements, subtract from the amount recipients receive and, in some cases, significantly diminish the size of a foundation's capital.[2]

It is the federal government, in fact, that has filled the power vacuum. Today no aspect of campus life is unaffected by federal presence. The Fair Labor Standards Act, for instance, which requires colleges to bargain collectively with their faculties' elected union representatives, and Executive Orders numbers 11296 and 11375, by prescribing affirmative action for hiring and firing, affect substantially who teaches, and thus indirectly what is taught and how it is taught. The Civil Rights Act, which regulates the racial, ethnic, and religious mix of employees and students alike, together with the financial aid programs of the Social Security Administration, the Department of Health, Education and Welfare, and the Veterans Administration and with new Internal Revenue Service policies that deny tax-exempt status to colleges that do not have race- and sex-blind admissions, determines *who* is taught.* The mandates of the Occupational Hazards and Safety Administration, by requiring sometimes expensive alterations, limit how colleges can spend money. The building codes of the Housing and Urban Development Administration, by stipulating how many square feet of living space can be allotted each student in federally subsidized student housing, affects the quality and nature of student life. The Family Educational Rights and Privacy Act (Buckley Law), which allows students access to all transcripts affects the quality and accuracy of student transcripts. The regulations of HEW that require government-created Institutional Review Boards to pass on any medical or sociological research about human subjects have considerable impact on the nature and direction of scholarly research.[3] Grants from agencies such as the Defense Department, the National Science Foundation, the National Endowments for the Arts and Humanities, the National Institute of Education, and the Fund for the Improvement of Post-Secondary Education pay the salaries of many faculty members and indirectly help to mold the structure and scope of curriculum and research. The reporting requirements of HEW, through its National Center for Education Statistics and their Higher Education General Information Survey, not only ensure that there are no secrets kept from Uncle Sam but also place an extra burden on administrative time and money.[4] This weighs especially on the smaller institutions.

Federal control of higher education has grown as a concomitant of the growth of federal aid. This aid has increased from around two billion dollars in 1967 to an expected ten

---

* Single-sex colleges are permitted by the IRS to discriminate on the basis of sex, but if coeducational colleges do so, they risk losing their tax-exempt status.

billion in 1980, and it has accelerated the change, already begun, in the way colleges make decisions. The process of institutional growth now is a highly political one, where the college president may have to deal with irate staff and faculty members as he tries to cut a program that is 75 percent federally funded but where the college can no longer afford its 25 percent contribution. Since allocations are based on the compromise of competing claims, the kinds of programs that get funded tend to be special ones, lying not at the center of the liberal arts but at the perimeter, such as the grant, by NEH, to develop an in-flight humanities channel, or the grant, by HEW, for research on how to watch TV.[5]

This diffusion of attention to the periphery has created centrifugal forces that campus administrators find hard to control. It has left, in the center, an area void of ideas and vitality. Whereas the old system provided focus on central problems by the construction of paradigms, the new one, by its encouragement of competing claims, blurs all the issues. Institutional growth, once guided by coherent principles, is now, like cancer, a mere haphazard multiplication of cells.

Supply, according to the eighteenth-century French economist Jean-Baptiste Say, creates its own demand. Just as a pusher hooks a junkie by establishing a dependence, so has the federal government, with its aid, hooked academe. Going cold turkey on this aid is viewed by most on campus as almost certain death. Yet the threat of withholding the fix is precisely the device used to ensure compliance with government mandates, for most of these mandates do not apply universally, but only as conditions attached to aid. Hence the government is perceived, whether it is true or not, as possessing the power of life and death over higher education. Within this framework, institutional autonomy becomes a charade, except at a few private institutions lucky or smart enough to remain independent. A few, like Rockford College in Illinois and Brigham Young University in Utah, have forsworn government aid specifically in order to remain free of control; but most have not, and instead of trying to extricate themselves are finding new ways to put themselves further in thrall. In 1978 Congress passed the Middle Income Student Assistance Act at the urging of the educational community, greatly increasing federal scholarship aid to middle-class students. John Silber, President of Boston University, is urging a proposal for the creation of a federal student loan program based on the model of social security. Retiring President Wiesner of MIT, whose institution already receives over 65 percent of its revenues from Uncle Sam, has urged greatly increasing federal subsidies to university research.[6] More hands than ever are reaching for the public purse even if it means further dependency. Clearly higher education in America is selling its birthright for a mess of pottage. Why is it doing this?

The answer, of course, is money. According to the conventional wisdom of the academy, demographic and economic trends make the growth of federal aid inevitable. The colleges need more money, lots of it, if they are to stay afloat, and only Washington has it in sufficient quantities to make a difference. It has become the green eminence in our lives. Specifically, this view attributes the squeeze to four factors.

First, the number of college-age students is declining. By 1990 there will be 20 percent fewer eighteen-year-olds than there are today, resulting in fewer students and less income from tuition.[7]

Second, costs, particularly in salaries and energy, pushed by inflation, are rising faster than revenues.[8]

Third, as tuitions rise, the cost of a college education approaches prohibitive levels, further discouraging enrollment, particularly from the middle class, which is neither sufficiently poor to qualify for financial aid nor sufficiently rich to pay its own way.[9]

Fourth, private colleges are facing increased and unfair competition from the subsidized state institutions, and, as a result, are losing students to them in even greater numbers.[10]

These four points, however, are completely misleading and do not in any way account for academe's current financial plight.

First, the economic downturn for colleges began a decade before the dip in student population. The decline in number of eighteen-year-olds did not begin until 1979 and the decline in the number of people between eighteen and twenty-four (the college-age population) will not begin until 1981.[11] *Yet the watershed year for college finances was 1970–1971!* According to the Association of American Colleges, "Beginning in 1970–1, deficits were apparently so common that *three* of the institutional groups (i.e., doctoral granting universities and both small and large liberal arts colleges) were in the red."[12]

Second, inflation, although great in the seventies, was more than offset by rising revenues. Private college and university revenue increased, during the period 1970–1976, by 52 percent while inflation went up 40 percent.[13]

Third, net college fees, rather than going up during this period, went down. The total cost of attending a private college, as a percentage of the net per capita disposable income, has decreased during the last ten years from 83 percent to 79 percent.[14] Moreover, as we shall see in Chapter 12, the net family contribution — what colleges actually expect students to pay — has declined steadily during the last twenty-five years.[15]

Fourth, competition for private schools from the state system, although great, is not substantially different from what it was during earlier, better times. The tuition differential, measured as a percentage of net family disposable income, has remained almost constant the last fifteen years.[16]

In sum, the economic plight of the academy today is not explained by demographics or changes in the national economy. Instead, the causes of these ills began, not because of a shortage of money in the seventies, but because of *too much money* in the sixties, and the institutional changes this glut helped to bring about.

To see this, let us trace the fortunes of one college from 1968 through 1976.

Micawber, as we shall call it, is a fine Midwestern liberal arts college. Enjoying the favors of a rich and generous man, founder of a publishing empire, it had, during the early sixties, grown in wealth and importance, increasing its endowment by twenty million and substantially improving the size and quality of its student body and faculty. It was, it seemed, a good young college on the way up.

In 1969 it initiated, under a new president and with federal help, a number of new and expensive programs, including an urban affairs department, a new system of visiting lectureships, the creation of a prestigious chair to be held by successful politicians, an individualized learning center staffed by education specialists, and an ambitious minorities program, which provided full tuition and expenses as well as complete counseling and tutorial service for seventy-five educationally disadvantaged students out of each class of five hundred. It also expanded faculty and greatly increased their rate of pay; it added to student services and to the curriculum; and it created, within the administration, two more deanships. At approximately the same time, it dropped the mandatory religion course, dropped freshman English from the syllabus, and loosened many of the liberal arts distribution requirements. All this was done, moreover, within a two-year period by faculty and administration initiative and without substantial prodding from the students. At the time, in fact, the college prided itself in being one step ahead of the students, by responding to anticipated, rather than actual, student demand.

As it turned out, however, the combination of these initiatives was more than Micawber could afford, and beginning in 1969–1970 it had a string of unbalanced budgets, which lasted until 1974. To offset these deficits it borrowed, in 1969, four and a half million dollars from its endowment; an action that, together with other questionable fiscal decisions, caused the college's benefactor to withdraw his support. The president resigned and was replaced by a man who tried to cut the minorities program. This resulted in an extended occupation of a college administration building and the new president's premature resignation. Meanwhile, because of a decline in the amount of funds available for financial aid, the loss of its traditional reputation as a church college, and racial problems, enrollment dropped from a peak of nearly 2,100 in 1971–1972 to something below 1,600 in 1976. In response to this, the trustees tried to trim faculty, but were met with such stiff resistance that only token cuts were made. To increase the cash flow, the trustees voted to follow an investment policy recommended by the Ford Foundation under McGeorge Bundy and adopted by Yale and other institutions. Known as the "total return" concept of investment, it was a scheme to invest the college's endowment in high-growth/low-yield stocks rather than in the safer high-yield/low-growth stocks. The idea was that the latter, although producing maximum income for the college, did not allow the college's endowment to grow with the rate of inflation; while that the former would permit this growth. To offset the lower income derived from the high-growth stocks, the plan called for selling enough of the stocks each year to assure the college of a 5 percent annual income. This, of course, was a way for the college, in a bullish market, to have its cake and eat it too — an endowment that kept up with inflation and at the same time produced a constant and desirable level of income. Unfortunately, they committed themselves to this investment policy at the onset of a number of bearish markets. The endowment shrank from thirty-five million in 1968 to less than seventeen million in 1975.

Micawber had discovered the ratchet effect: that it is easier to expand than to contract and that expansion does not necessarily make a college better off.

This is what happened to many colleges, beginning in the late sixties. This was, economically speaking, the heyday of academe, as enrollment grew by leaps and bounds and new sources of money were made available by the federal government, particularly for programs relating to expanded educational opportunities for the disadvantaged. As a result, colleges, too, grew like Topsy, expanding their faculty and physical plants. Unfortunately, they overbuilt, foolishly thinking expansion would continue when a glance at demographic tables would have shown them otherwise.[17]

At the same time many colleges, such as Micawber, discovered that rapid growth accelerated turnover in personnel and programs, which in turn cut the colleges off from their past and brought about institutional identity crises. They had given up their former role before they had decided what their new one would be. As a result, they found it increasingly difficult to attract students, and thus their tuition income dropped.

It was at this point, faced with deficit budgets and declining enrollment, that they began to cry that increased costs and unfair competition from the public schools were killing them and called on the federal government for help.

Today, all but the most prestigious private liberal arts colleges find themselves overbuilt. According to the *Comp-*

troller General's Report, a quarter of all private liberal arts colleges have 40 percent unused capacity. At the same time, the buildings, many of which were financed with HUD loans in the sixties, still cost the colleges, not only in energy and maintenance, but also in debt retirement. An increasing number of colleges are having trouble servicing these debts, and there are more frequent suggestions that the government simply write them off.[18]

Yet during this period of so-called retrenchment, when colleges are faced with such difficulties and are mortgaging themselves to Uncle Sam, *curricula continue to proliferate by a substantial amount.* According to the Association of American Colleges, between 1969 and 1976, while enrollment was increasing among private colleges by 9 percent, the number of courses offered increased (depending on the kind of institution) by 15 to 35 percent! In only one field (Russian) was there a decline in offerings. Moreover, according to the AAC, faculty grew faster than enrollment over this period.[19] Nationally, according to the National Center for Education Statistics, the number of faculty members (instructor rank or above) increased from 546,000 to 793,000![20]

Apparently higher education is following a policy of "proliferate or perish." It developed, during the sixties, expensive tastes and now, when it can no longer afford to live in the manner to which it has become accustomed, it continues to live in the old style anyway, charging everything to Uncle Sam's account.

This is a mystery. Why should colleges, particularly private ones, take from the federal government in order to increase their programs during a time when they are already overbuilt, and despite the fact that federal support entails federal control? As we shall see in the next two chapters, part of the reason is that they have adopted an educational philosophy that entails proliferation, but there is another reason as well: they do not fear government control because they have lost sight of what it is of value that they are giving up with their independence.

Most federal regulations that affect academe are attempts by the government to ensure compliance with some basic standards of social justice. For the academy to resist these regulations, therefore, would not only be unseemly for institutions that purport to be enlightened, but would also be a denial of their own moral sense as well.

What, however, if the situation changed? What if the nation were swept up once again, as it is periodically and was during the McCarthy era, by a wave of national hysteria that resulted in government mandates that were unjust or a threat to academic freedom? Strangely, this does not worry many on campus. President J. Martin Carovano of Hamilton College, for instance, said, "I am not afraid of government control. The government has always had the power of life or death over us. We are chartered by the state of New York and the state could, if it wanted, take away this charter tomorrow." Dr. Carl Kaysen, director of the Sloan Foundation's Commission on Government and Higher Education, when asked if the loss of autonomy of private universities would make them more vulnerable to a new demagogue, answered, "I think whether an institution is under private or public control has little to do with its ability to protect academic freedom. It is the power of the institution which determines how well it plays this role. A large state university, for instance, would probably be able to defend itself better than a small private liberal arts college. The chancellor might be able to get the governor of the state to call Washington on his behalf. The White House must answer a phone call from the governor of a state but does not need answer one from the president of a college, even if he is president of Harvard."

But these views are simply mistaken. Private colleges did have autonomy that public ones did not have, and it did make a difference. In the 1950s, for instance, two principal means by which universities could imbibe federal funds was through the National Science Foundation (created in 1950) and the National Defense Education Act of 1958. To receive money under these provisions, however, individuals had to sign what was called a disclaimer affidavit. This affidavit was a loyalty oath. Many institutions found this offensive and a threat, not only to academic freedom but also to civil liberty. Yet only thirty-one refused to participate in these programs and by doing so forfeited money for the sake of principle, and *all thirty-one were private colleges!*[21] They were, moreover, not all big powerful ones. Harvard and Yale were on the list, but so were Reed and Sarah Lawrence. Likewise, of nearly one hundred and fifty colleges and universities that, although not refusing to participate in this government grants program, did publicly register their disapproval, only a quarter were publicly supported institutions.

Almost all private colleges in this country began as sectarian ones. The First Amendment, therefore, guaranteed their academic freedom while the great variety of religions in America ensured considerable diversity between them. The differences, for instance, between a Congregationalist Harvard, a Quaker Haverford, and a Jesuit Holy Cross were considerable, as reflected in the curriculum, the code of student life, and the governance of the college. The sectarian diversity, moreover, assured that on moral issues of national significance there were many points of view articulated. American colleges and universities, particularly the private ones, served as countervailing moral forces to each other, to public opinion, and to the government. They ensured that national debate about important issues would not degenerate into a monologue.

During the 1960s, however, many institutions weakened their religious ties. It is not accidental, either, that they made this break at the same time they were attaching themselves to the pipeline of federal aid, and just as the spigot was being opened wider. This happened not because they needed the money — for they were at this time, as we have seen with Micawber College, flush with money and boom-baby enrollment — but because they had decided that the best education was the one with the most options. Religious affiliation limited options, and government money expanded them.

Paradoxically, however, these steps were taken at a time when students were protesting the cozy relationship between campus and the government. This was the time when laboratories were bombed, research contracts caused riots, and ROTC went underground. Yet today the Washington connection is stronger than ever — perhaps unbreakable — and today's undergraduates, when compared with those of the sixties, are docile and obsessed with achievement. This, however, may not always be so. Perhaps if the draft is reintroduced and students are forced to think about *their* relations with the government there will be a new awareness of the campus–Washington axis. When this time comes, will there be another, perhaps greater, explosion? Will they, as their predecessors did in the sixties, feel cheated by phony claims of academic independence, be skeptical of intellectual authority, and unwilling to accept opinions of professors whose paychecks come from a government they once again find reasons to distrust? Surely this new dependence, much stronger than the old one, will one day undermine, in students' eyes, the integrity of scholarship as it once did;

and the effects will be, once again, tragic for learning in America.

There is so little continuity in higher education that the new generation of administrators has already forgotten this lesson. They have forgotten what it was they began to give up in the sixties. Yet the fact that present federal laws are benign should not be a justification for surrendering academic autonomy. Laws change, and educational institutions should be built to survive them. The present laws are harmless in intent, surely, and there is no question that colleges as well as all socially responsible institutions in the country should try to achieve the kind of fairness the laws are intended to achieve. But colleges and universities should not willingly put themselves in the position where they could not, if they so chose, refuse to comply with regulations that compromise their mission. For it is their peculiar heritage, their special role shared only perhaps by the press, to serve as constructive social critics and to act as independent sources of moral judgment, not untainted perhaps, but at least different, so that during times of repression, hysteria, or crisis at least more than one voice is heard. They cannot perform this role, however, unless they are free to disagree with the conventional wisdom of the day and are able to survive economic sanctions and popular opprobrium for the sake of principle.

Twenty years ago at least a few private colleges had sufficient independence to resist a pernicious government policy. Fewer could do it today. Yet without them the country loses a mechanism of conceptual checks and balances and becomes increasingly vulnerable to the inertial forces of uninformed public opinion.

4

ADVISING
The Pedagogical Cop-Out

The schoolmaster timidly flatters his pupils, and the pupils
make light of their master.

— PLATO

Fatjack was hang-gliding again.

"Peel was such a great man," he was saying. "If the horse
hadn't thrown him there's no telling where he would have
taken England. As it was, repealing the Corn Laws made
England the world's most dominant power for one hundred
years. As Monypenny and Buckle say in the *Life of Disraeli...*"

His mind was soaring off, following the sun as it rose over
the British Empire, hedgehopping the successive electoral
reform acts, whizzing over the Crimean War, diving at a
pocket borough here and an Irish peerage there, sailing
through the smog of Dickens's London and weaving between the feuds of Disraeli and Gladstone.

Fatjack was what the students called him. A former football lineman, he had solid bulk of a superjock, a giant about
to burst through his skin like a boiled sausage. An athletic
phenomenon once able to run forty yards in a little over
four seconds, he was even now, at thirty-five and six-one
and two-hundred-and-eighty pounds, still formidable on a
squash or tennis court. His real name was John Percy Fosdick, and he was the Hugh Pecksworth Professor of History

at Farnsworth. Nineteenth-century British history was his specialty, and he was now giving a tutorial (for credit) to his star pupil, senior Ulysses Eng.

Fosdick wrung his huge hands together as he described Victoria's chagrin at Gladstone's refusal to rescue Chinese Gordon at Khartoum. Ulysses sat opposite Fosdick, stifling a yawn, eyes opened too wide as he tried to stay attentive. He had heard Fosdick's speech many times before. All Fosdick's students had. Just the mention of Wellington, Lansdowne, or Macaulay set him off hang-gliding, as the students called it, for an hour. As long as you could stay awake, tutorials with Fosdick were easy.

Macaulay, the nineteenth-century English politician and historian, was Ulysses' senior thesis topic. In fact, Macaulay had been Ulysses' undergraduate career. Ulysses discovered him during freshman year in the English composition course. His instructor had been a graduate student writing *his* thesis on Macaulay (under Fosdick) and all the essay topics — twelve in all — he assigned were on the life, writings, and speeches of Macaulay.

Having put such an investment of time and effort into one man, Ulysses decided to make as much use of this investment as possible. This he found easy to do. For at Farnsworth as elsewhere, few professors, especially in the humanities, gave final examinations anymore. Most required only a term paper on which to base course credit. Thus, instead of mastering the syllabus, the student, to pass the course, needed know only one thing. Ulysses' thing was Macaulay. He was amazed how many courses he could find for which his special knowledge was sufficient. Like a whistle-stopping politician rereading the same speech in each town, Ulysses was able, by making minor adjustments, to use the same essay in virtually very course he took as an undergraduate. He satisfied his general education science requirement by taking a course entitled "Darwin and his

Detractors" and for which his term paper was entitled "Darwin in Macaulay's England." Satisfaction of the humanities and social science distribution requirements in the same way was easy, since Macaulay was both a politician and a writer. Ulysses was unable to satisfy all the requirements for the major in history by application of such a narrow time slice: it was difficult for even the most lenient professor to understand, for instance, the relevance of Macaulay to the One Hundred Years' War; but in most cases his tactic prevailed.

He was able to pass a course in Far Eastern history by writing an essay about Macaulay's stint on the Supreme Council of India set up by the British government in 1834, and he was able to pass a course in American history by presenting a paper on the influence of Macaulay's abolitionist father on the American antislavery movement.

Ulysses had in fact discovered a marvelous game, which he called datagolf. The object of the game was for the player to make the rounds of the curriculum by using one set of data. Obviously, Ulysses had a high handicap. "Macaulay," he was fond of saying, "is putting me through college."

Fosdick, of course, helped. He had been Ulysses' advisor since freshman year. Because he was a member of the History Department, his influence had much to do with Ulysses' choice of major. Having received his Ph.D. in the sixties, when graduate students were allowed to specialize as never before, he had very narrow interests and knowledge, and he saw, in Ulysses, a budding young acolyte. He had, moreover, suspicions about the value of offerings in other departments whose work he did not understand, and he encouraged Ulysses to take as many courses in history as possible. In fact, out of thirty-two courses needed for graduation, Ulysses had taken eighteen in history; and although he had taken fourteen outside history, his datagolf with Macaulay had put him through eight of those.

History was one of the larger departments at Farnsworth. Although Farnsworth had, as Harvard does, thirty-seven major departments, 60 percent of the students, again as at Harvard, major in one of six departments, one of which is history.[1] So Ulysses, like his colleagues at other colleges majoring the popular fields, took mostly large lecture courses and got to know few faculty members personally.

Fosdick was Ulysses' only friend on the faculty. Fosdick was, in fact, very popular, if not respected, among students at Farnsworth. His other nickname, naturally, was "Fearless," the intended irony a hangover from his days as assistant dean of students, when it was discovered he could not say "No." Students who wanted the rules bent in their favor always went to Fosdick, if they could.

"To know only one thing is finally to know nothing," says John Ward, former president of Amherst College.[2] Yet that is all Ulysses Eng is learning. His miseducation is the result of the systematic refusal of anyone in the college to accept responsibility for his education. The president and dean made no attempt to tighten the general education program, to stem the proliferation of courses, or to encourage the giving of examinations, thus delegating educational policy to the departments and making Eng's datagolf possible. The departments, anxious to attract new faculty members by letting them teach what they wanted, and eager to attract as many students as possible by letting students study what they wanted, left educational guidance to advisors like Fosdick. And the advisor, for his own reasons, as we have seen, passed the buck to the student. The student, like Ulysses, impressed with his advisor's erudition and anxious to play the scholarly game himself, eagerly took the advisor's maladvice.

This chain of pedagogical buck passing and pathetic specializing is neither unique nor haphazard. A nearly universal phenomenon, it has surfaced at virtually every college in the country, and it is part of a syndrome built into today's curricula.

This syndrome got its start in the late sixties, when all but a few colleges abandoned the traditional liberal arts philosophy for a policy of options. From the end of World War II until the late sixties, most liberal arts curricula had four components: first, a mandatory set of courses to ensure competence in certain skills, such as writing, foreign language, and, in some cases, mathematics; second, general education courses, which were largely cross-disciplinary and designed to introduce students to the literary classics, the Western cultural and political heritage, and examples of scientific inquiry; third, a major, so that students would have the experience of going deeply into, if not mastering, one subject; and fourth, distribution requirements, which stipulated that students take some courses in areas unrelated to their major.[3]

In the late sixties and early seventies many colleges dropped the general education courses and the requirements in expository writing, mathematics, foreign language, and distribution.[4] One reason why they did was that the great proliferation in course offerings made these courses and requirements seem meaningless. A general education course or program is meaningful only if it is general. But as options were added to the catalogue they became less general. At Harvard, for example, in 1950–1951 there were four general education humanities courses open to freshmen, all with very broad themes such as "humanism in the West" and "epic and novel"; by 1979 there were sixteen offered, many with such specific topics as "civilization of continental and insular Portugal," or "oral and popular literature."

Likewise, distribution, expository writing, and foreign language requirements made sense when students had to choose from a small number of courses to satisfy them, but they made less sense when the number of choices mushroomed. For then students could satisfy these requirements by taking a course of only peripheral importance, meeting the humanities distribution requirement with such a course as "two avant-garde cinemas" (Yale) or the science requirement with a course on "biology and women's issues" or "hallucinogenic plants" (both Harvard).[5] They could, in short, like Ulysses Eng, take courses that satisfied the letter of the requirements but not their spirit.

In this way proliferation in courses undermined an important rationale for the old system. So when the old system came under attack by students who demanded more relevant studies, and by civil rights and feminist advocates who accused it of cultural or sexual bias, and by administrators who were anxious to respond to new demands, and by faculty members who found the teaching of general courses time-consuming and tedious, it was ready to crumble. And its abandonment set the buck-passer syndrome in motion.

This syndrome is what operates today. It has eight stages.

First, the college, when it gave up general education, simply got out of the business of educational philosophy altogether, for the old system was not replaced with a new one. Instead, faculty members were allowed to teach what they wanted and students to take what they wished. This trend affected every kind of institution, including elite ones (such as Yale and Amherst), accessible ones (such as Mankato State), single-sex colleges (such as Hamilton, Smith, and Mount Holyoke), public universities (such as the University of California, Berkeley, and City College of New York), and private ones (such as New York University). For to open a college course catalogue today is to be presented with syrupy rationales for the pedagogical cop-out. The 1978–1979 Yale catalogue "urges each undergraduate to design a program of study suited to his own particular needs and interests," and then goes on to suggest, but not require, that the student plan a course of study which shows a "reasonable diversity of subject matter and approach."[6] The 1978–1979 Smith College catalogue says, "The diversity of student interests, aptitudes and backgrounds, the range and variety of the curriculum, and the rapidity of change in knowledge and ways of learning make it difficult, if not impossible, to prescribe a detailed and complete course of study which would implement these goals and be appropriate for every student. The requirements for the degree are therefore quite general and allow much flexibility in the design of a course of study leading to the degree." Flexible indeed! All a student need do to graduate from Smith today is take thirty-two courses, of which sixteen must be outside the major.[7]

Second, the educational philosophy embodied in the general education programs provided a *rationale* for deciding what subjects needed to be taught, what departments were necessary to teach them and how large they needed to be. Without a philosophy and without a program, such a rationale no longer exists. If, for instance, a college no longer has a foreign language requirement, how can it continue to justify having German, French, Spanish, Russian, and Classics departments? It can do so only if these departments can continue to attract students. Many departments, especially those whose offerings are not perceived by vocationally directed students as necessary for their careers, can no longer feel secure. The departments know they must justify their presence on campus all over again each year, for if their enrollment drops, so do their pay and department size. Exacerbating this sense of insecurity has been the current fad among campus administrators, who, employing a "business model" to all decisions, look on each department as a separate entrepreneurial unit and thus encourage the faculty to respond to the ebb and flow of student demand. At many institutions, particularly the public ones, this encouragement takes the form of basing faculty pay and promotion on student evaluation of members' performance as teachers.[8] The sense of gloom that this insecurity produces could be cut with a knife. Terms such as *hunkering down, treading water, holing up* are the most common heard from faculty members today. As a recent study reported in *The Chronicle of Higher Education* noted, faculty morale is at an all-time low.[9]

Third, this insecurity puts irresistible pressure on faculty to placate a growing attitude of consumerism among students by offering them the courses they want rather than the courses they need. The absence of any general educational philosophy deprives the dean and faculty of any rationale on which to *limit* the number of courses. There is no longer a standard as to what is relevant to teach and what is not. Thus what is taught is determined by demand only. As dropping general education requirements has caused a decline in the number of those courses that emphasized universal themes and shared problems, the increase in electives that students are permitted to take promotes the growth of those courses that pander to narrow interests. The number of courses, as we have seen, is increasing at private liberal arts colleges four times faster than enrollment is growing, and most of these new courses seem to come right out of Disneyland.

Ivan Goldman, Professor of Journalism at the University of Montana, reported recently in *The Washington Post* that at Washington State, "Professors were running around tacking posters to trees to advertise their courses. In most instances the offerings were designed not so much to educate students as to entertain them: philosophy courses on Dylan (and I don't mean Thomas), psychology courses on J. R. R. Tolkien, English courses that study soap opera. No term papers, no final. Translated, of course the posters mean:

Come on in. This course is fun. It's easy, it's righteous. Hell, it's downright mellow. What's more, the prof dresses like a roofer and you call him Ray."[10]

Fourth, this same insecurity has encouraged teachers to give students high grades and grant them any request with respect to dropping or adding courses, granting extensions or incompletes; also to relax course standards regarding assignment of papers and giving of examinations. These developments we will examine more fully in the next chapter.

Fifth, the same faculty insecurity leads, ironically, to stronger departments. As long as there were general education requirements and a stable curriculum, the faculty as a whole, with the administration, was formulating educational policy, and the departments had little reason to want to extend their clout. Once these requirements were gone, the institution had delegated de facto responsibility for educational policy to the departments. But the departments, feeling less secure, were more concerned with their own survival than with educational ideals. Today they see themselves as special interest groups, and they perceive any attempt to reintroduce a general education program as a threat to their autonomy.

Sixth, as colleges have dropped emphasis on general education, students have, like Ulysses Eng, become more specialized than ever. At the University of Montana, for instance, according to Professor Goldman, a 1976 study revealed "that less than 26 percent of its graduating seniors that year took courses not relating to their majors."[11] In this way those who go to graduate school and become scholars enter graduate school more specialized than their predecessors. As the same trend toward excessive specialization has been present at the graduate level as well the last fifteen years, the new Ph.D.'s in academe today have far more narrow backgrounds and interests than their predecessors. The slide to specialization, as the Fosdick–Eng relationship demonstrates, is a self-perpetuating one, fostered by the view so many faculty members have that their principal function is to train replacements for themselves. Thus a real impediment today to the reintroduction of general education courses is simply the lack of faculty with sufficient breadth of background to teach such courses. Even President Bok of Harvard reports to the Board of Overseers that the problem facing implementation of Harvard's new Core Curriculum program "is to find enough professors who are trained to teach such courses and willing to make the attempt."[12]

Seventh, as the decline has been going on over a decade, the quality of faculties is much less than it was. The tendency to lower standards, which begins, according to many national studies, after fifth grade, continues through college. The Graduate Record Examination scores, for instance, have declined fifty-nine points since 1965.[13] So, despite the widespread glut of college teachers (which, according to some studies, means that by 1985 four out of every five new Ph.D.'s in the humanities will be unable to find work in their fields, and over 400,000 Ph.D.'s altogether will be out of work),[14] a common complaint among department chairmen is their inability to find competent scholars. "A department may get three hundred to five hundred applications for an opening," says Dr. Steven Cahn, Program Officer for the Exxon Education Foundation and Professor of Philosophy at the University of Vermont, "but after culling the obvious incompetents they may find a dozen people worth interviewing. Then half of these will be snapped up by Harvard, Yale, or Stanford."

Eighth, within this system virtually the entire responsibility for undergraduate education is delegated to the advisor, who finds himself in the role of educational philosopher by default.

These eight phenomena together comprise the buck-passer syndrome. And as with any syndrome, these causal links form a circle. For, as the faculty is filled with narrow specialists whose allegiance is to the departments and whose philosophy of education is limited to finding their own replacements, any attempt to reintroduce a general education program becomes less likely. Instead, the system feeds on itself. Like the symbiotic relationship between fungus and algae in lichen, which promotes growth through division, faculties and students encourage each other in their pursuit of narrow interests, furthering specialization and the formless proliferation of the curriculum.

A Harvard handbook for freshmen notes that "conferences with [the advisor] are very important."[15] Indeed they are, at Harvard and elsewhere, because he is the only one who is likely to be around to help the student plan a coherent course of study and plot his way through a Kafkaesque maze of options. The 1978–1979 Harvard *Handbook for Freshman Advisers* warns, "[I]n the fullness of time we will be fore-gathering each fall for a regular three-day meeting in which the regulations governing the new core curriculum will be explained: the foreign cultures 'fold-in'; the 'floater'; the 'limited by-pass option'; the half-credit core-count for the selected departmental full courses; and the double credit core count for the designated half courses."[16] Likewise, the advisor at Wesleyan University will need to explain to the incoming freshman the Departmental Major Program, the Standing Interdepartmental Major, the Departmentally Sponsored Interdepartmental Major, the University Major, the Collegiate Major, the options in the grading system, the Latin Honors Program, the Honors Program, the New Honors Program, advanced placement and credit, accelerated study, the Five Year Program, the Special Student Program, the High School Scholars Program, the *nine* study-abroad programs, the summer study program, Independent Study, Education in the Field, the Twelve College Exchange Program, the Teaching Exchange Program, the Teaching Apprentice Program, the Intensive Language Program, tutorials, and Combined Plans of Study.[17]

The *Report of the Select Committee on the Curriculum at Amherst College,* could be speaking for almost any college when it says, regarding its reform proposals, ". . . these programs do not replace the contribution of good advising. To the contrary, they invite a livelier participation by the adviser in the student's ordering of a course of studies."[18] How good, then, are these advising systems on which the colleges rely so much? The answer is "Terrible."

At Harvard, which takes more seriously its responsibilities in this area than almost any college and spends a great deal of money writing an advisors' handbook and selecting and training freshmen advisors, the system would, by any account, be considered a failure. The 1976 *Report of the Task Force on Student Life* noted that house tutors (who have an advisory role in the houses, for upperclassmen) were never given a job description. According to a report on the houses by Harvard's Office of Instructional Research and Evaluation, the system of house tutors was critically viewed by students and tutors alike. "The most important routine decision a tutor makes," according to one tutor, "is simply where to sit down at every meal." The students, when polled on the question of whether a tutor's advice is worth seeking, gave tutors a grade of 5.5 on a scale of one to seven, where one is "always" and seven is "never."[19] Moreover, according to the *Course Evaluation Guide* published by the Harvard Committee on Undergraduate Instruction, "Most freshmen will find they have entered a world where stringent rules and regulations, for the most part, do not exist," and "only rarely will one's academic adviser or senior adviser refuse a student's projected course schedule."[20]

Yet to travel from Harvard's advisory system to those at other institutions is to go from bad to worse. Yale, from 1966 through 1979, followed a set of recommendations (not requirements) that urged (but did not insist) that students take courses in several broad areas, including English composition and literature, foreign language and literature, history and philosophy of civilization, mathematics, natural science, and social sciences. Yale relied, of course, on faculty advising to see that students satisfied these guidelines. Then, in 1978, Yale discovered, when evaluating this "system," that it had been significantly ineffective. Yale found, for instance, that only 42 percent of all students had satisfied the foreign literature guideline, only 58 percent the mathematics guideline, and only 59 percent the natural sciences guideline.[21]

But what did they expect? All they had to do was to read *The Course Critique,* put out by the *Yale Daily News,* the undergraduate newspaper. "It is," says the *Critique,* "often possible to work around rules and regulations. . . . Don't rely on graduate student freshmen counsellors and faculty advisers for information; they generally know very little about undergraduate courses."[22]

In short, although the advisory system today is the principal device by which colleges and universities attempt to direct undergraduate education, it is a miserable failure. Is that a surprise? If the institution cannot say "No" to the student and cannot find an educational philosophy, why should it expect the advisor to do so? As Joseph Katz, Professor of Human Development and Director of Research for Human Development and Educational Policy at the University of New York, Stony Brook, says,

Advising is a perennial problem. There are forever calls to have faculty do more advising and forever complaints about the lack of time and attention that faculty give to it. Part of the problem is not that faculty are unwilling. It is also that they are not able. They are venturing into territory in which they do not have the requisite training (and they often do not feel very safe). Even when faculty are advising strictly about academic matters, they may not be able to disentangle imposing their own preferences or recruiting students to their field from considering what is in the best interest of the student.[23]

5

CURRICULUM
The Patina of Reform

Today advanced knowledge resembles a labyrinth still under construction. It lacks both wholeness and a center. Tunnels extend in all directions, crossing one another occasionally, and the best and the brightest are at work extending them.

— Steven Muller

The class is about to begin. The amphitheater is nearly full. Over 150 students, evincing the sartorial fashions of Goodwill Industries and Eastern Mountain Sports, wait, along with supererogatory faculty spouses and other auditors, for Professor Eikopf to appear. He enters by the stage door and stands behind the podium. He is a small, bald man with shining innocent eyes slightly magnified by rimless glasses. His looks somehow combine the narrow calculation of a petroleum engineer with the ascetic humility of a Buddhist priest. He speaks into the microphone in a low, well-modulated voice.

"Ladies and gentlemen," he says, "welcome to German 101. I am humbled by the number of you present. In this course we will be reading the great classical works of German literature, written by such men as Goethe, Schiller, and von Kleist, in translation. No prerequisites are necessary. Before we go on to the subject of the course, however, I want to cover an administrative detail. So many of you have chosen this course that, having no teaching assistant, I cannot hope to read and correct all the assignments you will be given this semester. Therefore, in all honesty, I would like to ask a favor of you. I would like to ask you to take this course on the pass/fail option, so that I will not need to spend a lot of my valuable time grading your papers. If, however, any of you feel you cannot take this course on a pass/fail basis, I will have no recourse but to give you an A."

There is a titter of laughter. This course policy is not a surprise to most. In fact, for many, it is a reason for being there. Few opt for the pass/fail grade, naturally, preferring the guaranteed A.

Professor Eikopf's courses are very popular. A couple of years ago he was given the Noah Webster Award. This prize is presented every other year to the professor who, according to a panel of college administrators, is considered the outstanding teacher on campus. He also knows what he is doing. He honestly does not like to waste his time grading papers and feels genuinely uncomfortable giving objective grades for work whose qualities can be only subjectively assessed.

Most important, he is trying to protect colleagues. Like so many colleges in the country, his college abolished the requirement that students achieve a certain level of proficiency in a foreign language before they graduate. As a result, enrollment in German, as well as in French and Spanish, dropped dramatically in the last decade.[1] Meanwhile, the dean of the college — aware of the decrease in enrollment for the entire college — is busy trying to cut the size of the faculty by refusing, whenever possible, to refill positions vacated by retiring or departing faculty members. The dean, in reviewing the staffing needs of a given department, looks to see how many "full-time equivalent"

(FTE) students are taught by each member of the department in a given term. If, say, the college average is fifty FTEs per faculty member per term, and the average number of FTEs per teacher in the German Department is twenty-five per term, then, when the next vacancy occurs in the department, the dean will not fill it. In this way, as Professor Eikopf knows too well, the German Department has been reduced from five professors to three. If they lose another, they will be unable to offer enough courses to provide a major in German.

The "battle of the FTEs" is a struggle for survival, where salesmanship is the name of the game and the strong departments are those most successful in providing "marketable courses" to meet student demand. Obviously a gut is more marketable than a tough course.

Although Eikopf is a fictional name, the straight-A professor really exists. His actions give meaning to the current buzz phrase "the decline of academic standards." There is no doubt that there is such a decline. Now everyone is aware of the problems at the secondary school level: since 1963 national average SAT scores have dropped forty-nine points in verbal aptitude and thirty-two points in mathematical aptitude, and our public schools are turning out thousands of functional illiterates.[2] The same situation obtains at the college and university level. As reported by *The Chronicle of Higher Education*, the Carnegie Foundation "argued that, instead of being shaped by a coherent educational philosophy, the content of general education had been determined by a number of internal and external forces — faculty interests, student concerns with the job market, 'relevance,' social fads, and the like."[3]

It is not difficult to agree with the Carnegie Foundation that general educator is "a disaster area." As noted in the previous chapter, this decline has brought about excessive specialization and the formless growth of valueless curricula. But that is not all. In addition:

• Giving extensions on papers and incompletes in courses has become a national epidemic. At Yale, according to a recent report by Associate Dean Martin Griffin, 22 percent of all students took at least one incomplete in the fall term of 1977. Most disturbing is the trend: while only 6 percent of the freshmen took incompletes that term, 20 percent of the sophomores, 33 percent of the juniors, and 31 percent of the seniors took at least one.[4] Evidently the Yale experience shows the rewards of procrastination.

• Grade inflation is also epidemic. According to the 1977 Ladd-Lipset nationwide faculty survey, as reported in *The Chronicle of Higher Education*, "80 percent of faculty at America's colleges and universities think there has been a widespread lowering of standards in American higher education, all but 6 percent of them agree that 'grade inflation' has become a significant if not serious problem of academic standards at their home institutions. Two-thirds admit to not applying as high standards in assessing student work as they think they should."[5] The Carnegie Council reports, "[B]etween 1969 and 1976, the proportion of students with A and B grade-point averages rose from 35 percent to 59 percent."[6] At Harvard, for instance, 83 percent of the class of 1977 graduated with honors as compared with 40 percent for the class of 1957. Also, according to a recent report of the Harvard administration, 85 percent of all grades given in 1977 were B minus or higher (compared with 70 percent in 1965–1966). At Yale, the percentage of A's rose, from 1968 to 1976, from 10 to 40.[7]

• Students are permitted to drop courses, in many cases well past the midpoint in the semester. This means a student can take a course, see how well he or she does and how hard the course is, and, if it is too hard, drop the course. At Connecticut College, for instance, students can drop a course anytime before final examination week. At one well-known liberal arts college 50 percent of recent registrations resulted in drops.[8]

• Many colleges delete from a student's transcript any failing grade. At Unity College in Maine, for instance, this is known as "non-punitive grading."[9] The idea is that successes, not failures, be recorded.

• Fewer professors are giving examinations in their courses. Most registrars report a dramatic decline in the number of final examinations scheduled. At Princeton, for example, Registrar Bruce Finnie confirms that fewer examinations are being scheduled than ten years ago. For fall term, 1979, he reported that no course offered by the Comparative Literature Department gave a final exam. At many colleges examinations scheduled are not given. Richard Shank, Yale Registrar, says, "During examination period I prowl the halls and find many empty classrooms where and when examinations are scheduled. Obviously many who schedule finals are not giving them." At Harvard, one of the few universities in the country where it is official policy that an examination scheduled must be given, of the 1,372 courses given in the spring of 1979, only 408 had scheduled final examinations.[10]

As these examples suggest, America's colleges and universities have grievously failed to maintain minimum academic standards. Surely such standards require that graduating students have taken courses in a range of subjects that a consensus of scholars believes are important and intellectually respectable; that the work done is of a certain quality and students have been sufficiently challenged to gain new confidence in their abilities and awareness of their weaknesses; that course policies recognize learning as a function of time, where taking twice as long to master a subject means learning half as much; and that students have mastered certain fundamental skills such as reading, writing, computation, and reading a foreign language.

Nothing is more trendy than education. Yesterday's heresy is today's creed. Five years ago everyone was still calling for more "relevant" courses and dropping "obsolete" requirements. At that time those who saw a decline in academic standards were either afraid to say so or were not listened to when they talked. Since the Carnegie Foundation issued its famous report, however, it has become respectable to decry the decline, to advocate quality and getting back to basics.

In the last year alone, for example, the Rockefeller Foundation has sponsored colloquia on literacy and the liberal arts and formed a commission to investigate the condition of the humanities; NEH has initiated a nationwide series of meetings on the "crisis in the humanities"; whole bureaucracies in Washington have been mobilized to search for new forms of "liberal learning"; a White House Conference on the liberal arts is in the works.[11] In fact, *millions* of dollars are being spent right now on reform. And at campuses across the country, curricular review committees are being formed, college presidents are writing pieces in national magazines decrying the present state, wars on illiteracy are being launched, and foundations' money is being spent for faculty and curricular "renewal."

Despite this momentum, however, the scandalous state of the liberal arts persists today. For most colleges have accomplished little. Reform attempts have been merely cosmetic. If more ambitious, they have either failed to pass the faculty or have been emasculated with amendments before passage. Thus Yale has reintroduced distribution requirements that are virtually meaningless within the context of their cafeteria curriculum; and Hamilton College, although still without any formal general education requirements, now has found the courage to *suggest* (but not stipulate) that students with their advisors plan well-rounded courses of studies (that is, they have adopted the voluntary compliance program Yale has just abandoned as ineffective).[12] Syracuse has revised its curriculum, creating the "Selected Studies Plan," which "leaves responsibility for curriculum planning largely up to the students."[13] Most of the rest have, like Mount Holyoke and Connecticut College, tried but failed to reach consensus on reform, or they have, like Smith College, shown no interest in reembracing the concept of general education at all.[14] A very few others, such as Harvard and Amherst, have succeeded in passing reforms more ambitious than most in the sense that their implementation requires the redesign of courses and not merely another overlay of distribution requirements. And these may indeed be the beginnings of the next bandwagon. But, if so, this is not much cause for rejoicing, for they are pathetically weak and their prominence today merely demonstrates how barren is the landscape of educational ideas on today's campuses.

The Harvard Core Curriculum proposal is a distinct response to the acknowledged growth of the course catalogue, now containing over 2,600 listings. "There is," says President Bok, explaining the rationale for the core curriculum, "wide agreement today that the General Education Program lacks a clear sense of purpose and permits students to sample from too large and varied an assortment of courses."[15] Yet instead of trimming the curriculum, Harvard has introduced the core, which asks students to take eight specially designed courses in five basic areas: literature and the arts, history, social and political analysis, science and mathematics, and foreign languages and cultures.

Core curricula are fine old educational policies, for the

idea lying behind them is that some courses should be required of everyone. The medieval quadrivium and trivium were core curricula. They ensured not only that every student mastered the important subjects, but also that all students shared a common intellectual experience. That is, the original idea was to ensure overlap by restricting choice. Unfortunately the Harvard program is a core in name only, for rather than restricting choice, it permits students to choose eight from approximately one hundred courses and does not limit the number of electives.[16] Moreover, so many amendments were added to this proposal to ensure its passage through a hostile faculty, that, as the confusions of their *Handbook for Freshman Advisers* implies, it is positively riddled with exceptions. Certainly little common educational experience is likely to result from it, for, rather than a core, it is a honeycomb.

The Amherst program can be seen as an improvement only when compared with what it succeeds. Replacing a completely laissez-faire curriculum, it asks freshmen to take three specially designed interdepartmental courses under the rubric of "Introduction to Liberal Studies." After freshman year, besides satisfying major requirements, the student must, with his advisor, plan his own "adjunct program," which consists of four thematically related courses of the student's own design.[17] In other words, it is an interdisciplinary minor of the student's own choosing. One wonders if Ulysses Eng could make an adjunct program out of Macaulay. In any case, how this ensures "breadth of knowledge" remains a mystery.

Even in ideal, moreover, the Harvard and Amherst programs — and others like them — do not signal a return to the traditional educational philosophy, for where the earlier program emphasized general knowledge, the new ones teach specific "methods of inquiry." Where the earlier programs developed basic skills through attempted mastery of a given body of knowledge, the new ones see skills as ends in themselves, as valuable possessions of "the educated man." Where the earlier program stressed familiarity with the Western "Greco-Roman-Judeo-Christian tradition" the new ones decry "cultural parochialism." And finally, where the old one sought to encourage the student not only to examine his own values critically, but also to engage in a broader search for universal values, the new one limits itself to teaching the student how to systematize his own moral and ethical views. In short, where the old program emphasized the form and content of knowledge, the new ones emphasize form alone. The old one gave the student both tools and material; the new ones give him only the tools.

The Harvard Task Force on the Core Curriculum states, "Our goal is to encourage a critical appreciation of and informed acquaintance with the major approaches to knowledge."[18] As Kenneth Lynn notes in *Commentary,* "*Approaches* to learning are the keys to the kingdom" in this proposal.[19] In fact this approach, quickly becoming the latest educational fad in the guise of "going back to basics," removes the student one step farther from reality, for rather than studying the world, students are asked to study how scientists and humanists study the world. It is reminiscent of the joke the English told to Americans during World War II: "We Limeys," they said, "dream about going to heaven. You Yanks dream about going to lectures on heaven."

In approach to problems of value — what President Bok calls "an awkward subject which fits uneasily within our scholarly tradition of objective analysis" — the new core curriculum is, Bok says, intended to "help students overcome parochialism" and (quoting the Core Curriculum Task Force) "to bring students to grips with important questions of choice and value by requiring them to think systematically. . . ."[20]

Similarly Amherst, ignoring its inconsistency in eschewing both "cultural parochialism" (you see what a buzzword it has become) and reintroduction of a foreign language requirement, offers its freshmen a program that should be called "introduction to methodological concepts," for the first group of courses on the subject of "Sign, Form and Meaning . . . will deal primarily with the . . . questions of how meaning may be expressed and interpreted and where these activities are located in liberal education." The second set on "Nature: Observation and Theory . . . will emphasize the creative and analytic processes through which science has defined, represented and interpreted nature," and the third, on "Social Life and Social Change . . . is not about specific societies or society-in-general, nor is it to introduce students to any particular learned disciplines. Rather the courses will be designed to suggest . . . that intellectual methods exist which allow a degree of understanding beyond uninstructed observation and common sense."[21]

The philosopher Gilbert Ryle made the distinction between "knowing how" and "knowing that": between knowing how to do things and knowing a fact or theory.[22] Obviously both are essential to living. Yet these new reforms restrict education to the former. This represents not only the transference, from graduate school to college, of the professional preoccupation with analysis, but also the adoption of pedagogical techniques that have been tried and failed in high school. High schools have for years emphasized both methodology and "values clarification" at the expense of knowing facts and being familiar with Western society and culture. As Paul Copperman says, "The goal of the new math was to teach children the concepts underlying the basic arithmetic operations. The goal of the new science curriculum was to teach children how to think like scientists. The goal of the new curriculum was to encourage each child to think for himself, to set his own learning goals. . . ."[23] Likewise, in the study of history in high school, as noted by the Council for Basic Education, "History has been diluted as it has become amalgamated with the social sciences and as concepts have superseded facts."[24] Thus, not surprisingly, there has been, according to the National Assessment for Educational Progress, a drastic decline in the secondary school student's knowledge of science, history, and our cultural and political processes.[25] Perhaps even more important, moreover, concentrating on techniques of study abstracted from their factual context has failed to teach high school students to apply what they have learned. According to the NAEP, "[Most seventeen-year-old students] can read, write and compute in well structured situations, but they have difficulty applying their knowledge to new situations."[26]

Yet despite the failure of this philosophy at the secondary level, the only significant educational reforms at the post-secondary level appear to be adopting it. If, therefore, Harvard and Amherst are the bellwethers of the next trend, the result could be a generation of students well trained in the techniques of scholarship, but with very limited knowledge of the world and little ability at applying what they know to their lives.

In any case, neither Harvard, Amherst, nor any other college on the educational horizon (with the possible exception of Yale) is even attempting today to come to grips with the other aspects of the decline or buck-passer syndrome. They leave untouched the problems of faculty morale and unwholesome competition between departments, of student consumerism and excessive specialization, of grade inflation and lowered course standards. More significantly, they fail to tackle the problem that has caused all the others: course proliferation.

Why, despite recent momentum in the direction of high standards, has there been so little real reform? And why are the reforms so far accomplished placing such a heavy emphasis on *analysis?*

The answer most commonly given to the first question is that the powerful academic departments have thwarted curricular renewal. They have become too strong and the dean can no longer tell them what to do. They now have full control of what they teach, of pay and appointments. The Harvard department has been likéned to an independent state, and as Frederick Rudolph notes in his work *Curriculum,* "Departments had grown naturally as efficient groupings of discrete centers of knowledge and faculty specialization. They had provided a logical organizational structure for passing out money and rationalizing the curriculum. But they also became imperial in their power and grasp. Unless handsomely funded and courageously defended, efforts to launch courses and programs outside the departmental structure generally failed."[27]

The answer most often given to the second question is that analysis is the only subject that *can be taught* today: for the growth of emphasis on ethnicity and cultural pluralism and the shrinking of the globe, by destroying agreement on values, makes teaching one morality or one cultural tradition both arbitrary and unacceptable to too many people; and the explosion of knowledge that has occurred in the past twenty years not only makes reductions in course offerings impossible but also has made consensus on what students should learn unachievable. Colleges are reduced, according to this view, to offering the more neutral "tools" approach to education, where rather than being told what cultural tradition or body of knowledge it is important to know, the student is equipped with the means, supposedly, to study the culture and/or science of his choice. As Jill Ker Conway, President of Smith College, notes in justifying her institution's laissez-faire philosophy, "We can no longer say, today, what courses ought to be taught and what ones ought not to be taught. We can no longer say, for instance, that students should study the Bible instead of the Koran. Those days are gone forever."

These phenomena, the power of the departments, the so-called explosion of knowledge, and the popularity of cultural relativism, are indeed impediments to the restoration of the liberal arts. They are, moreover, not unconnected. For the growth of the power of the department has not only contributed to what, as we shall see, is mistakenly called the explosion of knowledge, but also to the campus atmosphere which has made agreement on questions of value difficult to achieve. And conversely, the departmental structure itself is not an arbitrary grouping, but the product of a particular scholarly tradition; and it is this tradition that has not only helped to create departments, but has also generated the intellectual climate that has proved so hostile to general education.

Departments are relatively new to academe, but their intellectual origins are old. The first departments in this country were introduced at Harvard in 1825, ironically as a device to put an end to course proliferation![28] Yet in their divisions they reflected, and still reflect, the patterns of specialization that have been evolving since the late sixteenth century. Until that time Aristotelianism dominated scholarship, and this philosophy resisted specialization. Aristotle held that to know anything required knowing four things about it: what its composition is ("material cause"), what its structure and classification is ("formal cause"), what produced it ("efficient cause"), and what role it played in the system of nature ("final cause").[29] Thus, because to Aristotelians knowledge consisted in understanding things within a larger context, their view of reality was *holistic:* it was essentially indivisible. Within its conceptual scheme, specialization could not even be conceived.

Then, in the late sixteenth century, the "natural philoso-phers" such as Galileo and Kepler made an amazing dis-covery: that they could, by using mathematical reasoning alone, develop formulas which they could use to predict the occurrence of natural phenomena. Nature, they discovered, is quantifiable, just as Pythagoras had thought many cen-turies before.[30] The trouble was that the Aristotelians could not explain how this could happen, for neither a thing's structure or classification, nor its function were quantifiable. In other words, from the Aristotelian's point of view, all Galileo and Kepler could do was explain what produced a thing and what it was made of. They were at-tempting to *reduce* all of nature to efficient and material causation. To Galileo and Kepler and all later scientists, however, they had discovered a marvelous tool for under-standing nature. The fact that some aspects of things appar-ently could not be quantified did not bother them. These aspects they simply dismissed as unreal. The seventeenth-century philosopher John Locke, using a distinction he bor-rowed from Kepler, distinguished between "primary" and "secondary" qualities of things.[31] The former were proper-ties like motion, rest, and size; they were quantifiable and "really in the thing." The latter were qualities like color and odor; they were not quantifiable and were not qualities in reality at all, being merely appearances.

This new method of science made specialization possible. It concentrated, not on understanding things in the larger context of nature, but on *analysis:* learning about things by observing what precedes them in time and by breaking them down into their constituent parts.

There was, moreover, no end to the specialization pos-sible with this approach to scholarship. For if things can be known by breaking them down into their parts, then, since things are virtually infinitely divisible, the possibility exists to carry analysis on indefinitely: knowing more and more about less and less became a distinct possibility.

The currents of this tradition also encouraged moral neutrality and relativism. For scholarly analysis, as President Bok notes, strives to be "objective" and value-free. In making a sharp division between what is quantifiable and what is not, analysis has made a similar division between "fact" and "value"; for the latter is, like Locke's secondary qualities, unquantifiable.

Moreover, this scholarly tradition, geared to perceive the differences and not the similarities between things, emphasizes the differences between people rather than their similarities. The social sciences in particular take as gospel the (questionable) assumption that irreconcilable moral differences between people are commonplace. This thinking is also reflected in how universities judge themselves. There is a whole genre of psychological research, conducted by such men as Piaget, Kohlberg, and Perry, designed to trace stages of development of character and value. These are often cited to show the "good" effects a college education has on value development. Yet these studies all enshrine the view that all opinions of value are equally valid. William Perry, for example, outlines nine stages of values development. The lowest state — characteristic of the attitudes of many freshmen — he calls "dualistic," for persons at this stage see the world as black and white, good and bad, right and wrong. The highest stages, ones that it is hoped the students will reach by graduation, are the "relativistic." When they have reached these stages, they see, Perry says, "relativism . . . as the common characteristic of *all* thought, *all* knowing, all of man's relation to his world."[32]

Existing alongside and countervailing the analytic tradition, has been a synthetic, holistic one. Rather than believing things are best understood by taking them apart, as the analytic tradition does, this view supposes they should be examined within the contexts in which they exist and that it is by putting things together — making connections between things and simplifying — that we reach the truth. This synthetic tradition was largely an inheritance from the Greeks, particularly Plato and Aristotle. It was preserved for centuries as a part of church teaching. Thomism, the theology of the Roman Catholic Church from the fourteenth century until Vatican II, was simply the Christianization of Aristotle. It was maintained on campus in the form of classical studies, which formed the backbone of the liberal arts until the nineteenth century. Its emphasis lay on the intellectual goals of unity, continuity, and value. A heritage of the humanities, but not theirs alone, it pressed for the development of the whole man, for the inseparability of knowledge from value, and for knowing things not in isolation, but within the context of living.

It also persisted as a tradition within science. The goal of the unity of science and the belief that all of nature must be one system have been the sustaining ideas of scientific purpose. The crowning achievements of modern science, Newton's *Principia*, Darwin's *Origin of Species*, and Einstein's *General Theory of Relativity*, are so significant, not because they uncovered new facts (since they did not), but because they systematized and explained the more specific and often puzzling discoveries and experiments of their predecessors.

This holistic tradition, moreover, continued into the sixties. Its commitment to unity, continuity, and value was embedded in the general education requirements. Yet during the last fifteen years the abolition of requirements has banished this sense of purpose from campus, and today the field of teaching has been all but abandoned to analysis. The quantum jump in course offerings, by undermining general education, has therefore also dissipated the synthetic tradition.

This phenomenon of course growth, moreover, is *not* the result of an explosion of knowledge. Instead there has been an explosion of undigested and largely useless information, itself the result of "good minds made tiny by concentrating on tiny subjects" (as Roger Rosenblatt calls it) and by the great infusions of new money.[33] During the last fifteen years the conditions for specialization have flourished as research money has poured in. The federal granting agencies, particularly HEW, NSF, NEH, and NEA, have become the principal instruments in the promotion of overspecialized scholarship. "Too much of this money," said Elliot Richardson of research grants (when he was Secretary of HEW), "has gone into poorly conceived projects."[34] The same is true today. A 1978 study, published by the staff of the House Appropriations Committee, charged NEH and NEA with "cronyism"; that they have, in fact, been coopted by the academic community.[35] A 1978 report by the National Academy of Science claims that much of the 1.8 billion the federal government spends on social science research is "largely a subsidy for academicians."[36]

The result of this money has been a proliferation which has hindered, rather than helped, scholarship. So the humanities, instead of detonating with new knowledge, are, as is widely reported, perceived to be in a state of "crisis." The sciences have become embarrassed, not only with the easy accessibility of grant money, but also with the riches of a new technology that has gathered information faster than it can be understood. Although there are a few fields — notably genetics and geology — that have indeed achieved breakthroughs in the systematization of their discoveries, most have simply become glutted with information. Astronomy has made giant advances in X-ray telemetry and space exploration — and so has greatly increased its "data base" — but has found these advances to provide more puzzles than answers. All the while the accumulation of data makes the task of mastering it more difficult. Sheer quantity requires the expert to focus on an increasingly narrow spectrum of research.[37]

Finally, this information glut is exacerbated by the policy of publish-or-perish. Encouraging the nearly 800,000 faculty in this country to write, whether they have something to say or not, deluges the academic journals with pieces of questionable quality. There were, for instance, 3,250 articles on American literature published last year, double the number ten years previously. There were 850 articles on Melville alone. There are ten journals devoted exclusively to Shakespeare. A subscription to the *Chemical Abstracts,* which is a periodical digest of all the articles written in the field of chemistry, now costs over $5,000 a year![38]

At the bottom of all this activity lies the presupposition of the analytic tradition: that all useful knowledge of the universe and ourselves can be gained by armies of scholars engaged in minute inspection of isolated phenomena. As long as no subject is too narrow to be legitimate, new fields can always be created by dividing old ones. Low-level research, no matter how trivial, becomes grist for scholarship and teaching (as long as "it hasn't been done before"). So it is not surprising to find that some recent examples of scholarship could fit on the head of a pin. They include, according to the *Wall Street Journal,* "The Urban and Rural Jest (With an Excursus on the Shaggy Dog)," "Romanian House Decoration in Stucco," and "Haunted Sites in Indiana: A Preliminary Survey."[39] And with this approach, humanistic disciplines have been led into further emphasis on analysis. Philosophy is now almost entirely taken with the study of language. History has given up the study of events for the analysis of problems, using techniques borrowed from the social sciences. And literature, as always engaged in criticism and now flirting with linguistics, is not far behind

In this way all the fields of scholarship can, so long as there is sufficient money, keep on multiplying by division, in accordance with a kind of academic analogue to Parkinson's Law. The increased departmentalization of the faculty can be seen as simply another sign of this process. And unfortunately, still another sign is the kind of person it produces. Analysis is, after all, the activity of breaking something down. It is, like criticism, an anticreative activity, too often used as an intellectual weapon rather than as a means of finding the truth. So not only are our colleges turning out more specialists like Ulysses Eng, but they are also fast becoming centers hostile to creativity and unifying visions. In the recent piece in *Newsweek* commemorating Einstein's birthday, physicist John Wheeler notes that Einstein's genius was in making the complex seem simple. "Still more uncommon today," says Wheeler, "is the outsider generalist who, like Einstein, can lead the way surefootedly through the complex world of science and technology to goals that were overlooked or deemed impossible by most experts."[40] Surely this is the kind of person our universities should be trying to nurture.

Instead, the momentum of analysis produces someone quite different. It discourages imagination and encourages tunnel vision. It produces the expert, the person who concentrates on the cause and effect of things and not on their role within a larger system of nature. This person may be necessary for technology, but his limited vision is a threat to our future. It is such a person who, as an engineer, knows how to design a power plant but is ignorant of the dangers it poses to life. It is such a person who, as a chemist, develops an insecticide but has no idea or concern what effect this chemical will have in the food chain. It is such a person who, as a physician, prescribes pills to a patient without knowing what their full systemic effect will be. And it is such a person who, as a lawyer, knows how to win a case, but is indifferent to the social effects his victory may have.

The environmental movement has been largely a reaction to this kind of tunnel vision produced by our educational system. By implication the movement also advocates a return to the Aristotelian approach to nature, for the idea of ecology is that things can only be understood within the larger context of a system. This is what Aristotle taught, and Galileo and Kepler rejected.

This demand for a larger vision of life by environmentalists was translated, on campus, to a demand for more interdepartmental courses. Colleges have responded to this demand. Unfortunately, the faculties, by and large, have not been enthusiastic, for interdepartmental courses lie outside the control of their departments and too often are perceived as being in the penumbra of respectable scholarship. What the ecologists were asking is what the faculties largely could not deliver: that they reject the old vision of analysis and embrace a new one of synthesis. The ecologists wanted, not interdepartmental courses, but the rejection of specialties and the laying out of new boundaries between areas of knowledge. But the faculty, whose training was as specialists and whose routes to promotion lay within the departments, could not or would not respond. Thus the environmental movement on campus, once very strong, is now, like the civil rights movement and other relics of the sixties, moribund.

The society in which we now live is struggling to come to terms with the idea of limit. Ecologists are urging us to accept a new vision: that life is a cyclical, self-sustaining system and not an accretive, linear one dependent on unlimited growth. But this "growth" vision, which as a social philosophy is coming to grief as the world shrinks, has also been the vision of the academy. The analytic tradition knows no limits and has led to formless growth and narrow specialization. If the academy, therefore, is to come to terms with limit, it must reintroduce general, integrative courses that give meaning and shape to education; and it must find a principle on the basis of which to distinguish the important from the trivial and to limit the curriculum.

Saying what ought to be taught, of course, requires making value judgments, as, for example, emphasizing Western culture over others. But doing this is not necessarily arbitrary. On the contrary, not to emphasize Western culture but to teach varying cultures randomly is arbitrary, for, contrary to the beliefs of the analytic tradition, completely objective (that is, value-free) scholarship is impossible. The study of cultures, for instance, is an activity of sociology and anthropology. But these two are Western sciences, part of Western culture. To suppose we could study other cultures the way we study our own is to suppose we could simultaneously be members of other cultures and our own. Likewise, we are, whether we like it or not, speakers of the English language, and our educational and political institutions are Western, with a long and special history. It is to be misguided, therefore, to believe we should be indifferent to whether the Bible is taught in our schools, or the Koran. For the study of the Bible and not the Koran is the key to understanding Western literature, the origins of Western science, and the history of Western society and institutions. For our universities not to discriminate between the two, therefore, is for them to deny that we have a past and to risk cutting a new generation off from its roots.

The task of curricular reform is not accomplished with more money. It is not merely the political challenge of coping with departments. It is principally the intellectual task of converting a new generation of scholars to a belief in the necessity of general knowledge. Until this occurs, the student will continue to be neglected. For without an educational philosophy, but only a philosophy for research, colleges and universities are still delegating responsibility for education to the student and his advisor. So the student, left to his own devices, must work out his own curricular strategy to ensure he receives an education that not only trains, but also sustains, him.

6

STUDENT LIVING
Whatever Happened to *In Loco Parentis?*

Higher education appears to have been near the vanguard in
the decline of Puritan values in our society.

— HOWARD R. BOWEN

They teach us to live, when life is past. A hundred students
have caught the syphilis before they came to Aristotle's lesson
on temperance.

— MONTAIGNE

No one knows when Karen stopped eating. No one even
noticed she was getting thin until she fainted in psychology
class. The infirmary discovered quickly that she was ano-
rexic and began to force-feed her. Since Health Services
therapy did not help, she was sent home.

The Health Services analyst suspected the problem was
her mother, with whom she did not get along. Her mother
thought the problem was drugs, an overdose of something
she got at college. Karen didn't know, because she didn't
remember anything.

Some in the Student Affairs Office wondered whether it
had anything to do with the charges she brought against Jeff
Soames to the Student Disciplinary Committee. But since
she had left, that case was moot, and they would never know.

Karen's roommates, however, did know. They knew that she and Jeff had gone together for half a year; that they were both really straight; and that their shared innocence probably brought them together. They knew that Jeff lived in the same dorm and that he and his three roommates shared their bathroom; that the bathroom lay between Karen's and Jeff's suites and that its two doors would not lock because Jeff's roommates had removed the locks as a prank and the university hadn't gotten around to replacing them. They knew that through the bathroom the boys could enter the girls' room anytime, and vice versa.

They remember: Karen's trying to break off with Jeff and Jeff's anger at being jilted; Jeff's charging into their suite several times in a rage looking for Karen; Jeff's finding Karen twice and hitting her; Karen's bringing charges against Jeff with the Student Disciplinary Committee; the committee's knowing how to handle loud hi-fis and smoking in the wrong place, but not knowing how to handle real, nasty violence and doing nothing. Finally, they remember what happened one evening after everyone had gone to bed.

Karen had a ritual. Her roommates often teased her about it. She always carried ten pencils. At night, she would take them from the little plastic sleeve she kept in the breast pocket of her Gokey shirt and would, very methodically, sharpen them. Then she would line them up parallel on the bureau. After that she would get into her pajamas and go to the bathroom.

Since the bathroom afforded so little privacy, she always waited until she thought everyone else had gone to bed. Thus her roommates were awakened that night when they heard her scream. Brenda and Debbie got to the bathroom first. Karen was on the toilet, crying and clutching a wad of paper. Jeff was standing over her, slapping her face.

Jeff never bothered Karen again, and she never pressed charges. Instead, she stopped eating. Last June, Jeff graduated magna cum laude. Karen never returned to college. She works as a legal secretary now.

Karen's tragedy is not unique. Although more extreme than most, it exemplifies the degradation of student life today. For the good old college days are gone. Students now live in a ghetto, and the freshman entering this world is likely to find it quite different from the one he read about in the college catalogue. It is most likely different from the one he left and the one he will enter, too. For what distinguishes it from middle-class life and likens it to the ghetto are not simply the chaos and violence. These are symptoms of something more fundamental gone wrong. What is special about, and specially wrong with it, is the lack of privacy. To live in college today is to live in a fishbowl, where one's most intimate ablutions are shared, often unwillingly, with others.

"People," says Richard Sennett, in *The Fall of Public Man*, "can be sociable only when they have some protection from each other; without barriers, boundaries, without this mutual distance which is the essence of impersonality, people are destructive."[1] This exactly describes the causal nexus that shapes student life and that Karen so unfortunately discovered. For the lack of privacy there produces a psychic assault that both discourages intimacy and encourages loneliness, alienation, violence, narcissism, a more ambiguous sense of self-identity, changed relations between the sexes, greater isolation from the faculty, a decline of intellectual ferment outside the classroom, and, finally, the loss of a sense of community on campus. It is these, in turn, especially the alienation and loss of school spirit, that explain why vandalism and serious crime on campus are on the increase and why drugs have, apparently, been awarded tenure.

Altogether, these phenomena comprise the decline of the quality of student life that began fifteen years ago and continues to worsen today. What caused and continues to feed this decline? Conventional wisdom attributes it to the congruence of two irreversible social forces: recent events, such as the war in Vietnam, which undermined authority on campus, and the new postpill morality, which makes policies of in loco parentis both inappropriate and unenforceable. Yet these factors, although relevant, do not themselves explain what has happened and is happening. Far more important is the new wealth of both students and institutions, and the separation of living from learning that is entailed by the growing faculty interest in analysis.

To see how this is so, let us examine how and why this decline began and how the connection between the deprivation of privacy and student alienation is made.

Until the late sixties most colleges did maintain a policy of in loco parentis. They applied this policy through parietal rules that pertained to student living. These rules restricted visiting hours for members of the opposite sex, limited noise, proscribed drugs, and, in some cases, prohibited smoking and drinking.[2] They had, moreover, a number of attributes that made them easy targets for libertarian criticism. They were usually sexist in that women were subjected to more stringent rules than men. They were explicitly paternalistic. They smacked of "do as I say, not as I do," and seemed hypocritical. And if their intention was to restrict sexual activity, they were miserable failures. So it is unsurprising not only that they were considered anachronistic in a time when civil rights were on the rise, but also understandable that they should still be held in disrepute on campus today. When the dean of student affairs at Smith said recently, "Thank goodness the days of parietal rules are gone for good," she could be speaking for almost any college administrator.

Yet the role of in loco parentis was both smaller and greater than it seems: smaller because it was seldom intended to prevent sexual activity but rather to restrict it by providing students with a sanctuary; just as, in earlier times, colleges had been, like cathedrals, places of retreat from the temporal world. The rule was greater than it seems because it was not an arbitrary collection of dogma but part of a philosophy that had, as its purpose, something more than the inhibition of reproductive activity. To stand in loco parentis was part of the philosophy of liberal education, a philosophy that emphasized the inseparability of living from learning, and the importance of shared experiences both within the classroom and without. Parietal rules were the social corollary of general education requirements. Just as the latter focused on a common cultural heritage rather than on subjects that promote our differences, the former defined the community good instead of catering to individual needs. And just as general education ensured that students would share the same educational experience, parietal rules, by restricting visitors, provided an environment where students of the same sex would have opportunities to talk with one another about this shared experience. The intent and effect of the institution's role in loco parentis was holistic: by enforcing a common code of behavior in areas such as noise, drinking, and visitors, it protected individuals from abuse by their dormmates and it taught students to think about the community's interest as opposed to their own. And, by taking the decision for framing these rules away from the students, the institution's role in loco parentis did not force the students to oppose each other when their interests conflicted.

It is therefore not surprising that the policies of in loco

parentis should have been abandoned at the same time that general education was given up. And it is not surprising that similar reasons should be given for the demise of both: namely, the campus unrest during those times, the prevailing disrepute of campus authority, student resistance to anything deemed irrelevant, the women's liberation movement, and the advent of the sexual revolution.

But, though there is no doubt that these factors were important in the rejection of parietal rules, they did not, in themselves, bring about this rejection. For although there was much ferment on campus caused by the war in Vietnam, the civil rights and women's movements, and although this unrest surfaced as protests for more minority representation in the decision-making process, for black and women's studies, and against university complicity in the military-industrial complex, there were almost no riots or protests directed specifically against the university role in loco parentis. It did not happen that college authorities reluctantly gave in to student demands for more freedom in their living environment. Rather, at some campuses, enforcement of parietal rules was simply forgotten amid the confusion created by the war. At others change came with no more than a little nudging from the students. For the authorities had begun to question their own authority. They, like the students, were persuaded that young men old enough to be drafted were not only old enough to vote but also old enough to run their own lives; and they saw parietal rules as attempts to enforce an arbitrary morality, as sexist gestures, as inconvenient to enforce, and as generally possessing no merit.

They saw the rules this way because they had become converted to a new philosophy of student life. This new doctrine, which could be called the "philosophy of needs," was itself the product of three trends converging on the campus at this time: coeducation, the influx of new money, and the growing influence of the analytic tradition.

The great bandwagon to coeducation began in the late sixties. During the twenty years between 1945 and 1965 the number of institutions for men dropped only 20 percent. But during the next ten years it plummeted, declining in that decade alone by 60 percent. A parallel trend occurred in the decline in numbers of women's colleges.[3]

The reason why these declines occurred was not that colleges wanted to import date-bait for their students, nor that they had found a born-again belief in the equality of the sexes, nor that they were responding to the irresistible demands of young, sexually liberated applicants who would attend only coeducational institutions. The motive was primarily economic. As the better private liberal arts colleges grew in wealth during the sixties, their popularity grew as well, and admittance to them grew more competitive. Each succeeding entering class during this decade had at these institutions higher average Scholastic Aptitude scores than its predecessors. These colleges became accustomed, not only to a higher level of income, but also to higher average student ability.

Then, during the late sixties and early seventies, these colleges discovered to their surprise that there was a much smaller pool of potential applicants than they had thought, applicants who had both sufficient wealth to pay full tuition and scholastic aptitude equal to what these colleges had recently become accustomed to expect.[4] Rather than lower tuition or their admissions standards, therefore, they committed themselves to coeducation. This was seen, particularly by elite institutions, as a way to maintain the quality of their student bodies and alleviate their money worries at the same time. But once one institution went coed it put pressure on others to follow suit. For in doing so it was stealing applicants from single-sex colleges, which hitherto had appealed to a different pool of applicants. When Yale and Wesleyan admitted women, for instance, Vassar and Connecticut College were pressed to admit men, for the men's colleges would be for the first time attracting students who would otherwise have gone to the women's institutions. To protect themselves and increase *their* applicant pool, the women's colleges had to open their doors to men. This worked, of course, the other way round as well. Single-sex colleges fell like dominos between 1968 and 1972: Wesleyan, 1968; Connecticut College, Yale, Vassar, 1969; Harvard, 1971; Dartmouth, 1972, etcetera.

Yet as these colleges converted to coeducation, they dismantled parietal rules simultaneously. This occurred as an exact parallel to the demise of general education, for colleges were converting at this time to a policy of options, both within the curriculum and without. Building the curriculum on the model of a supermarket had already begun, and putting student life on the same basis was the next logical step. In doing so, of course, colleges were committing themselves to a far more expensive policy. For just as the absence of general education requirements caused expensive proliferation of the curriculum, so the absence of parietal rules caused expensive multiplication of alternative undergraduate lifestyles. Most colleges soon made it easier for students to live off campus. As a result many residential colleges became in effect nonresidential, some having less than 40 percent occupancy in their dormitories.[5] Many offered options among food plans, between eating on or off campus, and this deprived their food services of any economies of scale. Many institutions left responsibility for order in the dormitories to the students, resulting in expensive abuse of furniture and fixtures. All this added expense, however, was overlooked, for these were fat times with new money coming on campus in the forms of increased federal aid, swelling baby-boom enrollments, and the emergence on campus of a propertied undergraduate class.

Tom Wolfe noted fifteen years ago how much of America's wealth is spent by the young.[6] Many of these young went to college, in increasing numbers, in the sixties. They brought with them far more numerous possessions than their predecessors did ten years earlier. Stereos, water beds, and automobiles came to be seen by this generation as necessities. They were the penultimate consumers, trained by television to see life as a Chinese menu. It was not that they demanded options: rather, no other way of life occurred to them. Much of their choice, moreover, came through their mobility. If they did not like a place they could vote with their wheels. This scared revenue-conscious administrators to death and made them much more sensitive to student wishes. Students were transferring from one college to another at a rapidly increasing rate. Freedom, brought by wealth, was a new and subtle lever by which students could capture colleges' attention.

Yet, if money was the fuel, analysis was the furnace necessary to forge this new collegiate philosophy of consumption. The faculty interest in analysis, with emphasis on proliferation of minute research projects (of options, that is, for the faculty), deprived the institutions of any rationale to limit options in student life. Faculties, trained in the tradition of objective and morally neutral scholarship, feeling just as uncomfortable with the ethical and cultural slant of parietal rules as they did with general education, welcomed the opportunity to embrace the policy of options, which, by offering the student everything, committed the colleges to nothing.

It was, however, the implicit schizophrenia of the analytic

tradition which caused the institutions to claim they no longer would assume responsibility for how students lived their lives. For this tradition, descending from the discoveries of sixteenth-century physics, is dualistic. When Galileo and Kepler managed to reach truths of nature through mathematical reasoning, they inadvertently drove a wedge between mind and body, for neither these nor later philosophers could satisfactorily explain how a purely intellectual activity — mathematical reasoning — could be guaranteed to yield truths about the objects of sense. There seemed to be two very different things — reason and sense — between which there appeared to be no connection but which somehow maintained a reliable parallelism.[7]

Indeed, their relationship is a mystery. Why, for instance, should Einstein be able to work with equations on a chalkboard and, after arriving at $E=MC^2$, predict that, on the basis of his reasoning, the building of an atomic bomb was possible? This mystery of unexplained parallelism between thought and fact, evident from the fact that Kepler was converted to the Copernican theory of planetary motion over two centuries before his theory could be substantiated by physical evidence, led many philosophers and scientists, from the time of Descartes to the present, to make a distinction between the life of the senses and the life of the mind.[8]

Modern university faculties embraced this dichotomy because it provided the rationale for limiting responsibility. They came to believe their job ended at the classroom door. They were being paid to promote intellectual growth only; what the students did on their own time was their own business. The distance between classroom and dormitory increased as the distinction between learning and living became official policy.

The most important emergent symbol of this abrogation of institutional responsibility was the dean of students. This functionary appeared as parietal rules disappeared. Once there were no general policies for ensuring the well-being of the student body as a whole, the number of personal problems students reported began to increase. These problems — about roommates, visitors, noise, etcetera — could be handled only on an ad hoc, case-by-case basis, and only, of course, for those students willing to come to the administration about them. So the administration, rather than actively supporting a sense of community, created the office of dean of students, whose role was, on the whole, passive, reacting only to the expressed needs of the more vocal students. These deans looked on the quality of student life in atomistic terms, as individual problems to be solved by specific actions. The emphasis shifted from the promotion of the common good to the satisfaction of special needs. This position, which few colleges had fifteen years ago, has continued to grow in size and importance since. When Jill Ker Conway was asked what Smith College was doing to enhance the quality of student life, she replied, "We have recently added several new staff to the office of dean of students."

Yet the nature and existence of this office shows the barriers that have been placed between living and learning by erecting an institutional framework making it impossible to view student academic and emotional growth together. The dean of students is a specialist. His office is separate from, and does not usually report to, the chief academic officer. The job description of dean of students calls for a glorified counselor, a hand-holder, a fireman, a flack catcher. He is usually not a person with a strong academic background or interest, but rather an unsuccessful academic or someone trained in counseling or social work. He is usually compassionate and conscientious, but often anti-intellectual. He identifies strongly with the students, but is kept too busy trying to maintain a semblance of order in the dorms to reflect on how to instruct students to be more sensitive to the common good or how to create a sense of community on campus. And although trained to respond to the needs of the individual students who come to him, he is poorly equipped to instruct these students how to integrate their personal and intellectual lives.

The dean of students, in short, is presented with problems with which he is unable to cope. He has only an endless number of needs to satisfy, needs that increased as the advent of self-governing, coeducational dormitories, and crowding all conspired to rob students of privacy and laid the foundations for their feelings of loneliness, alienation, and hostility.

Many colleges made the change from single-sex to coeducational dormitories without adequate preparation and with little thought how this move would affect students. The results were dramatically bad and constituted a terrible invasion of privacy.

Take Harvard, for example. When it consolidated with Radcliffe, the Radcliffe administration insisted that the Radcliffe Quadrangle contain at least 50 percent Radcliffe students. Since Harvard men outnumbered Radcliffe women better than two to one, this meant that Radcliffe undergraduates not at the Radcliffe Quadrangle would be vastly outnumbered in the Harvard Houses to which they were assigned. If they were assigned to Mather House, they found that not only were they in the minority, but that, like Karen's, the typical suite for six women shared a bathroom (with two semiexposed toilets) with six Harvard men in the next suite.

At the Radcliffe Quadrangle one dorm was integrated by placing equal numbers of Harvard seniors and Radcliffe freshmen in coed halls with coed toilets. It was, according to one Harvard official, "a zoo." Likewise, the Radcliffe dormitories, many of which had been built with a sense for interior space and gracious living, were thoughtlessly revamped with new walls and partitions, cutting up common rooms to accommodate the new influx of Harvard men. The results were conditions which neither sex found tolerable. "Things got so bad," says Professor Stephen Williams, "that we found one whole dorm at the Radcliffe Quad completely abandoned by students. They just moved out. It was found completely empty."

Other institutions acted with a similar lack of planning. Many states, such as New Jersey, for example, require colleges to have separate bathrooms for the different sexes. But in the rush to ratify coeducational living, some colleges complied with the letter but not the spirit of this law. "We had a women's bathroom assigned to us," says one recent female graduate of Princeton, "but it was so far away we always used the men's instead."

The "third roommate" has become a campus institution. This person is, of course, the guest — roommate's boy or girl friend — who stays for extended periods of time, sharing living quarters with his friend and roommate. Although all colleges officially frown on this, few stop it because, as short stays of lovers are permitted, it is impossible to enforce. Few students want to make enemies of their roommates by complaining, and a few of those who do want to complain are threatened with physical violence.

As with Sam and Sally in Chapter 2, part of campus life today is the boy who visits his girl friend and stays weeks at a time in her room, either eating with her at the dorm dining room or being spirited food like a stowaway. "My girl's dormmates," says one Princeton undergraduate who had just returned from a two-week stay at Smith, "gave me dirty looks, but didn't say anything." The frustrated acquiescence to invasion of privacy, which that remark implies, symbolizes the essence of this widespread problem.

Crowding is not merely a function of the number of people per square foot. It is also affected by lifestyles. Some ways of living are more wasteful of space than others.

Real crowding — putting three into a suite meant for two, four into a triple, and so on — is part of policy at, surprisingly, the better colleges. The pressure for money tempts them to take more students than they should. (Ironically, the less popular institutions, which cannot attract all the students they want, are less crowded than the elite ones.) The University of Michigan, for instance, has added 4,000 students since 1968, yet not a single dorm.[9] Likewise a recent report of Yale University notes that its dorms were, in 1978, filled to over 105 percent capacity (a figure they admit to be very conservative): "Each additional student admitted to Yale College today means that somewhere on campus a three-room suite is converted from a triple to a quadruple with a very considerable increase in crowding and loss of privacy."[10]

The more widespread kind of crowding, however, is the result of wasteful use of space by students. As John Fox, dean of Harvard College, explains, "There is less real crowding today at Harvard than there was in the mid-fifties, and much less than existed in 1945. But there appears to be more crowding because of the way students use space. Take a typical Lowell House suite, for example. Used as a double in 1955 and 1978, it consists of two rooms and a bath. The first room one enters is the living room, containing two desks, two bookcases, and an easy chair. The second room, adjoining the living room, is the bedroom, which contains two bureaus and a double-decker bunk. Off the bedroom is the bathroom. In 1955, two fellows, one from Dubuque Iowa High School and one from Phillips Exeter Academy, would use the room as it was designed, sleeping in one room and studying in the other. But in 1978, two students, from the same two schools, would come to the suite with an expensive hi-fi and more furniture. They would take a look at the double-decker bunk and say, 'No way.' For they contemplated entertaining overnight their girl friends and wanted privacy. So they would put the double-decker bunk out in the hall and put one mattress in the living room. The bedroom became one student's room and the living room became the other's. This would create a noise problem (because of the hi-fi) and creeping squalor, because the rooms were being used in a way for which they were not designed. They also had less privacy, for the fellow living in the bedroom had to go through the living room to get to his quarters; and the fellow in the living room had to pass through the bedroom to get to the bathroom. This is why we have a warehouse full of double-decker bunks and this is why the casual observer believes we have overcrowding."

Privacy, because of these conditions, is being obliterated on campus. But without privacy, intimacy between people is impossible. The same conditions militate against a sense of sharing and growth through the society of others. In addition, two further factors, both consequences of the recent changes on campus, make intimacy more difficult for students to achieve.

First, the new freedom of students in choosing their courses of studies means they no longer share many common intellectual experiences. As they are all taking different courses, they have little to talk about with one another. At Hampshire College, where students design their own course of studies and yet where *communication* and *holism* are favorite words, a common complaint by undergraduates is that they have nothing to share. "We get so enthusiastic about what we are doing," says one, "that we want to talk about it. But back at the dorms we can find no one who understands what we are doing." In this way bull sessions, generated often in the past when friends gathered to cram for examinations or talk about assignments, are, if not becoming extinct, at least becoming less free-ranging. Whereas once they combined a mixture of logic, imagination, metaphysics, and hot air, they are today inclined to be serious and career-oriented. "At Princeton," according to one present undergraduate, "bull sessions are usually about what Harvard and Wharton business schools are looking for."

"Since colleges have abandoned responsibility for giving the curriculum any purpose or coherence," sociologist Martin Trow said in an interview, "students must provide this purpose and coherence themselves. About the only device they can find for this is their intended career. This may be one reason why careers are such a subject of conversation and concern on campus today." Yet although what students do in class may be applied to their careers, it cannot be easily taken to the dorms; and so rather than serving as a way to cement a sense of shared purpose, it seems, rather, to isolate them further and, through competition induced by careerism, to separate them.

Second, the advent of coeducational dormitories has significantly changed relations between the sexes and made intimacy, both between members of the same sex and between the sexes, more difficult to achieve. Friendships between members of the same sex are more rare today because they have less time alone together. In the days of parietal rules, a boy might be totally absorbed with his girl friend, but, when the visitors' curfew came, she had to leave. At some point he and his roommate had to talk to each other. The same, of course, applied to women. This is no longer true today. Now if a boy and girl are enthralled with each other, nothing prevents them from spending all their time together. And being together not only diminishes the time they talk with others but also tends to steer conversations they have with others to more neutral topics.

In mixed dorms this discouragement of bonding between members of the same sex is greatest. It is interesting to note that recent studies have found emotional growth to be more rapid in single-sex institutions than in coeducational colleges. Women, in particular, develop a better self-image at women's colleges than they do at coeducational ones.[11]

In a similar fashion, relations between sexes have changed. Earlier pairing has brought on precocious psychological disorders. One of the country's leading authorities on undergraduate emotional development, Professor Katz says, "The intensified relationships [of undergraduate living] have also brought with them the kinds of problems that in the past were associated with later adulthood, for instance, in marriage. These are problems of sexual functioning, break-up, abuse and exploitation, the discovery of inaptitudes [sic] in relating to other people."[12]

At the same time communal living discourages emotional intimacy between the sexes. "Fighting over the john," says one recent Harvard graduate, "did not make for good relations with the girls." Likewise, the instinct for survival discourages many from making the mistake Karen did, and finding in the same dorm a lover from whom one cannot easily escape. Often a kind of incest taboo emerges in a dorm, similar to what was found among young people growing up in kibbutzim in Israel: it becomes a kind of brother-sister tie rather than a romantic one. "The new dorm living in coed schools," says Alberta Arthurs, president of Chatham College, "increases the opportunities for friendship between the sexes, but greatly diminishes the opportunities for romance."

"Many undergraduates," said Princeton's Committee on Undergraduate Residential Life in 1978, "continue to ex-

press a considerable degree of dissatisfaction with their residential life. . . . Paradoxically, the University's success in
creating an open, 'optional' system has also resulted in a
more fragmented undergraduate student body. This system
allows, and to some extent encourages, groups of students to
go their separate ways. Consequently there is much less interaction among students than is desirable."[13] This committee could be speaking for most colleges in America. As
Professor Katz says, "Outstanding is the lessening of the
sense of social connectedness (and social objectives). . . .
Students are again more isolated from each other and some
of them, particularly at highly selective institutions, cope
with this by studying hard, while others react with a tendency to discouragement and more slovenly performance."[14]

Few colleges are making any attempt to improve the social life of undergraduates. Occasionally a dorm will sponsor
its own mixer on student initiative. At some campuses fraternities and sororities fill this function, but these institutions, suffering financially from inflation and an antisnob
snobbism lingering from the sixties, are by and large in
decline. So whether boy meets more than one girl not only
depends more than ever on student initiative, but also often
requires considerable luck. For all these reasons — the lack
of privacy, the crowding, the loneliness, the decline of the
bull session, the lack of social life — almost all sense of
community has disappeared from campus. Students are, as
the Princeton report suggests, simply a collection of individuals going their separate ways.

In this atmosphere of flux where students have no sense of
sharing, unstable elements predominate. According to psychologist Nancy Goldberger of Simon's Rock Early College,
who is conducting research on undergraduate emotional
growth, "The least mature students are [among campus]
leaders . . . in that they are often partners and instigators

of disruptive activity, [while] the bulk of the student body . . . is more conformist and easily swayed by their peers. . . ."[15] It is no wonder, therefore, that many colleges are experiencing a rise in meaningless violence and vandalism, that academic cheating and serious crime are on the rise, that standards of behavior at college are in a disgraceful state, and that drugs continue to be a serious problem. A 1979 report by the Carnegie Council on Policy Studies in Higher Education notes that the ethical decay on America's campuses is accelerating, that many colleges are "reluctant to insist on ethical conduct by students," and that "most institutions of higher education, to a small or large degree, exhibit . . . these destructive aspects."[16]

There is much evidence to support this. "We worried a lot about the sudden surge of vandalism at our campus," said one Macalester College official in 1979, "until we learned that the same things are going on at other institutions." A small compensation, but true. The Carnegie Council reports that theft and mutilation of library materials was found to be a serious problem at over 80 percent of all institutions it studied. The annual loss rate at undergraduate libraries at the University of California, Berkeley, Northwestern University, and the University of Washington is between 4 and 5 percent, where every percent point represents a $63.4 million loss.[17] Lansing Lamont, in his recent book *Campus Shock,* notes, "Over a two year period, in the 1970s, libraries at Princeton saw their losses double; in one year alone more than a hundred journals at two of Princeton's science libraries had been mutilated."[18]

A 1974 poll revealed that 42 percent of Amherst College students and 30 percent of Johns Hopkins students admitted to cheating on an examination or paper. At research universities, according to the Carnegie Council, such cheating has increased from 5.4 percent in 1969 to 9.8 percent in 1976.[19] Lamont cites similar evidence:

Polls at Michigan and Dartmouth disclosed that from half to more than 60 percent of the students had violated the honor code at least once. A 1976 student survey at Stanford found that those who believed cheating was never justified had dropped in fifteen years from three-fourths to roughly half the student body.[20]

Serious crime, moreover, is on the rise. The University of Michigan found its crime rate went up 287 percent between 1965 and 1970, says Lamont. In 1974, "the more than 10,000 individual crimes reported were equal to the number in Syracuse, New York, which has four times as many people."[21] At Princeton recently, authorities there admit, government drug enforcement officials successfully completed a major drug bust.*

What we are witnessing is not merely a decline in moral standards, but also something that signals a serious erosion of the undergraduate psyche. Much of student attention has always been focused on the self, for three reasons. First, the passage to adulthood requires self-discovery and the separation of one's own ego from that of one's parents. Second, "Know thyself" has been a pedagogical dictum since the time of Socrates. Third, the classical problem of personal identity has occupied a central place in the history of Western ideas since the time of Descartes.

The classical problem of personal identity is twofold:

---

* Is this aberrant behavior explained by the conditions of student life? The famous experiments on crowding which John Calhoun conducted with Norway rats in 1958 suggest it is. Calhoun learned that crowding among rats caused many behavioral disorders, including aggression, pansexuality, and sadism, and upset the usual pattern of courting, sexual relations, and child rearing. This environment he called the behavioral sink. Others have noted that such conditions bring about physiological changes — such as enlarged adrenal glands — which suggest an excessive amount of stress. See Edward T. Hall, *The Hidden Dimension* (New York: Anchor Books, 1969), chap. 3, and Edward O. Wilson, *Sociobiology* (Cambridge: Harvard University Press, 1975), p. 255.

first, to say what the self is, and second, to say how it can be known.

What is the self? Cartesian dualism, which the analytic tradition inherited, makes the self seem elusive. For if I am both mind *and* body, then I am apparently two things and have no singular identity. This ambivalence is built into Western speech. For I say both "I sat down," when I *mean* "my body sat down," and yet I also say, "I disagree," when I do *not* mean "My body disagrees." The word *I* is apparently used by us ambiguously.[22] Furthermore, whatever "I" am persists through time. But we know that the molecules of which I am comprised do not persist, but are constantly being replaced. Likewise my mind's link with the past is entirely through memories, which are fallible and limited. I can forget things or misremember them. It cannot be my mind, therefore, that makes me the same person that existed in infanthood, for I do not remember being an infant. Hence the puzzle.[23]

The second problem, trying to say how the self can be known, is the problem of how anything can be aware of itself. The eye cannot see itself, only a reflection of itself. The finger cannot point at itself. The philosopher Kant noted that for these reasons direct self-knowledge is impossible. We come to know ourselves, said Kant, by indirection, as something other than the object of our consciousness. So the self is like the photographer who is never in the picture. We may know him by inference from what he does, and we may see him indirectly, by noting his shadow in some photograph, but we may never see him in his pictures.[24]

The reason why classical philosophers thought this an important problem, and not just an interesting intellectual conundrum, was that the self is the repository of moral and legal responsibility. It is the self we reward or blame for actions. If the self does not persist through time or cannot be known, then questions of virtue and crime, praise and punishment, become moot.

For the same reasons the problem of personal identity is important today. Not only is it vital to the emotional and intellectual growth of young people that they learn about themselves, but it is necessary that they have a sense of personal identity so that they may have a sense of personal responsibility, and vice versa. Yet our society in general and colleges in particular are so structured as to obfuscate the self and make the path to its discovery as difficult as possible.

Social observers such as Christopher Lasch and Richard Sennett have noted that narcissism is the endemic character disorder of our times.[25] It is distinguished not merely by an obsession with the self but also with an inability to achieve self-knowledge. The narcissistic individual is not interested in his own actions but in his own needs and feelings. He is trying to achieve self-knowledge just the way Kant said was impossible: not by observing himself indirectly through what he does, but by trying to observe himself directly; trying, that is, to peer into his feelings in order to find the "real self." This form of impossible introspection is encouraged, Sennett notes, by a society that abandons rules and puts little emphasis on stylized patterns of behavior. Rules of life, like rules of a game, provide the distance — in the form of roles — through which we can achieve some perspective on ourselves.[26]

Yet the factors that obfuscate the self and responsibility in society are present, in spades, on campus. When colleges abandon the rules of curriculum and student life the students are deprived of means for achieving self-distance and instead are encouraged in fruitless introspection. The "deans of students" philosophy of needs abets narcissism. The lowering of standards and the loss of rules has weakened students' conceptions of personal responsibility. The college, as corporation, with its rapid turnover of personnel, and the unwillingness, on the part of virtually everyone, to assume responsibility for its policies, exemplify unaccountability. Rather than performing the ancient precept of promoting self-knowledge, colleges are thwarting this discovery.

Despite the very fashionable recent talk in academe about curriculum reform, these problems of student life are almost totally ignored. It is true that Yale, to its credit, is making a modest cut in the size of its student body to alleviate crowding and that Princeton is contemplating establishing a house system to facilitate the socialization of its student body.[27] But these are Band-Aid measures, which fail to come to grips with the enormity of the problem. Almost all other colleges, moreover, studiously ignore their responsibilities in this area. They don't even want to talk about them, preferring the easier route of phony curricular reform. Even Harvard, which has been more conscientious than most, has done little. The thirty-two recommendations of its 1975 Student Life Task Force were almost completely ignored by the administration, while the recommendations of its sister, the Core Curriculum Task Force, as the world now knows, received great attention.

This reluctance to tackle the problem of reform is the result of many things. The majority of administrators in academe are defeatist and believe that historical currents are too strong to be reversed by individual action, that resisting the new morality is quixotic, and that any move to reintroduce rules into student living would be fiercely resisted. Others simply look for a cop-out and find the rationales of historicism and moral relativity a good justification for inaction. Still others, especially the younger administrators who were themselves reared in the new plastic environment, have embraced the philosophy of needs and sexual freedom and do not understand why they should want to reestablish a sense of community and a new, more wholesome college life. Faculty, meanwhile, stick to research and to a narrow definition of their responsibilities as educators. The poor students do nothing, because, being obsessed with their own economic future, they believe they ought not to rock the boat and because, having no knowledge of how things used to be, they do not know what they are missing. The institutions' cash flow problems, meanwhile, themselves largely generated by the policy of options, contribute to the physical decay of the student environment and provide grounds for the specious argument that reform is too expensive. Finally, society itself is not complaining — yet. As Sennett notes, many of the jobs awaiting students carry with them an institutional definition of their personalities and so the perceived need is not for graduates with a strong sense of their own identities, but for perfectly malleable individuals who can fit without friction into arbitrary and fluxing corporate categories.[28]

Yet these rationales for inaction are wrong. Defeatism is unjustified. The present state of affairs is *not* inevitable and *is* reversible. The national mood is changing. More people are craving more structure, a stronger sense of identity, responsibility, and roots. As long as that craving is unmet, we are in danger, for it may be satisfied in unwholesome ways. The phenomena of the cults and communes demonstrate that many today miss a sense of community and are willing to give up thinking to get it. The success of est, which teaches persons to accept responsibility for what they do, and similar programs of self-help, show that many are looking for a more clearly defined sense of identity. The popularity of *Roots* and the revived interest in genealogy shows that people feel needlessly cut off from their past. On campus students are increasingly willing to accept reasonable constraints on their freedom. "This university could impose almost any rules it wished," said an undergraduate at Wesleyan University recently, "but they don't know it and so do nothing."

Alberta Arthurs of Chatham College recounts how, in response to some unfortunate incidents in the dormitories, involving unwelcomed visits by off-campus people, she decided to lock the dorms and require all students to carry keys. Her entire staff urged against the action, convinced that students would raise a protest. "Instead," she says, "we did not receive one complaint. Not a peep."

The need for reform is obvious, and students are willing to accept it. The real impediment to reform lies with administration and faculty attitudes, which are further fossilized by a lack of imagination. Academics imagine themselves between Scylla and Charybdis, having to choose between a return to paternalism and arbitrary enforcement of a narrow moral code on the one hand, and nearly complete permissiveness on the other. Yet there is a whole spectrum of alternatives open to them. New policies should not be thought of as directed to student life alone. They should be thought of — along with curricular reform — as *educational* policies whose purpose is to promote the intellectual and emotional growth of undergraduates and to restore a sense of community to campus. So long as reform of the curriculum and student life are taken together, many alternatives exist. There are many ways to design the curriculum so that it furthers a sense of sharing; and many ways to design a pattern of living that encourages scholarship, reinforces the community, and protects individual well-being.

7

CAMPUS INDECISION-MAKING
The Slippery Slope

Presiding over an academic faculty was like being pecked to
death by ducks.

— STRINGFELLOW BARR

The scene resembled the pit at the commodities exchange.
The room was filled with angry people, all of whom were
shouting at once. The floor was strewn with paper. Most
were standing, some on furniture, and many were waving
papers in their hands. At one end of the forty-foot room was
a small, pudgy man, immaculately dressed in a three-piece
gray pin-striped suit, standing in front of a chalkboard on
which were written many figures. He was waving his hands
in an apparent attempt to restore order, but everyone was
ignoring him.

The small man was David Oil, president of Farnsworth
College. This was another weekly meeting of his Policies
and Prescriptions Committee.

President Oil had created the committee the previous
year. Its charge was planning the budget, and thus the future, of Farnsworth College. It was not working the way
he had hoped.

Ordered by the trustees to come up with a balanced budget (although otherwise they did not much care what he

did), President Oil had asked each of his campus constituencies — the faculty, the minorities, the students, the "biweekly" (blue-collar) staff, and the "monthly" (white-collar) staff — to choose, by their own means, six of their number to represent them on "P & P," as it was called. These thirty people, together with Oil's staff of deans and vice-presidents, formed the committee.

It operated on the principle that, as Oil put it, "the squeaky wheel gets the grease." Therefore, all members, big wheels as well as small, were invited to squeak. And squeak they did.

The trouble was, they found it hard to balance a budget this way. Each week, Oil would appear before the committee with a "revised, tentative proposed budget." Each week each member would attack it as being unfair to his or her constituency, and each week Oil would be sent back to his office to prepare another draft.

The result was that, the previous year, they had been unable to balance the budget. Unable to reach agreement on how expenditures could be kept within the limits of revenues, they agreed, instead, unanimously, that they would expand revenues. Once that alternative had occurred to someone on the committee, its task had seemed very simple. They would solve their problems by raising more money. Their enthusiasm for this alternative, eliciting as it did vestiges of the old school spirit (they had, after all, adjourned on Oil's exhortation, "Let's all go out now and sell the school!"), swayed the trustees, who, even though businessmen, were not without romance, to accept the plan.

Unfortunately, they had found more money and more students harder to come by than they had thought. Their revenues were up, but not enough. Farnsworth had a deficit budget.

Now they were at it again, and this time the trustees would not be so easily swayed. In fact, they were damned mad. Yet it was not going any better. They needed to make a 10 percent cut in expenditures to balance the budget. At their first meeting, Oil had suggested that it be made across the board, that everyone suffer a little so no one would suffer a lot. But this had satisfied no one. The faculty representatives had pointed out that their pay was already below the national norm; the minorities complained that they were already reduced to token numbers; the custodians observed that this would mean the gym would have to be closed on Sundays, and so on. What Oil would have liked to have done was to end Farnsworth's teacher education program altogether, since over half of their graduates were unable to get jobs anyway, but he knew he didn't dare. Not only the faculty representatives but the faculty union would be down his neck; and the other constituencies would support the faculty. For if they let him make a cut there, who knows where he might make one next?

Oil's job was tough, but by creating the P & P Committee he had made it tougher. He was hoisting himself by his own petard, and the trustees, by their indifference, were letting him. Their philosophy was to let him have enough rope to make a mess of the college, *then* hang him.

So Oil stood in front of his own committee, ignored and despised simultaneously. Yet this time he was eager to get their attention, for he thought he had a solution to which none could object. He knew he could not make any cuts in the personnel budget, for salaries were sacred. The economies had to be made, therefore, in the capital budget. He now knew how to do this; how to make the 10 percent cut so no one would be hurt. He would take it out of the library book budget.

This is a true account of what happened recently at a small liberal arts college. It is also, in fundamental aspects, typical of the way decisions are made by colleges today.

The "squeaky wheel" represents a profound change in governance. No longer can decisions be made by one person, sitting in Old Main, after conferring with a few colleagues. Colleges have become pluralistic democracies, where decisions are made by committees chosen to represent competing interest groups. In this system people are picked as president not because they are competent, imaginative, articulate, or (heaven forbid!) because they exhibit initiative. Persons with such qualities have little chance to make it past search committees whose members are chosen to represent every conceivable side of all significant campus issues. The system ensures that presidents shall be innocuous and safe, have few ideas, present a good image, and, by promising to do as little as possible, will not make enemies or further divide the campus. Even if a president wanted to show initiative, however, he would find the way made difficult. So much power has filtered to students, the faculty, and staff that his area of discretion has been reduced by a Mandarin bureaucracy, a consumer mentality among students, a faculty sometimes unionized and usually divided into strong and competing departments, economic constraints, and the inchoate jumble of federal programs and regulations.

Besides increasing the level of bureaucratic inertia, this new method of governance institutionalizes the ratchet effect for spending. It makes profligacy easy and frugality difficult. It encourages the proliferation of options in the curriculum and student life. It discourages long range planning and, by promoting ad hoc solutions to problems, disrupts the continuity of institutional growth. It puts a premium on self-interest and further erodes the sense of community on campus. It treats all interests as equal and discourages institutional commitment to any set of values. It makes a virtue of deficit spending and tempts institutions to rely still further on government aid.

In short, this new form of pluralistic governance acts to entrench still further the profligate policies of consumerism that pervade America's campuses. It does so because it is, surprisingly, the administrative analogue of the faculty's interest in analysis. Together, they form a new academic ideology, which has brought the present decline about and now makes reform so difficult.

What is this new academic ideology? To understand it, let us first take a look at the old one and see how the former grew out of the latter. This way it will be clear just why the new ideology is antithetical to quality education, and why genuine reform is a long way off.

The years immediately following World War II were a time of academic renewal. The GI Bill brought veterans into the colleges in large numbers, infusing higher education with a new dynamism. In 1945, a prestigious Harvard committee issued a report defining and supporting the concept of a liberal (general) education (the famed "Red Book"). This report was highly influential and had a ripple effect across the entire country. The essence of Harvard's message was that a liberal education was a general, as opposed to a special, education. A general education, the committee held, should introduce students to a common historical and cultural background and should scrutinize the underlying ideals and assumptions on which modern society is based. In effect, general education became humanistic education.[1]

As we all know, institutions in those days had been thoroughly elitist by today's standards. Only one person out of five went to college, compared with one out of two by 1970.[2] Higher education was for the wealthy and, to a lesser extent, but ideally, for the gifted. So the fusion of the meritocratic ideal and the concept of a liberal education as essentially value-oriented produced a vision that was, at least unconsciously, Platonic.

Plato developed his philosophy largely as a response to the Sophists. The Sophists were itinerant teachers who claimed to teach citizens of fifth-century B.C. Athens and other city-states how to win debates and, generally, how to succeed by appearing to be clever. As theoretical support for their teachings, the Sophists developed a philosophy of relativism. There was no central, objective truth: anything that anyone believes is as true as what the next person believes. All ideas are equally true.[3]

So the Sophists were the first egalitarians of ideas. In response to this, Plato held that not only is there objective truth, but the highest truth has ethical value, and the pursuit of truth is an intrinsically good activity. Knowledge is virtue and vice versa. In fact, the only activity that has intrinsic moral value is the pursuit of truth; and the order of reality — the truths that we pursue — is hierarchical. This insight in turn led Plato to a principle of social organization: a society comes closer to the truth (and thus is a better society) if and when the wisest rule, the bravest are soldiers, those with green thumbs grow food, and so on. This meant that the best society is one where everyone does what he or she does best.[4]

Plato presented many arguments in refutation of the Sophists, arguments that were so convincing that they seemed to bury relativism for all time. Stripped to their essentials, they said that if relativism is true then there is no truth, no knowledge (an implication some Sophists, such as Gorgias, were willing to accept). But we know there is knowledge; we have perfect examples of it in mathematics. Besides, if there were no knowledge, relativism, as it pretends to give knowledge, would be false.[5]

For many centuries Plato's philosophy has presented the

paradigmatic rationale for scholarly activity, and it is not surprising that it perfectly expressed the values of the early postwar establishment. Classicism at that time was still very strong. At Princeton in the forties and fifties, the Classics Department was the most influential on campus. Under chairman Whitney Oates, it helped Robert Goheen, a professor of classics, to the presidency of the university and Francis Godolphin, another classicist, to the deanship. President Pusey at Harvard, arriving in 1953, was another classicist.

By saying that knowledge is virtue, however, Plato did not set a high value upon scholarship only. His doctrine also entailed that the pursuit of knowledge and the pursuit of virtue were inseparable, and that what students were taught and how they lived were equally important to the scholarly community. Plato, in short, provided a justification, not only for saying what students ought to be taught, but also for saying how they ought to live.

The private liberal arts colleges at that time at least pretended to be committed to one value: the pursuit of knowledge (and thus virtue). Their ideal was of a community of scholars sharing this value and through sharing becoming a harmonious whole. The method of college governance at that time reflected this vision: if, ideally, relations between members of the community were based on trust, there was no need to provide institutional safeguards to protect individual rights.

There were already at work, however, during this period of 1945 to 1960, powerful demographic forces undermining the Platonic ideology. These forces as a group constituted what Riesman and Jencks called the Academic Revolution.[6] In essence, the Academic Revolution was a transference of allegiance by the members of the scholarly community from the particular colleges and universities that employed them to their professions or professional fields. The loyal Mr. Chips was replaced by the highly mobile professional.

The Academic Revolution had been going on for over a hundred years as just another facet of the trend toward specialization. In fact, it was another manifestation of the momentum of the analytic tradition, which began, as we saw in Chapter 5, much earlier, but which was accelerated by the post–World War II growth of colleges and universities, the foundation of many state colleges and universities, and the demand for faculty members, which in turn stimulated the Ph.D. mills, academic salary increases, and competition between institutions for teachers. As a teacher became more in demand, he saw himself as a philosopher or linguist first and only secondarily as a member of a particular college community.

Also, these new academics, having received a highly specialized schooling in graduate school, regarded themselves as specialists training other specialists in the same field. Thus a professor of philosophy would teach philosophy to students who would become teachers of philosophy, and so on, apparently forever.

Then, too, as professors became increasingly itinerant, few had the opportunity or the incentive to become involved with questions of curriculum and academic standards, or to develop a profound education philosophy.

The violence of the last decade — the Kennedy and King assassinations, the escalation of the war in Vietnam, the invasion of Cambodia, the antiwar demonstrations, the race riots, the campus riots, the Kent State tragedy — destroyed the apolitical, Platonic innocence of the campus. It was a time when it was difficult to put one's mind on scholarship. Students came to college hostile to any institution or individual that did not take a stand against the war or for civil rights. They demonstrated. They demanded more participation in college governance. They demanded more relevant — that is, more political — courses. They demanded better grievance procedures and asserted their "rights and freedoms." They demanded veto power over endowment investment decisions and the abolition of grades and "outmoded" course requirements, including English essay writing, foreign languages, religion courses, comprehensive examinations.

The faculties and administrations, largely sympathetic to the students' political concerns and fearing violence, gave in to these demands to one degree or another, usually without much debate.

At the same time the civil rights movement was accelerating. Most colleges and universities, again responding to student concerns, carried along by the momentum of the times, and making use of newly available federal funds for the purpose, began aggressively recruiting disadvantaged minority students, whose preparation for college was in many cases far below that of other students. This gulf was bridged by a more liberalized application of grading standards.

These events transformed campuses into the antitheses of the Platonic ideal. The supposition that truth was objective was replaced by ad hominem suspicions and a belief only in "commitment." The close-knit community of scholars dissolved into a Babel of conflicting groups, each using the campus as an arena in which to pursue its interests and ideas. Governance by an autocratic, if benevolent, president gave way to pluralistic democracy.

The Platonic ideal itself was given up, not only because events made it apparently too irrelevant, and not only because it was simply not understood by the new students, but also because a majority of the faculty and administrators, themselves children of the Academic Revolution, did not share it. When the students began to attack the system as elitist, the faculty and administration had little ideological ammunition with which to defend the status quo. It was as though the majority were ashamed of the existing system and the more quickly things were changed the less embarrassment for all. The students had exposed a gaping void in educational philosophy.

During this period the social scientist began to assume more influence on campus. These were political times with political problems that were thought to call for political expertise. The social scientists were seen as possessing it. The campuses appeared transformed into microcosmic versions of the country at large, and they apparently needed reorganization along the lines of a state or federal government. Faculty constitutions were rewritten, students' bills of rights were composed, and judicial committees were set up to settle disputes. It is not surprising, therefore, that during this period social scientists and lawyers emerged in positions of power in college administrations. Derek Bok, a lawyer, replaced Nathan Pusey at Harvard. Kingman Brewster, another lawyer, became president of Yale. William Gordon Bowen, an economist, assumed the presidency of Princeton.

The social scientists approached the problem then facing the campuses with a new ideology, and this ideology quickly became the new orthodoxy. It saw the campus as a pluralistic society of competing interest groups, each fighting for its slice of the pie. The college resolved these disparate claims on its purse by a process that could be described as adversarial resolution. This was the policy followed at Farnsworth by President Oil. As decisions were made on the recommendations of committees where all relevant interests were represented, priorities were established by compromise among the different factions. This process in turn rewarded those who organized politically and brought further fragmentation to the campus.

Somewhere in the profusion of competing interests the

goal of the pursuit of knowledge was submerged. At best it surfaced as *one* of the values being touted. If all interests were equal, so were all ideas. If there was sufficient demand for courses on auto mechanics for women (which Goucher College offered recently), then such courses were deemed valuable, presumably as valuable as courses on Shakespeare.

If Platonism was at the heart of the old academic ideology, sophism was at the heart of the new, for this new egalitarianism of ideas was based on a new relativism, a relativism that was derived from the methodology of the social sciences.

Social science is the study of man's actions, values, ideas, emotions, and institutions. The scientific approach to these subjects requires the scientist to be as objective as possible. Objectivity in any discussion of human values requires that the scientist remain neutral with respect to the ideas of the peoples studied. But to remain neutral in any discussion of values is to refrain from making any value judgment. Ideas are so many "data" to be quantitatively measured, not subjectively or qualitatively assessed. This is what it means to be "value neutral."

The social sciences are, or aspire to be, sciences; they have a scientific methodology. Although there are many scientific methodologies, the majority of social scientists have adopted a form of radical empiricism.[7] According to this doctrine, the only sentences that are scientifically acceptable are those that are directly verifiable by experiment. But no value judgment is verifiable, and therefore, it is held, no value judgment is objectively true or false: one is as true as another.

This means that sentences such as "The pursuit of knowledge is better than the pursuit of sex," "Shakespeare is a better writer than Larry Flynt," and "Writing essays on Macaulay, although dull, is good exercise," are no more or less true than such sentences as "The pursuit of sex is better than the pursuit of knowledge," "Larry Flynt is a better writer than Shakespeare," and "Writing essays of any kind, but especially on Macaulay, doesn't teach a person anything of value." It also means that such sentences as "The academic establishment's insistence on the study of Western heritage represents a cultural bias" may very well turn out to be true because, depending on how "cultural bias" is defined, it may be verifiable.[8]

This methodology was borrowed from the teachings of the logical positivists. They dismissed whole categories of propositions as meaningless. For instance, they held that all moral statements were meaningless.[9] When I say, "Stealing is wrong," they said that I am not saying anything at all; what I am doing instead is expressing my feelings of opposition to stealing, just as though I were uttering a Bronx cheer or saying "Boo!" Such statements have no "cognitive content" and there can be no rational argument about them. Moral utterances, therefore, express only emotional attitudes, which have no objective validity.

Logical positivism was given up long ago by most scientists and philosophers, including many of the positivists themselves. It was noted that the principle proved too much; it was too restrictive. Many obviously scientific statements, such as "Electrons have no mass," were not directly verifiable. Many other classes of meaningful statements could not be verified, for instance these: "Mr. Micawber was sure something would turn up," and "Queen Elizabeth the First had the foresight to keep the English fleet in drydock over the winter preceding the Spanish invasion." Finally, the verification principle itself was not verifiable and therefore was, according to itself, neither scientific nor meaningful![10]

Yet this positivist doctrine, germinated but failing to flower in philosophy, has taken firm root in the social sciences. It has done so because it provides a simple (if over-simple) distinction between fact and value, which allows social scientists to make the (sometimes bogus) claim of scientific objectivity. They can claim they are dealing with facts and are neutral with respect to values.

The growth of a pluralistic social framework and egalitarian ethos on campus during the sixties found its perfect rationale in this positivistic ideology from the social sciences. Its message was clear: all ideas are of equal value, and therefore everyone should have an equal voice in the determining of academic policy.

The current state of higher education in America is, as we have seen, the result of a complex series of events, and colleges' responses to these events, which have occurred during the past fifteen years. This period can be viewed as one in which colleges began at a peak; but, attempting to climb higher, they inadvertently stepped on a slippery slope. Every effort they have made since to climb up that slope has only caused them to slide farther.

Clearly the slide down the slippery slope cannot be reversed by taking the same steps that started it in the first place. To reverse the slide and achieve a more profound reform, therefore, requires that these and other institutions of higher education reject the new ideology. They must eschew the temptation to be all things to all people, by rededicating themselves to the pursuit of knowledge and the study of values. They must renew their commitment to the inseparability of living and learning. They must discourage divisive pluralism in their own communities by adopting new mechanisms of decision making that reward partisan advocacy less than current mechanisms do. Finally, they must resist government encroachment by a determination to do without aid whenever possible, and through this paring develop more streamlined and less diffuse academic programs.

This does not mean that colleges and universities must become enclaves of autocracy and intellectual snobbery. Rather, they should strike a balance between the requisites of scientific objectivity and the adoption of values, and between the egalitarian demands of a democratic society and the needs of scholarship. This will occur, however, only when academe comes to perceive that it is not necessarily a microcosm of the nation but an entity somewhat apart and different, a community of scholars, diverse to be sure, but engaged in a common pursuit. Paradoxically, it will serve us best not by copying society but by remaining a constructive critic of it; not by responding to ephemeral political and economic pressures, but by remaining sensitive to the long-range requirements of its mission.

In the next chapter we will see how these things might be accomplished.

8

THE ONE-ROOM UNIVERSITY
Higher Education in an Age of Limits

It was a saying of his [Aristotle's] that education was an ornament in prosperity and a refuge in adversity.

— DIOGENES LAERTIUS

Tis only from the selfishness and confin'd generosity of men, along with the scanty provision nature has made for his wants, that justice derives its origin.

— DAVID HUME

They were sitting in the potato patch that lay between College Hall and the equestrian statue of Aquila Farnsworth. Rodney Haynes was reading.

"So you see," he went on, "that there are no provable ultimate moral disagreements."

"You're being too pompous, too abstract, pedantic," Debbie Potilla broke in. "Don't you mean we never really disagree about right and wrong?"

"No I don't mean that," replied Rodney, as he absent-mindedly clawed the moist dirt with his fingers, "I mean that when we disagree about right and wrong we are really disagreeing about some fact. . . ."

"That doesn't make any sense," said Stan, who at that moment was ducking to avoid the jet from the sprinkler as it passed him.

"Look," said Rodney, trying to be patient, "I'll explain again. Suppose you and I are disagreeing about whether capital punishment is right or wrong. You believe in it and I don't. That looks like a moral disagreement, right? But perhaps you're for it because you believe killing criminals will deter others from committing crimes, and I am against it because I don't believe it will deter. So our disagreement, which looks like a moral one, is really a factual one. It is over whether capital punishment deters. So," he concluded, "what I am saying is that whenever people disagree about a moral issue, you can never *prove* that the disagreement is not really a disguised factual one."

"That's a Sophistic argument," said Justin. "You're just playing on the fact that it is impossible to disprove the existence of anything, including centaurs, unicorns, flying saucers. . . ."

"Let me play the devil's advocate," said Hank Seneschal. "Suppose you're married and suppose I sleep with your wife. We agree about the facts, we agree what's happened, right? But suppose I say what I did was right, because I believe your wife and I love each other; but you say it is wrong because adultery is wrong. Isn't that an ultimate moral disagreement?"

"Not really," replied Rodney. "First, you can't *prove* our disagreement doesn't rest on some disguised disagreement about some fact, say about the consequences of breaking promises — which, after all, is what adultery is. Second, you seem to be confusing self-interest with moral reasoning. If it were a moral position, you'd have to say adultery is always right, for everybody in love, and I doubt you'd want to say that. Third, adultery is considered an evil in practically every society . . ."

"Not every," Stan broke in.

The bells of Morehead Tower began to chime. That meant it was two o'clock.

"Time to hit the dirt," said Hank. "We've got fifteen rows yet to weed. Who's reading next week?"

"Helen," someone said.

"Your turn to choose," said Hank. "What are you going to write about?"

"I've been trying to decide," said Helen, adjusting the straps on her bib overalls. She was a large girl wearing a large button that said, "Stassen in '88." "You know that story about the businessmen who raised cats for fur? Supposedly they found a completely self-sustaining business. They skinned the cats and fed the meat to rats. Then they fed the rats to the cats. I want to prove it can't be done. There is energy loss to account for. It violates the first law of thermodynamics. That's one idea. The other is to explain why that old husband's tale, that hot water freezes faster than cold water, is wrong."

So ended another class at Farnsworth during the 1988–1989 school year. The class was "Core Course 8," otherwise known as "Remedial Bull." It was instituted in 1986, a year after Farnsworth began giving all incoming freshmen a new psychological aptitude test known as the Imago-Levity Inventory. This test showed that less than five percent of all students had any imagination whatsoever, or knew how to laugh. For instance, 57 percent of all students, when asked to draw a picture to go with the caption "The cow jumped over the moon," refused to do so because, they said, the situation was "too improbable." Ninety percent did not see anything funny in the section on the traveling salesman (some thought it sexist, others couldn't see how anything to do with sex could be funny. "Sex is like drinking water," said one. "What's so funny about that?"). Likewise the section on the limerick (again, "too improbable," and many thought humor and verse were incompatible). The classical humorists, from Lewis Carroll to James Thurber, left them cold. Only Jonathan Swift provoked any response.

This, it turned out, was not just Farnsworth's problem. It was a national phenomenon. A presidential commission, studying the "decline in innovation" that had caused America to drop behind most of her economic rivals, had discovered it. "There is," they said, "a crisis of creativity (in America) because a whole generation of students has grown up without imagination or fantasies." The general mood of pessimism was blamed, of course, but television was made the major culprit. "People can no longer imagine without a picture in front of them," as one of the panelists on the commission said.

But, although inability to understand jokes could be attributed, in part, to an inability to indulge fantasy, that was not the whole story, for the eighties was the third straight decade of dead seriousness in higher education in America. The sixties had been a time of high moral dudgeon. The seventies had been unrelentingly careerist, where students were guided too often by a philosophy of opportunism. The eighties had seen the emergence of an underemployed and spiritually starved generation who in their struggles for economic survival had sought refuge in philosophies of alienation and nihilism. The cynicism of Doonesbury, a product of the war in Vietnam, which had seemed funny in the seventies, was, by this last generation, seen simply as *true*.

Now, however, as the eighties drew to a close, a new mood was sweeping the country. The nation was beginning to discover that it could live, and live rather well, perhaps even better, with limits. America had finally matured. It had exorcised the frontier, the wilderness, the myth of the endless matrix of nature from its collective unconscious and discovered, as crowded countries of the world discovered long ago, that real wealth, their future, lay, not off the map, but within themselves. "What we are is what we've got" became the byword. The country began, for the first time, a serious inventory of its inner resources.

This manifested itself in a new round of government and foundation studies, university task forces and public soul-searching. It was discovered, for instance, not only that young people had no imagination or humor, but that they were desperately conformist as well.

Naturally, the educational system received much of the blame for this development. From a decade's perspective, the colleges and universities of the seventies appeared to have taught something quite different from what, at the time, they had claimed to teach. They had claimed, at that time, to eschew "cultural parochialism" and to teach objectivity. But now it seemed that they had in fact espoused a set of values, not only the values of professionalism and careerism, but also, more silently, they had acquiesced to the conventional wisdom of the day on virtually every political issue, including the role of government, the Equal Rights Amendment, Affirmative Action, abortion, capital punishment. In short, the universities had been politically liberal during a time when liberalism was still the national philosophy, and, although this philosophy may have indeed been the best one for the times, the fact that, during this decade, not a peep was heard on campus from the dissenting side on the moral issues of the day suggested that they did not provide a climate where these issues could be openly debated. They set an example for conformity of thought, which that generation of students took with them.

This complacency continued until the dormitory riots at Berkeley and Brown in 1985; the ones that, according to President Kennedy, "made Watts look like a picnic." It was at this time, too, that Farnsworth underwent a major transformation. Struggling with deficit budgets, declining enrollment, deteriorating buildings, and increased costs during the first half of the decade, they had, by 1985, reached the end of their corporate rope. The catalyst, that year, was the third national diesel fuel crisis; the one that was so severe it cut food production in half, stopped most interstate trucking, and caused the food riots in Manhattan. Farnsworth's food services were unable to serve any fresh vegetables, and they knew the next year would be worse. So under a new president, Melony Blanchard, they charted a radically new course.

They plowed up the quad, planting vegetables, making food gardens, which were tended by students, faculty, and administration alike. They assured all faculty members that no tenured person would be released, but introduced a new core curriculum, cutting out three quarters of all the courses from the catalogue. Strangely, the task of reaching a consensus on the core curriculum, something that had seemed impossible ten years previously, had, under the pressures for survival and the new "wartime" spirit of "chipping in" engendered by the energy crisis, turned out to be easy.

Also adding incentive to faculty acquiescence for reform was the fact that by trimming the curriculum, faculty workload was reduced, providing more time for teaching, advising, and research. At the same time a new sense of community developed as the gas shortage made commuting, either by faculty or students, much more difficult. Regular car pools developed. Many Farnsworth people moved closer to school. For the first time the college had a waiting list of faculty members volunteering to live in the dorms and serve as resident tutors. These tutors organized weekend work forces of students and faculty to paint the dorms and together with the entire faculty and administration drew up a new code of student life, trimming options and reinstalling some simple rules concerning student living.

With the simpler curriculum and student life, Farnsworth was able to eliminate several administrative positions. Other such posts it filled with faculty members. A professor of physics, now an overstaffed department, took on, for a raise in pay and drop in course load, the position of part-time registrar, and the college discovered that his interest in teaching and "liking numbers" brought to that office many fresh ideas for the study of college and student performance. It was he, for example, who initiated the highly successful program to correlate data gathered by admissions with undergraduate performance, so that, for the first time, the decisions of the admissions department could be measured.

This transition occurred with remarkable smoothness, since the idea of making Farnsworth a "self-sustaining and ecologically viable academic community" had wide appeal. As Joseph Ditto, Professor of Medieval History, noted, "The new Farnsworth fits squarely within the academic tradition. After all, the grandparents of the modern university were the monasteries. They were the centers of learning in the Middle Age and they were, like Farnsworth, communities of scholars sharing a contemplative life and, by growing their own food, existing as self sustaining societies."

It was in the same climate that the course on Remedial Bull was created. It was a freshman expository writing course, where students had to write a thousand-word theme a week. But it was more. The rule was that every other week the student could write on any subject of his choice, as long as, first, it was a subject entirely new to the student, and second, it had been done before. The first condition was to encourage the student to do significant reading in new areas and to give him confidence in solving problems. The second condition was to encourage the student to find new solutions to old problems. As the course prospectus said, "The task of scholarship in the 1980s should not be to find new problems, but to solve old ones."

On alternative weeks, the instructor would assign essay topics. Hank Seneschal would usually ask students to defend a position that was opposite to the one they were predisposed to take. This is what he called his Socratic method. Thus he asked a women's rights advocate to explain and defend Dick Diver's remark in F. Scott Fitzgerald's *Tender Is the Night*, that women have "made a nursery out of a continent."[1] He asked one staunchly conservative student who had a visceral suspicion of "big government" to disprove Parkinson's Law, and he asked Rodney, a believer in relativism, to prove that there was no real disagreement about values in the world.

The principal purpose of the course, however, according to the Farnsworth faculty resolution, was "to teach students how, once again, to have fun with their minds." The supposition was that intelligence was too often thought of simply as a tool, honed for serious and narrow purposes. This view, it was now thought, offered little sustenance to those who, in the 1990s might, after graduation, find themselves working in a bureaucracy writing memos the ultimate destinations of which they would never know, or to those who would find themselves underemployed and forced to work at jobs that held no intellectual challenge for them. Instead, it was thought, education for the 1990s should be less purposeful, less serious, and more innovative. It should teach people how to be creative even in an air-conditioned environment; it should encourage a variety of talents; it should nurture the imaginative use of free time; it should counteract the idiocy of television. In short, it should teach people to be happy with themselves and others, and it should teach them to live better on less. The Farnsworth Faculty Task Force, in designing this course, noted the many historical precedents which demonstrated how the right education could make the poor life rich: that Spinoza was a lens grinder, Leibniz a librarian, that Socrates was an unemployed veteran, that Hawthorne worked in a customhouse, Trollope in a post office, Einstein in a patent office, and so on.

To achieve this purpose, Remedial Bull was intended to reintroduce students to the bull session. "Slinging the bull" was, they now decided, an "important oral tradition," which had been inadvertently lost during the "decade of adjustment," as the eighties were now called, and when it was lost so was the idea of using the mind for play. Remedial Bull was designed to encourage students to recapture this tradition and this sense of play through writing papers and having arguments about "perfectly useless" issues, such as why some hard-boiled eggs are hard to peel and others are not, or whether a tree falling in the wilderness makes any sound.

There is a model teacher for every decade and in every decade there are other teachers who are waiting in the wings for their time to come. During the sixties the model teacher was the professor of anthropology who used class hours to help students paint political posters. During the seventies, it was the professor of economics teaching courses on accounting. In the eighties it became the Renaissance man or woman, the sadder but wiser professor who cared for his students' character and knew something about life. Wisdom had replaced intelligence.

Hank Seneschal was the model for these new times. He had been a teacher on and off for twenty years, but only recently had his time come. "For two decades," he once wrote, "I've been waiting to play my role." That is not quite true, but he had led a checkered career, one that could not have been plotted with SAT scores, grade point averages, Graduate Record Examinations, and foundation fellowships. He was English, for one thing, going up to Cambridge after four years as an officer in the British army. He had lost a front tooth during that tour, not in combat but in a drunken game of "Moriarty, Are You There?" at the officers' mess in Suez in the late fifties; a tooth that, in perverse vanity, he refused to replace with an artificial one. He had been sent down from Cambridge for helping to place an automobile on a steeple; had emigrated to Canada, taking a degree in philosophy at the University of Toronto; had taken a degree in journalism at Columbia, had worked for *Business Week*, and finally, had left *Business Week* in the early seventies, after writing an unflattering piece on Stavros Niarchos, to become a teacher of journalism at Farnsworth.

He did not last, however, failing to get tenure because of an incident he "provoked" in 1976. That year, it seems, one of his students, living off campus, vandalized her apartment to the tune of $5,000 and refused to reimburse the landlord. As the college did nothing to encourage her to pay the damages, Hank took matters into his own hands. He gave her an "F" in the course and told her that he would not change it until she paid the landlord. He justified this, he told the college, "on the solid Socratic grounds that if a student did not know right from wrong, she should not pass a college course." The college authorities, naturally, were incensed. The Grievance Committee overruled Hank, expunging the "F" from the student's record; and Hank's contract was not renewed.

In the intervening years, until Farnsworth asked him back, he worked as a television repairman (always having been good at that kind of thing) and, after saving some money, sailed around the world alone. When three students successfully sued Farnsworth in 1983 for neglect of the dormitories, Hank was hired to supervise the renovation of the building and grounds. Then, in 1985, when the college made a systematic effort to make the most of its resources, it found Hank had all the qualifications for reinstatement on the faculty. So now he taught Remedial Bull and supervised the grounds. This combination, although new on American campuses, where specialization has been a byword, is an ancient one, for the position of Fellow of the College and Keeper of the Buildings and Grounds is found at every Oxford college. There he is called the Domestic Bursar.

Hank's course, in fact, was modeled in many ways after his experience at Cambridge. As under the unwritten rules for High Table, no student was allowed to write on any subject in his field. As in an Oxbridge tutorial, the tutor simply asked a question of the students and left to them what reading they would do to answer it. But his expectations were high, and woe to the student who had not read thoroughly and thought through his topic before putting pen to paper. He also followed another English practice, in part. Aware that students, when graded on essays, tend to be too cautious, to sit on the fence on major issues for fear of finding themselves differing with the instructor, Hank would grade every other essay. The ungraded essay would receive only copious comments. "What you should strive to do," he told the students, "is to achieve the same degree of originality and risk in those essays on which you are graded as on those on which you are not."

This is a portrait of a good college and a good teacher in the 1980s. It is an example of how colleges could meet the lean times ahead, and it demonstrates that, during the 1980s, American higher education will face not only challenges, but opportunities as well. For enrollments, and possibly revenues, are going to be less than in the past. And while no one can enjoy the prospect of the bankruptcy of some colleges and the deficit budgets and declining living standards of others, consolidation could have a salutary effect. It could prevent further haphazard multiplication of programs that lie at the periphery and not at the center of the liberal arts, and it could provide added incentive for the academy to work for the consensus it failed to find in the seventies.

Farnsworth, for example, had, under President Oil, continued to expand during the seventies in the face of declining enrollments and revenues. The entire campus community at that time refused to believe a day of reckoning approached, and the faculty, infected with the scepticism of that time, could not believe resources were really limited and was unwilling to make the personal sacrifices necessary to keep Farnsworth afloat. In this way Farnsworth was like most other colleges at that time and like the country as well, for the decline of the liberal arts was, in a sense, like the energy crisis. The energy crisis was inevitable in the long run, but it began prematurely, not because of a sudden shortage of energy, but because of an excessive increase in consumption. Consumption had simply grown faster than had energy supplies. So when, in the eighties, a real decline in energy began, the problem that had already emerged in the seventies became greatly aggravated. Only then was the country ready to accept that the solution was not more gas, but more efficient use of it. The country, for the first time, accepted the idea of limits to growth. Americans became forced to agree to a division of energy and a scale of national priorities.

Likewise, the decline of the liberal arts was the result, not of shortage, but of plenty. Too much money had caused proliferation of options, radical change, and abrogation of those rules that defined the community and thus discouraged the pursuit of unity, continuity, and shared values that comprise the essence of the liberal arts. The solution, therefore, it was discovered, was not more money or more students, but a willingness, on the part of the academy, to accept the idea of limit, to work to achieve a new consensus of academic priorities, and to express these priorities in new policies governing the curriculum and student life.

But such an epiphany occurs only in crisis. For Farnsworth, for instance, it took the food crisis of '85 and the rash of colleges entering receivership at that time to force a closer inspection of their policies. For the first time, then under a new president, they realized their choice was between real reform and receivership. Only then did they begin to order their priorities and through this review discover that small can indeed be beautiful.

None of this, of course, may happen. It is possible that our colleges and universities will continue as they have continued, indulging their philosophy of consumption by continuing to grow, by becoming increasingly expensive, and by asking the government to foot an ever larger proportion of their bills. If they do, educational quality will continue to decline and what little independence and diversity still remaining within the system will be lost.

The reform that the Farnsworth model represents, moreover, is not the only one or only good one. It is not a paradigm of an ideal. There is no such thing as *the* correct educational philosophy. No society can be so certain of its needs or its future that it can afford to put all its educational eggs in one basket. It is, therefore, diversity that must be preserved at all costs. This is achieved, not by transforming every institution into a microcosm of the nation, for this transformation not only requires expensive duplication of programs, but because, ironically, it also diminishes the real differences between institutions. Rather, each college should strive to be simple, unique, and homogeneous. In this way the system as a whole will exhibit diversity.

National educational policy for the past fifteen years has rested on a fallacy, what philosophers call the "fallacy of division." This is the error of believing that the parts should be like the whole. It is believing, for instance, that because a leaf is green, all its parts (atoms?) are also green; that because a cake is sweet, all its ingredients are sweet. Our colleges and universities have made this error in believing that because ours is a pluralistic society, each campus should exhibit this pluralism as well. But this policy has failed, not only because it results in less real diversity between institutions, but also because it has been nearly impossible to achieve on any given campus. Typically "diversity" has been interpreted as meaning economic and ethnic diversity. But there are many ways in which people of different races are similar and many ways in which people of the same race differ. What many colleges have done is to achieve economic and racial diversity at the expense of a diversity of talents and interests. At many colleges, for instance, as with professional schools, the pressure of applicants has forced admissions committees to put greater weight on quantitative measures of academic ability, as determined by SAT scores, thus selecting an elite — diverse perhaps ethnically, but not so diverse in interest and ambition. There is little difference between the white youth headed for medical school and the black youth headed for medical school.[2]

The aim of higher education in the eighties, therefore, should be to achieve real diversity, diversity not only of race and income, cultural and religious tradition, but diversity of talent and interest as well. No one institution, moreover, can afford to attempt a complete mixing of these elements. Instead, each institution, relatively simple and homogeneous, concentrating on what it can do best and on whom it can serve best, should concern itself with making a unique contribution to the heterogeneity of the system. This, most emphatically, does not mean a return to any form of racial or economic segregation. What it does mean is that every college can no longer be all things to all people.

Many conscientious people are concerned that educational reform in the direction of higher academic standards signals a return to elitism and to the denial of access to higher education to those people who have only recently gained this access. *Elitism* and *academic standards* have become flag words used in waging emotionally charged arguments over the direction of higher education. Such arguments, however, are unproductive and largely misdirected. Unproductive because, as they raise ideological prejudices, they change no one's mind. Misdirected because this is an irrelevant issue. For while no one institution can simultaneously raise its academic standards and widen its admissions criteria, there is no reason why the system of higher education cannot contain both "competitive" and "accessible" institutions. In fact, such a system is necessary. Perceiving elitism as an issue, therefore, rests on the false premise that all our colleges and universities must be alike. For if they were all alike, the country would have to choose between quantity and quality, between all institutions being accessible to everyone and all institutions being restricted to the best and the brightest.

This point is graphically demonstrated by comparing the American system with a European one. The Italian university system, for example, is and has always been highly centralized and monolithic. So when, in the sixties, students attacked it as elitist and demanded that it be more accessible to all Italians, it did not possess the flexibility to accommodate more students in one place while retaining a semblance of quality at another place. The system was too brittle. To meet egalitarian demands, academic standards were seriously compromised.[3] In America, by contrast, thanks to the large numbers of institutions, this flexibility exists. The demand for open admissions can be satisfied by one institution while the demand for quality can be met by another.

Regardless of the educational philosophy an institution chooses to follow, it must still cut costs, wean itself from dependence on the federal government as much as possible, emphasize teaching more than it has, encourage its faculty to develop wider interests, reintroduce higher academic standards, and reassume responsibility for the quality of student life.

Doing this, of course, faces both political and institutional impediments. These impediments must not be underestimated, nor should they be overestimated, either. The changing conditions of society may weaken those impediments, and more determination and a renewed sense of mission on the part of all segments of the larger academic community can overcome them.

Government, especially the federal government, must be made more sensitive to the peculiar needs and vulnerabilities of colleges and universities as institutions.

Foundations should discourage development of peripheral programs, limit research fellowships, and concentrate their resources on providing colleges with the incentive to refine their institutional objectives and to establish a meaningful order of priorities.

Graduate schools of arts and sciences should, in their admissions policies, deemphasize narrow specialization. They should stress a commitment to teaching and character development.

Professional schools — particularly of law, medicine and business — should deemphasize grades in their admissions requirements and put greater emphasis on a broader range of talents and to a commitment to higher ethical standards.

Trustees and regents must take a more active role in defining their institutions' missions, in supporting the presidents' reform initiatives, and in introducing more effective and less political decision-making procedures. To do this they must be better informed. Most trustees are businessmen and therefore accustomed to evaluating the performance of a corporation by looking at a balance sheet. Whereas this is sufficient when gauging the performance of a profit-making entity it is insufficient for gauging the performance of a college. Too often the reports trustees see do not contain the kind of information on the basis of which they can determine trends and shifts in the institution's performance. Even the kind and quality of financial data most trustees receive is inadequate. They deserve better information and should insist on it.

Alumni should take a more active interest in the fortunes of their alma maters. This interest should not be restricted to financial support; they should also know what is going on and how their money is being spent or misspent. More colleges should create alumni "boards of visitors" to provide the administration with fresh perspectives on all aspects of college life.

Administration should be streamlined: something which is entirely possible when the decision-making process is depoliticized and the number of options in the curriculum and student life are trimmed. Students, in particular, should have an advisory role only. The cardinal principle here is that power should belong only to those who can be held responsible for their decisions. Putting a college junior or senior — someone who will leave campus in a year — on an important committee is inviting irresponsible governance.

College presidents should provide the initiative for reform. This should not be delegated to deans or committees. The general rule should be: presidents act; committees react; faculty enact; deans implement. Highest priority should be given to reform of both the curriculum and student life. In the latter, single-sex dorms should be made more available. Student security and privacy should be more actively protected and the college should assume a significant role in organizing student social life.

Faculties, with administrations, should begin to reverse the decline in standards. They should trim the curriculum and prevent further proliferation by the simple device of prohibiting the introduction of any new course by any department until that department has dropped an old one. Decisions for extensions and "incompletes" should not be the faculty member's alone; a central office should oversee this, to ensure a uniform and fair policy. Dropping courses should be prohibited after a reasonable time — say two weeks into the term. All grades, pass and fail, should appear on the transcript. All but upper-level courses for majors and expository and creative writing seminars should have final examinations. To discourage grade inflation, a professor's pay or promotion should be partially determined by his ability to keep the grade point average of his classes within certain specified limits. At the same time the curriculum should be given sufficient structure to reduce faculty insecurity and reduce competition between departments. The college's commitment to ethical conduct should be demonstrated by the firm application of strict punishment for cheaters: for example, any such conduct should go on a student's transcript automatically, and all serious infractions (or second offenses) should incur permanent expulsion.

Faculty advisors should be better trained and supervised. To provide incentive and prestige to this role, they should be given a lighter course load and/or greater pay. Not everyone in the faculty should be an advisor.

What should parents and students do? What is *their* relationship with the college? Strangely, most colleges have vacillating attitudes toward both. Colleges treat students alternatively as children and as adults, and they cannot decide whether their parents exist or not. Typically, on matters of curriculum and living, colleges treat the student as an adult but send the term bill to his parent; they address all correspondence to the student, but send it to him care of his parents and begin all letters with the condescending salutation, "Dear Jerry." They send grades to parents only with student permission but organize parents' committees to make parents feel more "involved."

The rite of passage in America, always ambiguous, is now, by these policies, hopelessly muddled. What students and their parents can do about it and how the student can ensure himself a profitable and happy undergraduate career is the subject of Part II.

II
THE SURVIVAL OF
THE STUDENT

9

GOING TO COLLEGE
What It Does for the Student and What It Does to Him

One of the benefits of a college education is to show the boy its little avail.

— RALPH WALDO EMERSON

Education should be as gradual as the moonrise, perceptible not in progress but in result.

— GEORGE JOHN WHYTE-MELVILLE

Will It Make Him More Creative?

Some people go to college for the same reason others climb a mountain: because it is there. Others are persuaded by a form of Pascal's wager: that going can't hurt, but not going might. A friend of mine, whom I shall call Dave, thinks it can hurt. What's more, he's right.

Dave is a scientist and a genius. He invents useful things like the "Miracle Methane Converter," a handy machine that turns garbage to gas. He builds houses for the fun of creation — the way others build model airplanes. A lifelong friend of a famous architect, he has built, on his land and with his own hands, two houses, including the furniture that goes with them. He plans to build four more. He is an expert on pre-Columbian art, having dug much of it up himself. In his fifties, he quit a large chemical corporation around ten years ago to work for himself. He doesn't make a lot of money, but he gets by. According to almost any measure, he would be called a success.

Right now he is sitting in his house, drink in hand, in the lap of a life-sized statue of Buddha. A large man himself, sitting in front of the bronze he gives the impression of a split image, a double-barreled guru. "College is a waste of time," he is saying. "The professors are a lot of dingalings. They've never done a creative thing in their lives. They only write about each other's work. I had to unlearn almost everything college taught me before I could accomplish anything. It took me a decade to overcome the handicap of a college education."

Dave has a Ph.D. from MIT.

He is right, too. According to most studies, a college education does not encourage or improve creativity or imagination. According to one study of seven dissimilar institutions, it was found that "in five of them the dropout rates were higher for students identified as creative than for students not so identified."[1]

If Dave is right about creativity, is college in general a handicap? Why go?

Will It Make Him More Money?

For several generations of Americans, the reason for going to college was to earn more money. According to a 1968 national study conducted by the American College Testing Service, earning a higher income was the first choice among male freshmen of reasons for attending college.[2] Taken strictly as an investment, like buying a bond or putting money in savings, it made good sense. In the 1950s the money spent on a person's higher education yielded, on average, a lifelong return on investment of 15 percent. In the 1960s the rate of return had shrunk to 10 to 13 percent, but education was still a sound investment. Today, however, it hovers around 5 percent, well below the rate of inflation and the prime interest rate; and several studies claim that a college education, for the average American, is no longer a path to greater income at all.[3] The report of a study conducted by Dr. Dean K. Whitla, at the Harvard University Office of Instructional Research and Evaluation, which investigated the benefits of attending college at five very different institutions (one being Harvard), noted, for instance, ". . . the income differential favoring the college graduate has all but disappeared."[4]

The disappearance of the college education as a sound investment decision was put forcefully by Caroline Bird in *The Case against College*. A college education, she says, is "the dumbest investment you can make." For example, suppose a 1972 Princeton male freshman had invested the $34,181 his diploma cost him at "7.5 percent interest compounded daily, he would have at retirement age of 64 a total of $1,129,200 or $528,200 more than the earnings of a male college graduate."[5]

Why is college no longer a good economic investment? Not primarily because it has become more expensive, for as we saw in Chapter 3, net college costs have not gone up faster than the rate of inflation. Rather, the lifetime earnings of college graduates have been in decline since the sixties, and the lifetime earnings of noncollege graduates have increased. The reason for this is simple. There has been a slackening of growth of those occupations that require a college degree, while at the same time there has been a great growth in the number of those graduates. There is an excess supply of educated labor.[6] According to the Bureau of Labor Statistics, unemployment among high school graduates and dropouts has decreased during the last few years, while unemployment among college graduates has increased. Between now and 1985, one quarter of all college graduates will be working at jobs that do not require a degree. The Organization of Economic Cooperation and Development predicts a surplus of 950,000 college graduates in the next ten years. Likewise, fewer people are willing to do necessary menial and physical labor, so the rate of pay for such occupations has increased faster than the rate for others.[7]

These pessimistic projections do not mean that a college education is not necessarily a good investment for you: that depends on your family background (children of college graduates derive more benefit from college than children of nongraduates), intelligence, talents (both potentially significant factors in upward mobility), and drive.[8] Moreover, Ms. Bird's argument does not take account of what I call the Stanley effect.

Stanley is the son of friends of ours; the youngest of four children. His three older sisters all went to good private colleges, which cost their parents about $7,000 a year per child. Stanley decided not to go to college. So his parents, "to be fair," and having the money, gave him the equivalent amount of money they would have spent on his education: around $30,000. Stanley did not put the money in the bank, as Ms. Bird advises; he did not buy bonds. He bought a sports car, gave some nice parties, bought expensive presents for his friends, took transcontinental plane trips. In a year the money was gone. The Stanley effect, therefore, is this: Ms. Bird's argument works only if the student can persuade his parents to give him the money they would have spent on his education (assuming, also, he does not qualify for financial aid or a low interest loan) and only if the student does in fact put the money in the bank and not touch it for forty-five years (and only if the bank is still in business at that time and savings have not been wiped out by inflation).

So college may still be a good financial investment; but the point is: don't count on it. Going to college cannot be justified on economic grounds alone anymore.

What Other Kinds of Reasons Are There?

In the last fifteen years there have been many attempts to measure the nonpecuniary value of a college education. These are the so-called value-added studies. They evaluate the effect of higher education on such things as students' emotional and intellectual growth, changes in attitudes and behavior. They are all attempts to find what benefits, besides money, are derived from a college education.

What do these studies tell us? That is hard to say. They do not always agree, and most contain one or more of the following weaknesses: first, they are all conducted by academicians and therefore probably contain a pro-academy bias. Would you believe an evaluation of the social contributions of the oil industry conducted by the Mobil Oil Corporation? Second, almost all the researchers — as does the entire academy — have a liberal bias, a bias in favor of change, against authority, in favor of relativism and against traditional morality, against established religion and in favor of "adjustment" to change, and so on. So when a researcher says, for example, "Our study . . . suggests that college attendance results in constructive growth,"[9] one does not know what this means until one takes the particular biases of the researcher into account. Third, most of these studies compare the changes in college students between freshman and senior year. But the ages eighteen to twenty-two are ones of tremendous growth for everyone, not just college students. Lacking a "control group," these studies cannot tell us, in most cases, whether the "positive growth" they record between freshman and senior years are due to the college experience or simply to surviving twenty-two years. Fourth, as we have seen, life on campus has changed greatly during the last decade, yet many of these studies were done in the early seventies. What they report, therefore, although once true, may no longer be accurate.

With these caveats, these studies are still useful. They do show patterns, both good and bad, and they do confirm the conclusions reached in Part I. Below is a summary of this research, drawn largely but not entirely from a 1977 compendium of these studies prepared by Howard R. Bowen for the Carnegie Council on Policy Studies in Higher Education.[10] Showing my own biases, I have divided them into three categories: "some good things a college education will not do," "some bad things it will do," and "some good things it will do."

Some Good Things a College Education Will Not Do

1. A college education is not likely to improve writing skills. According to the Whitla study, which compared freshmen and seniors in writing at five different colleges, "While we would like to report that all seniors composed more forceful and logical essays, made fewer syntactical mistakes, and even spelled better, we cannot . . . a group of natural science seniors who were very able by SAT standards, did very poorly — worse than their able freshmen counterparts."[11]

2. A college education is not likely to improve one's ability to reason. Ability to reason is defined here as "the ability and disposition to think logically on the basis of useful assumptions; see facts and events objectively — distinguishing the normative, ideological, and emotive from the positive and factual; weigh evidence and evaluate facts and ideas critically; think independently; analyze and synthesize." Although some studies found college produced a "small increase in rationality," one researcher found that "male dropouts showed slightly greater gain [in ability to reason] than those who persisted in college four years."[12]

3. *Ability to learn is not enhanced by a college education.* A Whitla study, designed to test whether seniors could master new material more quickly than freshmen could, discovered that "seniors did not learn at a significantly faster rate than freshmen."[13]

4. *As we have seen, a college education does not increase a person's creativity.*

5. *There is no evidence, that a college education will make students more wise or prudent.*[14]

6. *As we have seen, a college education will not, on average, significantly improve earnings.*

7. *Going to college does not ensure that a student will be associating with the best and brightest elements of society, nor that he will be living in a heterogeneous social environment.* Educators have long noted that a student's peers are the single largest determinant of what and how much he learns. As Woodrow Wilson said, "The real intellectual life of a body of undergraduates, if there be any, manifests itself not in the classroom, but in what they do and talk of and set before themselves as their favorite objects between classes and lectures." Yet, according to Bowen, "Millions of young people who are not attending college are more capable, actually or potentially, than many who are."[15] Likewise, on diversity, according to Professors Cliff Wing and Michael Wallach in their important study on admissions, *College Admissions and the Psychology of Talent*: "Our research indicates, first, that [admissions practices] revolve tightly around intelligence test scores and grades; second, that talented attainments of high orders of quality ranging across a wide spectrum of valued fields of human endeavor as ex-

hibited outside the classroom count for relatively little; and third, that such attainments could count for much more, in the sense that favoring students who display them would lead to a class 50 to 60 percent different from the class actually admitted."[16]

8. *College graduates, on the whole, are not more satisfied with their jobs than those without a college degree.* In a 1969 survey of job satisfaction, for instance, while 97 percent of college graduates were at least reasonably satisfied with their work, fully 94 percent of high school graduates were as well (although job satisfaction has been declining for everyone, see below, Chapter 14).[17]

Some Bad Things a College Education Will Do

1. A college education will not teach intellectual honesty and probably teaches intellectual dishonesty. Studies done ten years ago showed colleges' influence in this regard to be neutral, but, as we have seen (in Chapter 6), plagiarism and other forms of cheating have been endemic since the early seventies.[18]

2. As we saw in Chapter 6, there is much evidence that the college experience increases a feeling of alienation, anxiety, and unhappiness. This is supported by a poll conducted by Dr. Whitla, which concluded that "anxiety increased modestly between freshmen and seniors" and "happiness decreased between freshmen and seniors at the Private College."[19]

3. The college experience makes students more aggressive and less sociable. The Bowen report notes that "in another set of studies, which measure sociability and friendliness . . . seniors appeared to be 'less sociable,' 'less socially adventurous,' 'less socially integrated,' 'less friendly' and 'more aggressive.' They also appeared to have less need for affiliation and less need to be nurturant to others. Comparative attitudes of freshmen and seniors toward developing 'ability to get along with different kinds of people' supply another bit of evidence on the matter of sociability. In a series of studies, relatively fewer seniors than freshmen rated interpersonal skills as an important goal."[20]

4. *The college experience has not contributed to development of a need for achievement, while it has increased the desire for personal power.* The Whitla study, for instance, could find no evidence that the college experience (in 1977) enhanced the sense of need for achievement and speculated, "It is conceivable that young people have become more sceptical about the chances for accomplishment." The same study discovered that while 24 percent of private college freshman males were motivated by a desire for power, 35 percent of private college male seniors were so motivated.[21]

5. *Coeducational colleges diminish women's self-esteem and self-confidence and all colleges increase women's fear of success.* In 1979 the *Chronicle of Higher Education*, summarizing the results of a study on coeducation financed by the Ford Foundation and the Rockefeller Family Fund, stated, "Men and women enter college with similarly high aspirations, . . . but women lose much of their ambition during undergraduate years. In addition women students at six of the country's most prestigious colleges have lower self-esteem even though their grades are about the same." Likewise, the Whitla study notes that fear of success increased among private-college women.[22]

6. *A college education does not improve a person's ability to reason about ethical issues and discourages moral conduct.* The Bowen study notes that "current critics of higher education seem to hit the mark by stressing a breakdown of conventional standards of personal morality on the campus" and goes on to suggest the reasons for this are, first, "the influences of higher education that make students intel-

lectually more flexible and tolerant, as well as less authoritarian and dogmatic, also operate to make students more flexible, permissive, and relativistic in their personal and social value judgements. Second, higher education probably has been more effective in promulgating social values as *ideas* about war and peace, international affairs, human rights, human equality, and the environment than it has in strengthening individual value systems of *personal* morality."[23] As we saw in Chapter 6, this decline is nearly universal.

7. *A college education weakens personal commitment to established religion.* The Bowen report notes, "As measured by the Allport-Vernon and Allport-Vernon-Lindzey scales, the relative strength of religious values declines during college. Virtually all studies using this scale have reached this conclusion." A typical example of the degree of this trend was the change in attitudes of a sampling of National Merit Scholarship winners (polled in 1962). When asked, "Do you personally feel that you need to believe in some sort of religious faith?" 88 percent of freshmen gave affirmative responses, while only 51 percent of seniors gave the same answer.[24]

Some Good Things a College Education Will Do

1. *A college education does improve, somewhat, a person's verbal skills, including his ability to mount effective oral arguments, his quantitative skills, and his vocabulary.* The average increases in scores, for instance (on a special test designed by the Educational Testing Service), between sophomore and senior year were 31 points in mathematics, 35 in "effectiveness of expression," and 27 in vocabulary.[25]

2. *A college education does result in an increase in substantive knowledge.* The average improvement on scores on

the Graduate Record Examination between freshman and senior years is 100 points.[26]

3. A college education does motivate people to continue to learn for the rest of their lives. This "residue" of a college education is significant, and is reflected in the college graduate's greater participation in political, artistic, educational, and cultural activities. A 1975 study revealed that 79 percent of college graduates had read a book all the way through in the last six months (!), as compared with 46 percent of those with only a high school diploma.[27]

4. A college education increases, somewhat, a person's aesthetic appreciation. For instance, a 1969 poll revealed that 57 percent of seniors believed that college had increased their enjoyment of literature, and 53 percent thought that college had heightened their appreciation for art, music, drama. In a 1963 poll conducted by researchers J. W. Trent and L. Medsker, 50 percent of college women liked classical music, as compared with 13 percent of noncollege women. There is, however, according to studies, less evidence that a college education improves reading tastes.[28]

5. College-educated people are much better informed about, and participate more actively in, public events; they are more inclined to vote. A late sixties study revealed that college graduates scored 65 percent on a quiz about domestic events and 95 percent on a quiz about foreign events; high school graduates' scores were 45 percent and 77 percent, respectively. Another study reported that while 74 percent of all college graduates polled reported having voted in the 1972 presidential election, only 48 percent of all nongraduates reported having voted in that election.[29]

6. A college education makes people more politically liberal. Is this good or bad? I think generally good, but like most people, I suspect, I couldn't give an unequivocal answer to this. It is too bad, however, that a college education does tend to promote political conformity. A 1975 Gallup Poll notes that while 24 percent of college freshmen considered themselves "left of center, moderately liberal," fully 42 percent of college seniors considered themselves such.[30]

7. *A college graduate is more adaptable.* Numerous studies confirm this. Researchers J. N. Morgan, I. A. Sirageldin and N. Baerwaldt, for instance, constructed an adaptability index called "Concern for Progress" (that tested such things as ambition, receptivity to change, attitudes to scientific discoveries and willingness to use new products), and discovered that scores on this test ranged from 14 for those with only a grade school education to 22 for those with a college degree.[31]

8. *College graduates are better parents.* They spend more time with their children and are more willing to make sacrifices for them. One study discovered that "college-educated wives devote about 25 percent more time than other women to child care, and also that the husbands of college educated women spend about 30 to 40 percent more time in child care than other husbands." College graduates also spend a higher proportion of their income on their children. According to one study, however, college graduates are more likely to find that their children have behavioral problems and are also more likely to feel inadequate in dealing with their children's problems.[32]

9. *Children of college graduates have a higher measured intelligence.* Virtually all studies confirm this.[33]

10. *College graduates are healthier, eat better, and live longer.* A 1968 study of 270,000 Bell Telephone employees revealed that "men who enter the organization with a college degree have a lower attack rate, death rate, and disability rate for coronary disease at every age, in every part of the country, and all departments of the organization." A 1966 study by the Bureau of Labor Statistics revealed that among

families earning $15,000 a year, the families of college graduates spend $50 less per year on tobacco. Still another study shows that college graduates have a lower mortality rate. The mortality rate for male college graduates is .87 (where 1.0 is the average) and for male high school graduates it is .95.[34]

11. A college education is a necessary stepping-stone to the professions. For those 10 percent of undergraduates who will go on to professional school, a college education is a necessary prerequisite.[35]

Bad Reasons for Going to College

In Part I, we saw the many ways in which American higher education is in decline. In the empirical studies just cited, we saw the tangible effects that this decline has had on the undergraduate population. Many of these effects are horrifying and bode ill for the country's future, for they show that not only are our colleges in trouble, but that they are seriously damaging our children as well.

Does this mean, as Caroline Bird suggests, that all but a small minority of Americans would be foolish to go to college?

Not at all. They only imply, first, that the decision to go, and especially the decision to go right after high school, should no longer be automatic, should be carefully made on the basis of sizing a student's talents, aspirations, skills, emotional strengths, and weaknesses, and may be, on the basis of this review, difficult to make; and second, that there are bad reasons as well as good ones for going to college, and that what may have been, in the past, a good reason for going may now be a bad one.

These studies strongly suggest there are three bad reasons for going to college: (1) to make more money; (2) to be more creative; and (3) to grow emotionally. If a student's principal aim in life is to make a lot of money, he may still benefit from going to college, especially if he has a good chance to be one of the top 10 percent of college graduates who make graduate school; but he should, even then, consider other options as well. He might, for instance, make more money as a television announcer (a growing industry where average salaries for experienced people range around $40,000) than as an architect (an overcrowded field with about equal average salaries).

If the student's aim is to be an artist or writer, he might be better off not going to college. Not only does a college education not develop creativity or writing skill, but, after college, those jobs — laborer, postman, housewife, or meter reader — that do not require a degree and that therefore make fewer mental demands on a person are far more congenial for the aspiring moonlighting writer or artist.

For the student with emotional difficulties, for the student who wants more independence from his parents, or for one who simply feels the need for more maturity, college is unlikely to be helpful. There is no good evidence that a college education improves, and much evidence that it hinders, emotional growth. So long as he is in college, the student remains a quasidependent of his parents (in most cases). For more independence and maturity he might be better off joining the army or merchant marine; going to college, perhaps, later.

Thus, unless the student is bound for professional school, there is no good practical reason for going to college. A college education today has almost no direct, immediate, positive effect on a person's life.

Good Reasons for Going to College

The good effects of college are long-term and indirect, but they constitute excellent reasons for going. Empirical studies show that college can teach us to appreciate a wider variety of things, to be more adaptable, to be more aware of the past and more concerned with the future, to be healthier, better parents and better citizens. Perhaps the most important personal benefit of a college education is gaining greater knowledge and appreciation of science, literature, and the arts; and the single greatest social benefit is promoting concern for the well-being of future generations.

In short, these studies show that the most important part of undergraduate education is a general education. This conclusion, moreover, is confirmed by other studies. Dr. Whitla, for instance, reports that "72 percent of the alumni felt that the private college had had a strong overall influence on their lives" and that the primary source of this influence was "the broadening, liberalizing" impact of . . . the "liberal arts factor." Bowen states that "regarding the purposes of a college education, all studies show that seniors place substantially greater emphasis on general or liberal education and less emphasis on vocational education than do freshmen. . . . Similarly, in considering the goals of higher education, alumni tend to give substantially greater emphasis to general education than to vocations."[36]

In sum, there appear to be just two good reasons for going to college today: to enter the professions and to receive a general education. These goals, moreover, are not incompatible.

10

CHOOSING A COLLEGE
Why It Matters

MIU is the only institution of higher learning to offer a natural and systematic method to purify the nervous system, thus enabling the student to expand his awareness, and to progress toward higher states of consciousness . . . all first year students at MIU take a course in Einstein's theory of Special Relativity, with over 90 percent achieving a very high level of understanding.

— Maharishi International University,
"Awarding of Degrees"

In principle no legitimate profession, occupation, vocation or station in life can be precluded from Dordt's educational concern. Wherever insight is required, there Dordt College is called to supply it. . . . In this way Dordt College, by remaining aware of the demands of the times, can carry out its educational task of providing leadership that is not only uniquely Christian, but also dynamic and relevant.

— Dordt College Faculty Statement of Mission

How Not to Choose a College

I did not think about college until the fall of my high school senior year. I was at Carmel High School in Carmel, California, at the time. A newcomer to California, I decided not to stay. Although this was the early fifties, California was already a very mellow place, and I was too much a hair shirt to feel comfortable there. There had, I thought, to be more to life than wearing cashmere cardigans and driving a convertible to the beach to watch "submarine races." I decided to go east to school.

The only school I had heard of in the East was called Harvard. I had been there once, when I was eight. My mother had taken me to see the glass flower botanical exhibit at the University Museum. All I could remember about Harvard was the glass flowers, which had impressed me. I applied there because of the glass flowers. It was the only college to which I applied.

At that time Harvard was the target of Senator Joseph McCarthy, who accused the institution of harboring "pinkos." When my high school teachers heard I had applied they tried to dissuade me, suggesting a safer place, like Stanford, instead. "Harvard is riddled with Commies," they said. That made the place seem even more attractive, for the only Communists I had seen had been uniformed ones in occupied Berlin and Vienna. They had been driving tanks and made those cities very exciting indeed. I tried to imagine Russian soldiers walking among the glass flowers, as I had seen them wandering among the formal gardens of Sans Souci.

"Don't go to Harvard," my friends said. "You'll learn to hate life." That, of course, was a challenge. You don't *learn* to hate life, I thought. You either do or don't, and I didn't.

"You should go somewhere else, somewhere more fun, like Dartmouth," my parents worried. "You are already too bookish, and Harvard will make you more so." Seeing nothing wrong with books, I remained obstinate. I applied, took the College Boards (having never heard of them until December of my senior year), was accepted, and went. I did not become a Communist, did not learn to hate life, and did not spend all my time reading books. I was glad I went.

I was lucky. For this is an example of how *not* to choose a college. It is wrong to make a choice on the basis of such scanty information. It is wrong not to visit the campus, meeting with professors, alumni, students, and even dropouts of the college, if you can. It is wrong to develop an idée fixe early and apply to one college only. It is wrong to make a choice for negative reasons, as I did, or because of the glass flowers, for that matter.

To make a sound decision you should have the right information. Yet that is increasingly difficult to find. As we have seen, colleges and universities have changed so rapidly in the last few years that traditional characteristics of particular institutions and the usual differences between types of institutions — public and private, church and secular, etcetera — have disappeared. At the same time more colleges are resorting to deceptive advertising in their frantic efforts to attract students.

The Carnegie Council reported in 1979 that at a small, respectable, private church-related Midwestern liberal arts college, an admissions officer told a prospective student about a new vocational program the school offered, which he could take; and he told the student, who had a low high school grade point average, that he would "probably" be admitted. The truth was, the program was planned but did not yet exist, and the admissions officer knew it. Also, the college had an open admissions policy, so the officer knew that the student would be admitted. This is a double example of what the Carnegie Council calls bait and switch and negative sell, increasingly common tactics used by admissions officers on the unwary student.[1]

For more colleges are turning to the hard sell. They are advertising on television and radio, holding slide shows, running newspaper ads and sending unsolicited 45 rpm records in the mail. More colleges are paying commissions to admissions officers or their representatives for every head they bring in and in this way are promoting unethical recruiting. "Inflated and misleading advertising," says the Carnegie Council, is becoming a national problem.[2] This misdirection may take many forms. Besides claiming the existence of programs that do not exist and pretending to be more selective than they are (very common), many colleges make false claims about the availability of financial aid, hide their plans to drop programs or faculty members, and cover up their current financial difficulties.[3]

Nowhere is this deceptive advertising more evident than in the typical college course catalogue. Originally intended as a single statement of policies and programs, it has become the principal means by which a college advertises its wares. The result is that too often the catalogue no longer gives the applicant an accurate picture of what to expect. In a 1975 national study of catalogues, for instance, the Carnegie Council found that "81 percent of the catalogs did not list the instructors of their courses; 72 percent . . . did not tell when their courses would next be offered or how frequently the courses were given; 56 percent . . . did not tell anyone of the following — which faculty were part-time, which were on leave, and which were not teaching; 18 percent . . . neither explained which, if any, high school courses were required for admission nor directed interested parties to another source for that information" and "5 percent . . . did not describe the contents of the courses listed."[4]

What You Should Know About a College

Today, when a college investment may amount to nearly forty thousand dollars, it is vital that applicants and their families know more about the colleges to which they apply. In fact, a college education should be treated as an investment, and you should know just as much as you would know about any other prospectus before you take the plunge. This information, we see, is not likely to be volunteered by the admissions officer. You will not find it in the college catalogue. The high school counselor will not know it. You must find it yourself. You must *ask;* but first, you must know the questions to ask. Here are some suggestions:

1. What you should know about the college as an institution. What kind of financial shape is it in? Has it had deficit budgets lately? Has it released many faculty or staff members recently? What has been its history of tuition increases? Some colleges have a tuition increase insurance plan: they guarantee, for a fee — around $300 — that they will not raise your tuition for four years. What has been the turnover among the administration? High turnover means trouble.

2. What you should know about the curriculum. Does the college have a sound general education or core program? Remember, a large majority of seniors and alumni consider this the single most important characteristic of a college.[5] What programs are actually going to be open to you? What subjects do students actually major in? This will tell you, perhaps, what are the stronger departments, where the crowded courses are, and something about the interests of the undergraduates. What are the most prestigious departments and what are their academic biases? As we shall see in Chapter 13, virtually every department is strong in only one area of its field. You should know where this strength is before you attend. What are the sizes of the courses? The average size means nothing: find out the sizes of the biggest classes and the sizes of the classes you are interested in.[6] What are the size limits of courses, and what are your chances of being admitted? What are the prerequisites? Of the courses in which you are interested, does the professor have special requirements? Who will teach the courses in which you are interested?

3. What you should know about the faculty. How many will be on campus next year? Are teaching? How much is the faculty paid? The American Association of University Professors provides guidelines; this is an index of faculty quality. Is the faculty unionized? If so, this is a sign, especially at a private college, of bad blood on campus. Has the

faculty struck lately? What is the size of the larger departments and the smaller departments? Too great an imbalance means a poorly coordinated curriculum. It is simply
growing in response to demand.

4. *What you should know about the students.* What
kinds of students are admitted: that is, what are their vocational interests? Every college has token diversity; few have
real diversity. How many students drop out and *why?* Few
students today drop out of college because of the money.
More common reasons are the social life, the lack of desired
courses, the anonymity of the institution.[7] What kinds of
jobs do they get later? Some colleges, such as St. John's in
Annapolis, Maryland, and Santa Fe, New Mexico, keep detailed records on this.

5. *What you should know about student life.* What are
the living options? Can you really have the dorm you want?
What are the sizes and configurations of the rooms? Are the
dormitories built on the corridor principle or the entry principle? The former are like prisons; the latter like apartments.
Naturally, the latter are much more in demand: they afford
much more privacy and quiet. How are room assignments
made? By lottery, by choice, or by computer? Remember,
many colleges say they make them one way when in fact they
are made another. At Harvard, for example, assignments to
houses are supposedly made by computer, but according to
one official intimately involved in this system, "There was a
lot, I repeat, a *lot* of individual tinkering with this process.
Many people were given special treatment." What are the
conditions of the dorms? How are the dorms run? Remember, "self-governing dorms" are to be avoided. What are the
dorm policies? Have there been many "incidents" there
lately? What is the social life like? What kinds of extracurricular organizations are there (newspaper, literary magazine, dramatic society, political associations)? How active a
role does the college take in organizing the social life? Are

there fraternities, sororities? What are they like? What is the surrounding community like?

6. *What you should know about alumni.* What is their giving record? A low level of giving may mean the college has changed greatly from what it was, that it has a poor administration, and that its past reputation may be no guide to its present state.

7. *What you should know about admissions.* Knowing the average Scholastic Aptitude Test scores of entering freshmen may not give an accurate indication of your chances to be admitted. To most colleges students "self-select," that is, they don't apply if the average SAT scores to the college look too high for them. In fact, many colleges whose applicants have high SATs take almost anyone who applies. Therefore you should ask: not what is the SAT profile of those who *enter* as freshmen, but the SAT profile of those who *apply* and those who are rejected. Also, find out how many were rejected. Finally, what is the college's acceptance ratio: that is, what percentage of the students the college accepted actually enrolled? That is, how many turned the college down?

8. *What you should know about financial aid.* According to the Carnegie Council, 17 percent of all college catalogues "neither explained what types of financial aid were available and how to get them nor directed interested parties to another source for that information."[8] You will need to find for yourself, therefore, what your chances are for financial aid (see below, Chapter 12).

How Do Colleges Differ?

How do colleges differ and how important are these differences? Dr. Clark Kerr, former Chancellor of the University of California and Chairperson of the Carnegie Council on Policy Studies in Higher Education, said, "It is the general impact of all colleges that matters more than the differential impacts of one type of college versus another type."[9] This conclusion has been supported by many studies and, indeed, has been part of the thesis of Part I; for what differences there are, are diminishing. Nonetheless, studies have revealed that, *on average*, there are some differences between institutions, and it is useful for the college applicant to know them, for knowing them may help answer many of the above questions. If this sounds paradoxical — that it matters more whether you go to college than where you go, yet that choosing a college should be done carefully — it may be explained by analogy. Choosing a college is like buying a car. Any car will get you to your destination. But while one car is inexpensive, gets good mileage but is noisy and uncomfortable, another may be comfortable but very inefficient and still another may be small, quiet, efficient, and comfortable but require many repairs along the way. In short, where you go to college is not a matter of life or death; rather it is a matter of expense, comfort, efficiency, and style. Some will fit you better than others.

Elite vs. *Accessible Colleges.* As I write this, the Harvard class of 1954 has just held its twenty-fifth reunion. *Newsweek* and several other national publications covered it. "This class," said *Newsweek*, "boasts the likes of writer John Updike, Sen. Edward M. Kennedy, the heads of two major museums, the president of Colgate, historian Christopher Lasch, lawyer F. Lee Bailey, more than 100 other attorneys, upwards of 80 doctors, more than 70 professors, and at least 95 men who earn — they say — over $95,000 a year."[10] The obvious implication of this article, and many like it, is that it indeed does matter a great deal where you go to college, that there is some immutable pedagogical pecking order, a great chain of learning, with Harvard and the other ivies at the top along with Stanford, Cal Tech, and a few others, while stretched out below, in order of diminishing clout, are the smaller liberal arts colleges, the great state universities, the church colleges, the lesser state universities, and the community colleges. This view perceives the educational system as a vast social filter, a filter that elitists believe is for the placement of talent and Marxists believe is to protect the capitalist class, but that in any case acts, like the agent of a Calvinist God, to assure our predestination. According to this view, where you go fixes you, for better or worse, for life: it determines what you do, how much money you make, how successful you will be, and even whom you marry. If you are admitted to a prestigious college, you may never need to worry again; if you don't, you are fated either for a life of obscurity or a life of incessant struggle to survive, or both.

This view is widespread today. It is believed by anxious parents and it is promoted by high schools and prep schools that rate themselves by the prestige of the institutions to which their graduates are accepted. The prevalence of this view accounts for the terrible anxieties of high school senior year; for the grotesque increase in enrollments, in recent years, at the prestigious institutions; for the terror, disappointment, and brief but illusory victories that come in the mail each April. Yet this view is largely mistaken and is becoming less true each year.

What are the effects of attending a selective institution? In 1977 Alexander W. Astin, professor of higher education at the University of California, Los Angeles, President of the Higher Education Research Group and one of the country's leading authorities on student development, published the results of a ten-year study he had conducted of 700,000 students at 300 colleges and universities.[11] This work is perhaps the best-documented account of how different kinds of colleges affect students. What he found was that attending a selective institution is indeed a mixed blessing. It does not, he discovered, increase your chances of getting a higher starting salary, although it *may* help you land a job that pays better over a lifetime. Attending an elite college increases your chances of being admitted to medical school but hurts your chances of making law school. That, moreover, elite colleges do not offer overwhelming advantages is also supported by Bowen, who notes that students at the better colleges do not learn more (if differences in initial ability are taken into account), nor is what a student learns correlated with "the student-faculty ratio, library books per student, the average ability level of the student body, and the affluence of the college."[12]

Students at elite colleges, Astin notes, tend to be more liberal, less religious, more self-critical, less interested in money, to have higher self-esteem, to drink more and smoke more but be less likely to get married. They tend to be more verbally aggressive and more interested in sports than average. They have a better chance of getting into college teaching, nursing, business, and engineering. They are more likely to be satisfied with their colleges and are less likely to drop out.[13]

There has, moreover, been a change in the *kind* of person elite colleges have been accepting. Dr. David P. Campbell, Vice President of Research and Programs at the Center for Creative Leadership in Greensboro, North Carolina, in studying twenty successive years of Dartmouth College admissions decisions (1947–1967: the longest such "longitudinal" study ever done), discovered, for instance, that over this period Dartmouth had, quite unconsciously, changed its implicit criteria for admission.[14] During the late forties and early fifties it favored students with business interests. But as Dartmouth became more popular and more selective and the average SAT score of its applicants began to rise, the admissions committee began to favor students, not with business interests, but with interests in science and scholarship. That is, while in the earlier years Dartmouth students were more likely to become businessmen and make a lot of money after graduation, in the later years the Dartmouth student was more likely to become a college professor.

Small vs. *Large Institutions.* There are far greater differences between small and large institutions than there are between selective and less selective ones. Astin and Bowen note that students at smaller colleges learn more, mature faster, become more involved in campus life, are more likely to be challenged, less likely to demonstrate, more likely to be liberal. Attending a large university affects the student less in almost every way. It also discourages the development of altruistic values. Students at the larger institutions are, however, more satisfied with their social life. Perhaps most important, the amount of student-faculty contact is determined, not by the student-faculty ratio, but rather by the size of the institution. That is, students are more likely to know faculty better at a small college, regardless of the college's student-faculty ratio, than they are at any large university.[15]

Private vs. *Public Institutions.* There are few public four-year liberal arts colleges. That is, aside from community colleges, almost all public institutions are large. Although there are few differences between the large private institutions and the large public ones, the differences noted above — between small and large — also hold between small private colleges and large public universities. As Astin says, "Practically all the effects associated with college attendance are more pronounced among students at private institutions. Thus, increases in artistic interest . . . and religious apostasy are greater among students at private institutions."[16] Astin adds that students at private institutions see more of the faculty, are happier with classes, are more aggressive. Attending a private institution, he says, "substantially increases the student's chance of pursuing a career in science."[17]

Religious vs. *Secular Colleges.* There is less difference between these two than one might imagine. Religious institutions do change a student's values less than secular ones do, and, although religious interest drops even at the church colleges, it drops less. Students tend to be more conservative, more altruistic. Astin also reports, "Religious apostasy is reduced in the nonselective Protestant colleges and increased at the selective colleges. Selective Protestant colleges have a *positive* impact on musical interests and hedonism [smoking, drinking, etcetera], and they increase a student's chances of persisting to graduation, enrolling in graduate school, and becoming a college professor."[18]

Coeducational vs. *Single-Sex Colleges.* There is a great difference in the effects of these kinds of colleges, and most evidence favors the single-sex institution. The disappearance of single-sex institutions, therefore, from the standpoint of the interests of the student, is one of the most unfortunate trends in higher education today. As Astin says, "Some of the most dramatic effects were associated with attending men's or women's colleges." He reports that at such institutions students have stronger academic interests, see more of the faculty, have more self-confidence; they are more satisfied with every aspect of undergraduate life except social life (though women seem more happy with their social life at single-sex colleges than men do). Men at single-sex colleges are, says Astin, more likely to participate in athletics and to get good grades. Women are, as we have seen, more likely to develop high aspirations and to attain positions of leadership. Attending a men's college greatly increases one's chances of being admitted to law school and of achieving business career plans.[19]

Residential vs. *Commuter.* As you would suspect, almost

every effect that college has on a student is accentuated by living on campus. Dormitory students are typically more involved in campus activities, develop more self-confidence, are less religious and more liberal, drink more, smoke more, stay up later than their commuter counterparts. The most unfortunate effect of living off campus, however, is the tendency for students who live at home or in apartments to drop out before graduation. According to many studies, students who do not live at college do not pursue their studies as far, nor have as high ambition as other students do.[20]

Eastern, Western, and Southern Colleges. Most western colleges are public ones; many eastern colleges are private. In the West, good students are more likely to attend a public institution. Students at eastern colleges, according to Astin, are less likely to marry while in college, more likely to persist in their studies, and more likely to graduate with honors. Students at western colleges are more likely to be happy with their choice of college. Attendance at a western college or university reduces a student's chances of admittance to all professional schools except law school. Western students have a better chance of being admitted to law school. Students at southern colleges are more conservative in all things but race. On matters of race, they are more liberal than their northern counterparts. Students in the South are more likely to be involved in campus activities and to get lower grades; they are more likely to be religious and less likely to live a hedonistic lifestyle.[21]

College Calendars. In my opinion, the college calendar is one of the most important, yet most overlooked, determinants of the quality of instruction and the quality of student life. Yet today, colleges, either in an attempt to appear more distinctive or as a means to accommodate more students, are modifying the calendar, often with little thought for how it affects the quality of instruction or student life. You will therefore hear, as you investigate colleges, of the "Colorado College Plan," the "Dartmouth Plan," and so on, and you should know what these are.

There are essentially four kinds of college calendar today, with variations: the quarter, the semester, the 4–1–4, and the block.

1. The Quarter. This is an old system, which most public universities use. It divides the year into four ten-week quarters, separated by two- or three-week vacations. In the typical system students may attend any quarter, although most attend fall, winter, and spring and do not attend summer. This calendar is a good one for processing a large number of students, as state universities must, but a poor one for learning. Ten weeks is simply not long enough to learn some subjects. The continuity of instruction is interrupted and often students are not on campus long enough together to get to know one another. Lately, to accommodate more students, some elite colleges have introduced it, and this is a bad sign. The "Dartmouth Plan" is a quarter calendar, with one very unfortunate variation: freshmen must spend the first three consecutive quarters on campus, but, after that, need spend only eight of the next twelve on campus. It is a system that, according to *Esquire,* "almost guarantees that after freshman year, no two students will spend more than six consecutive months on campus simultaneously."[22]

2. The Semester. This is, of course, the old tried and true calendar, still used by a majority of colleges. It is my favorite. Typically, the school year is divided into two terms of fifteen weeks. The first term will begin in late September and finish at the end of January. The second term will begin in the first week in February and end in the first week in June. This calendar provides sufficiently long terms to permit teaching the more sustained topics and it allows more continuity in undergraduate life.

Recently, however, many colleges, like Yale, have gone to a modified semester system. With this calendar, the year begins early and ends early. The first semester runs from Labor Day and finishes before Christmas; the second begins after Christmas and ends in early May. The supposed advantages of this calendar are that students will not be required to work over Christmas vacation, and, by beginning summer vacation early, they will find their summer jobs before students from other colleges take them. These advantages are more theoretical than real. At Yale, for instance, the fact that the fall term ends just before Christmas is the major reason why undergraduates take such a phenomenal number of "incompletes" in their courses that term.[23] That is, knowing they have a vacation following the term, they ask the professor to allow them to finish their course work over vacation. As for jobs, few summer jobs start in May, and many require the student to stay after Labor Day. So if the early start to summer vacation is an advantage, the early end is a disadvantage.

3. *The 4–1–4.* This is one of those "innovations" that emerged in the sixties and is still popular among small liberal arts colleges.[24] It was a response to student demands for relevance, and thus its popularity rests on the fact that it permits the college to give academic credit for nonacademic work. In this calendar, there are three terms: fall, interim, and spring. The fall term is twelve weeks, beginning just after Labor Day and ending before Christmas. Interim term is the month of January. Spring term begins in the first week in February and ends in the middle of May. Students are required to take four courses in each of the fall and spring terms, and one in each interim term (hence, "4–1–4"). The rationale for this system is that the interim

term is for experimentation, for faculty and students to try new things. In fact, this term is one during which there is little academic or other accomplishment. Typical interim term activities are a trip to Europe or a campus course on "Star Trek." Faculty members are encouraged by the administration to make their courses fun and games, yet this is a gimmick that wastes both faculty and student time (although quite popular with students). Faculty members are burdened with an extra course preparation and are forced to choose between teaching a serious course (which neither students nor dean will like) or a frivolous one. Students could better use this time, either as part of fall and spring terms, or in the summer for employment.

4. The Block. This is the latest innovation, widely known as the "Colorado College Plan."[25] In this calendar, students take one course at a time, as the school year is divided into nine three-and-a-half-week blocks. The advantage to this plan is the flexibility it permits. Courses do not have to be on campus — they can be anywhere the professor and students want to go. Flexibility, of course, means discontinuity, and this is one of the disadvantages of the plan. There is much coming and going: the campus becomes a way station, and students have fewer friends sharing the same course with them at the same time. But the greatest drawback of this system is a pedagogical one. Few students have the concentration span sufficient to study one subject intensively for one month and learn as much as one would taking it over a four-month period, and the instruction, coming prepackaged, does not encourage the student to make connections between what he learns in one course and what he learns in another. It is difficult for the student to do much writing in such courses and there are certain subjects that simply cannot be taught with it. I have, for instance, taught a course on Immanuel Kant's *Critique of Pure Reason* in the semester, the quarter, the 4–1–4, and the block plan. In a semester, the entire book could be covered. In the 4–1–4 we covered the material, but not so thoroughly. In the quarter, we skipped some sections. In the block course we could not finish the book, and the students could manage only half the writing that students who took the semester course could accomplish.

Summation of Differences. In sum, there are differences between types of colleges, although many of these differences — between elite and accessible institutions, between private and public, religious and secular, coeducational and single-sex — are diminishing. Students learn more, grow faster, and find jobs upon graduation more easily at single-sex colleges, but they are less satisfied with their social life. Small liberal arts colleges do a better job in almost every respect than large institutions. Students at church-related colleges tend to be more conservative, but in general the differences between them and other students is small. Students at elite colleges do not learn more but may earn more in later life. Students at private colleges are better satisfied than students at public ones, less alienated, but more prone to drink and smoke tobacco and pot. Dormitory living accentuates both the bad and good effects of student life. Colleges and universities do reflect the peculiar values of the regions in which they are situated. Colleges on the semester calendar are more likely to provide students with a congenial living and learning environment.

How should this information affect your choice? It means that a student who wants independence and anonymity above all else, who is strong emotionally and somewhat aggressive, would be happiest at a large university. But a student who is not very self-confident, who is most interested in learning and growing, would be best off at a small college. It means that going to a small private institution is still worth the extra money for most students, but that going to a large private university may not be worth the extra cost. It means that every student should seriously consider a single-sex institution, if he can find one.

Getting Your Questions Answered

There is no substitute for asking. You should speak with as many people as possible: high school guidance counselors, admissions officers, other administrators, students now enrolled at the college you are considering, parents of these students, and (especially) dropouts. If at all possible, visit the campus during term-time, and snoop around. Don't be satisfied with a guided tour. Visit faculty members, especially those who may be teaching the courses you are interested in. Visit a dorm.

In addition, there are many publications that can help. The American College Testing Service, for instance, publishes a book entitled *College Planning/Search Book,* which contains valuable information, not only about all the colleges and universities in the country, but also about admissions and financial aid.[26] At some larger universities, such as Yale and Harvard, there are course critiques available, written by undergraduates and very frank.[27] From the college, of course, you should obtain, not just the catalogue (announcement), but also the schedule of courses for the following year. This, which is given to enrolled students automatically, is seldom given to applicants unless they ask.

As you gather this information, however, keep the following points in mind.

1. Fewer colleges will be choosy in the 1980s, so don't be put off if you read that the average test scores of entering freshmen at the college in which you are interested are higher than yours. Remember, many students hurt themselves by self-selecting.

2. Few college guides contain any history of the institu-

tion. This information can be valuable. Knowing where a college has been may be a guide to where it's headed.

3. That a college lists "both coed and single-sex dorms" or other options does not mean they will be available to you. Check.

4. Not all colleges listed as church-related are *really* church-related.

5. Dropout rate figures are important.

6. If a college has few graduation requirements, it means that features of the "Buck-passer Syndrome" — haphazard scheduling, competition between departments, and probably grade inflation — are present.

7. Don't believe any college that claims to have an effective advising system. Stay away from ones that claim to rely heavily on it.

8. If a college offers many options — off campus learning, individualized instruction, internships, externships, special calendars, different living plans, and so on — this probably means it is in financial trouble. The better, more secure institutions do not need to attract students this way. There is an inverse relationship between the soundness of the institution and the number of special programs it offers.

9. Check, in the course catalogue, on the rules for dropping and adding courses, and on grading and transcripts. What you find may shock you!

10. Are the language departments offering many courses on literature in translation (where no knowledge of a foreign language is required)? Is the Classics Department offering courses on modern civilization? Is the English Department offering courses on political issues? If so, this is a sign of an uncontrolled curriculum.

11. A course catalogue is unlikely to tell you what courses are available next year, whether you are likely to be admitted to the course you want, what the real (as opposed to

nominal) prerequisites of courses are (the real are often less stringent than the nominal).

What the Statistics and Empirical Studies Don't Tell You

The essential message of all the world's religions is this: that the world may be corrupt, but individual salvation is still possible. That is also, in a sense, the message of this book. The educational system, on average, is corrupt and not working as it should. That was the message of Part I. The message of Part II is that within this system, individual salvation — that is, a good college experience — is possible.

To realize it is possible requires knowing the limitations of empirical studies. Throughout Part II, I cite results of such studies on the effects of attending college. These figures can be useful, but one should keep in mind that they are averages, and you are not average. No one is. This information, therefore, should be used as a series of danger signals or signposts, but not as a map.

It is easy to persuade ourselves that our lives are beyond our control, that we are directed by larger social or historical forces, that what happens to us is more important than what we do. At the same time, we are too inclined to believe that the choice of college is the most important decision we will ever make, and that, after this choice is made, we have set our lives on automatic pilot and never need to touch the controls again.

Yet both these views are mistaken. The choice of college is not the most important decision of a lifetime. It is only one of many; and we are, at all times, in control of our lives. We are not the victims of statistical averages, mean deviations, or sociological laws. We are controlled by ourselves, and we must never take our hands off the wheel.

11

ADMISSIONS
Unnatural Selection

Some colleges, including a number of respected institutions, have been less than fully responsible in the way they handle admissions.

— The Carnegie Council

We must insist on diversity. Diversity in a species, as Darwin pointed out, insures survival in a wider range of environmental hazards. The analogy probably holds for education; when we do not know any one best way, or are not even sure of a few good ones, then diversity . . . should be stimulated. This does not mean lowering standards; rather it means expanding them.

— DAVID P. CAMPBELL

The Mystique of Admissions

I am sitting in the office of an admissions officer of a major, elite university. The university is famous for having altered its admissions policy to put less emphasis on high school grades and aptitude tests and more emphasis on other forms of personal achievement. Several national publications had recently called attention to this, running headlines such as "College Searches for Diversity of Talent." I asked the admissions officer how this new policy was working out; whether, despite their claims, SAT scores were still the major determinant of admission.

"Not at all," he replied with the sigh of a man who has

answered the same question a thousand times. "We look at many things, sometimes deliberating an hour on one application."

He picked up a pile of manila folders from his desk and began to thumb through them.

"That's what I'm doing now," he went on, "evaluating applications." He opened the top folder. "Here's a boy, 550 on his SATs. He won't make it." Then opening another: "Here's a girl from Cleveland, scored 750s; she's going to make it." Then another: "This boy has 650 — he's borderline," and so on.

Was this man talking out of both sides of his mouth at once? Not at all. Typical of most admissions officers, he was trying to be honest and to do a good job. The fact is, he literally didn't know what he was doing. He thought he was considering a wide variety of factors when in fact he was not.

As Professor Cliff Wing of Duke University told me, "Most admissions officers remember the exceptional decisions, but not the routine ones. They remember the boy with low scholastic aptitude whom they admitted because he was a concert pianist, but they forget the hundred with low SAT scores whom they rejected."

Few admissions departments in the country, despite protestations to the contrary, operate scientifically or systematically. They do not consciously work with clear-cut criteria, preferring the more nebulous, "holistic" approach instead. That is, they consider the "whole person," but won't say what that is. At the same time they do not test themselves to see if they are doing what they think they are doing. Despite claims that they are searching for diversity, they do not, for instance, give applicants vocational or interest inventory tests. They do not do long-range "longitudinal" studies of the people they admitted and the ones they rejected to see whether there are any unconscious patterns to their admissions decisions.[1] Few admissions officers, for instance, know how many students they admitted ten years ago are now house painters and how many they rejected have won Pulitzer prizes.

Instead, for reasons which we shall see, they operate on a year-to-year basis, never looking very far ahead or far behind, cloaking their deliberations in a veil of mysterious rhetoric about the need for diversity, all the while they are choosing students who exhibit a remarkable degree of similarity.

We have seen in the previous chapter how the Dartmouth admissions office, over a long period, shifted, without knowing it, from admitting people with a business interest to people with a scientific interest. Dr. Campbell, the author of that study, has also discovered that our elite institutions, on the average, discriminate, without knowing it, greatly in favor of the firstborn.[2] This discrimination is especially severe at entrance to graduate school, and in this way is reflected in the number of firstborns who hold the important positions in our society. Thus, while about 45 percent of all persons in the United States are firstborn, 94 percent of all astronauts, 60 percent of all chemists, 58 percent of Danforth Fellows, 54 percent of physicists, and so on, are firstborn. At the other end of the scale, 32 percent of tradesmen, 31 percent of electricians, and 22 percent of encyclopedia salesmen are firstborn. Another study has found colleges tend to favor the "morning glories" over the "late bloomers." And many studies have revealed that colleges and universities tend to admit students with fewer interests and to reject those with numerous interests.[3] Those people, according to one study, who have the widest variety of interests in our society are policemen, salesmen, and department store managers; while those with the smallest number of interests are astronomers, mathematicians, artists, and authors![4]

How Admissions Decisions Are Actually Made

It is a universal ritual for American colleges to claim, as Connecticut College does, "Many factors are taken into consideration in the selection of a freshman class," and as Colorado College does, "Students are selected for admission not only on the basis of their academic abilities and promise, but also because of their potential cultural contributions to campus life." Typical of this claim is the April, 1979, article that appeared in the *Wall Street Journal* with the headline "Elite Colleges Consider Many Factors in Search for a Mix of Students," and that noted that "Duke wants a 'diverse' student body. . . . Stanford wants 'academic ability and high energy level' and Harvard wants 'the best possible mix of a student body where students teach other students.' " This is what they say they do. What do they really do?

Professors Wing and Wallach have conducted the only complete, systematic study of the admissions process, and although it was done ten years ago it appears to reflect accurately present practices.[5] They divided colleges into three categories: minimally selective, moderately selective, and highly selective. Colleges in the first category accept virtually everyone who applies. Public institutions in the first category usually admit this fact, while private colleges in the same category try to hide it.[6]

Colleges in the second category typically accept around 60 to 70 percent of those who apply. Most of these are small liberal arts and church-related colleges. The third category, comprising perhaps only 180 to 200 elite colleges in the country, reject around 50 to 80 percent of all applicants.

What Wing and Wallach found was this: that by using one criterion alone — the student's score on the verbal portion of the SAT — they were able to predict, with better than 80 percent accuracy, in a cross-section of all colleges and universities and of highly selective institutions, whether the student would be admitted or not. When they also knew the student's mathematical aptitude score and his high school grades, their accuracy approached 90 percent.[7] As few admissions committees could predict their own decisions better than that (that is, if they had to decide all over again, they would not pick the same freshman class), Wing and Wallach were able to explain almost all admissions decisions by these simple criteria alone. They also discovered that the less selective the college, the more it relied on SAT scores in its decisions. The moderately selective institutions, apparently, accept virtually everyone above the thirtieth percentile.

The more selective institutions, on the other hand, are apparently in a better position to consider a variety of factors in admissions. They receive far more applicants with high SAT scores than they can admit and must find some way to decide, for instance, what students with 700 SATs to accept and what ones to reject.[8] Still, Wing and Wallach found that even the highly selective colleges rely almost entirely on SAT scores and high school grades in making their decisions. In a detailed study of the Duke University admissions process they discovered:[9]

(1) the committee discriminated against students who expressed no interest in professional school;

(2) accomplishment in the extracurricular areas of writing (say publishing an article while in high school), editing (being editor of the school newspaper), and science (winning a science prize) helped a candidate's chances, but only moderately;

(3) accomplishment in drama (acting in the school play) and leadership (being president of the class) did not help gain admittance;

(4) accomplishment in art (having held your own ex-

hibition) and employment (having held a job while in high school) actually hurt a candidate's chances.

In sum, Wing and Wallach found that colleges are apparently biased in favor of students who show academic talent early; they are biased in favor of preprofessional studies; moderately selective colleges are not at all interested in a diversity of accomplishment, talent, or interests; highly selective institutions are only slightly interested in diversity and what grades a student gets in high school and how he scores on the SATs, particularly the verbal section, almost completely determine where he will be admitted. Finally, Campbell's studies have suggested that the tendency of elite colleges to emphasize a more narrow and more scholastic set of criteria has increased since the fifties; undergraduates today probably exhibit a more narrow set of interests than they did twenty years ago.[10]

Why Don't Admissions Committees Practice What They Preach?

Why do colleges preach diversity while they practice conformity? For a number of reasons.

First, in a democratic, egalitarian society, they cannot openly practice elitism. Nor can they openly admit to a stated and fixed set of criteria for nonacademic accomplishment. To do so would be to invite second-guessing and endless politicking over what characteristics — artistic achievement, scientific, literary, and so on — should be given what weight. The easiest way to avoid this is to preach diversity, practice scholasticism, and remain vague about the details.

Second, as we have seen, few admissions offices bother to test themselves and therefore do not know what they are doing. Many institutions, the smaller colleges and public universities in particular, lack the resources to spend a lot of time selecting students or keeping detailed records on what they do.

Third, faculties and administrations like the emphasis kept on aptitude scores. Faculty members are interested in teaching only the students who are willing to concentrate on academic interests. They are, remember, looking for their own replacements. Administrators are well aware that most people measure the worth of a college by the average SAT score of its entering class. After all, most college guides rank colleges by this measure.

Fourth, at bottom lies the fallacy of the analytic tradition: the supposition that quantitative measurement is "objective" while nonquantitative measurement is subjective; that so long as people are measured objectively, the college is not making a value judgment, but that to measure people on the basis of their individual accomplishments is to base the decision on a questionable and arbitrary value judgment. In basing their decisions on SAT score and grades they are presuming that these devices, and these alone, measure what is socially valuable. Is this a valid assumption?

What Do SAT Scores Tell Us?

Numerous studies, conducted by researchers at the American College Testing Service and elsewhere, have been done to find an answer to this question. This is what they tell us.

1. Someone who scores high on the SAT test is likely to have high grades, in high school, college, and graduate school.[11]

2. Getting high grades in college increases one's chances of being admitted to professional school. That is, grade-getting begets grade-getting.[12]

3. According to Astin, the grades a student gets determines the size of his salary in his first job. For students going on to business, teaching, and engineering, for instance, the difference, according to Astin, of one letter grade is worth between $500 and $900 in starting salary.[13]

4. There is no connection between high grades and later life accomplishment. The best students are not necessarily the most creative or accomplished later, no matter what criteria are used to measure later life accomplishment. As the ACT reports, "Unfortunately, college grades are generally poor predictors of real life success."[14]

5. Having high grades in college does not mean a person is more likely to be a good scholar. Professors Wing and Wallach note two studies where groups of scholars were graded with respect to their creativity by a variety of means (such as articles published, respect of peers, number of times their work was cited by others), and found that the most creative were not the ones who had, earlier in life, the higher SAT scores or grades. They conclude, "When viewed in the light of meaningful criteria of life accomplishment, academic grades and the intelligence tests that predicted them fare quite poorly within the upper part of the academic skills spectrum."[15]

6. Those who score high on the SATs are less likely to be creative artists than those who score low on the SATs.[16]

7. Those who get high grades in college are more likely to have emotional and personal problems in later life.[17]

8. Achievement outside the classroom is a far more accurate sign of how productive and creative one will be later in life. Many studies conducted by the ACT in the late sixties confirm this.[18]

In sum, the SAT scores measure one thing: how good a person will be at getting good grades. The college admissions process, therefore, by relying so heavily on test scores, is making a very fundamental mistake. It is implicitly assuming either that SAT scores measure something socially valuable other than grade-getting, or that the latter is the only intrinsically valuable activity. Both of these assumptions are wrong; but by making them, our colleges are choosing a student population which is good at getting grades, picking students who will go to professional school to be good students. Thus today, when there is general concern that too many college students have narrow vocational interests, that too many want to go to professional school, when too many seem to think that grade-getting is an end in itself, it is well to remember that the admissions offices chose these people. The selective colleges are choosing these students over those with wider interests. In doing so, moreover, they are determining, in part, who will be the cultural, intellectual, and political leaders of the country. They are, by this practice, assuring that the country will be led by an elite that possesses but a narrow range of talents and interests, an elite that tends to think and act alike. If survivability depends on adaptability, therefore, this practice will, in the end, diminish our ability, as a culture, to survive.

12

FINANCIAL AID
Good News and Bad News

No man ought to looke a given horse in the mouth.

— JOHN HEYWOOD

I fear the Greeks, even when bringing gifts.

— VIRGIL

Satan Sam

My grandfather, "Satan Sam" Wragg, went to college — the University of the South at Sewanee, Tennessee — when he was fourteen. He received financial aid known as a sister-ship. His father, a small-town country doctor, was murdered when Sam was a small boy. That's why his older sister, Great-Aunt Penie as we knew her, went to work to support her younger brother. She became a clerk at the Atlanta *Constitution* and put Sam through college and graduate school. She never went to college and never married. She stayed at the same job her entire life and was never promoted. She took a keen interest in the career of her brother, and that, I fear, was her only pleasure.

Many families three generations ago had their Aunt Penies, the maiden aunts who dedicated their lives to their brothers. Many families today can thank for their well-being the fact that one of their male ancestors was the beneficiary of a sistership.

Things have changed since my grandfather's day, and like most change, this has been both good and bad. It is good that no longer do families need to make heroic sacrifices to send their children to college, that women in particular are not expected to forsake careers in favor of their male siblings, that a college education is accessible to minorities and the poor. It is good that the cost of education has declined, steadily, in real terms, for everyone for three generations. Yet at the same time these gains have exacted tremendous social and financial cost. The system of financial aid that made these improvements possible is, as we saw in Part I, increasing the reliance that educational institutions are placing on the federal government and thereby weakening them and making them more expensive and less efficient; and as we shall see, it is changing, in the wrong ways, our social behavior. We are, in short, paying less for education today, but we are getting less from it as well.

The Good News

A higher percentage of women attend college today than men; more blacks and other minorities are attending than ever; and the cost to the family of attending college has declined for fifty years and continues to decline.[1]

It is one of life's ironies that, when the cost of a B.A. at some institutions approaches $40,000, it is still more affordable than ever. That is because higher education has never been so heavily subsidized. In 1929–1930, for example, 65 percent of college costs were paid by the family. By 1959–1960, only 48 percent was paid by the family; by 1969–1970, 39 percent and by 1975–1976, 32 percent. Likewise, federal aid to students has been making quantum leaps. In only four years, between 1974 and 1978, for example, it more than doubled; from $1.8 billion to $4.9 billion. It was expected to be more than $6 billion by 1979–1980.[2]

Thanks to these subsidies, all families, at every income level, are being asked to spend less on education each year. A family of four, earning $12,000 with one child in college, for example, was expected to pay $1,805 for college in 1956–1957; in 1979–1980, the same family would be expected to pay $270. A family earning $30,000 in 1972–1973 was expected to contribute as much as $7,960; by 1979–1980, that is down to $4,130.[3]

As a result of these trends, fewer people find finances prevent them from attending college. In 1966, 28 percent of high school seniors not planning to attend college gave financial reasons for not going; in 1972, it was 24 percent, and by 1975, 8 percent.[4]

As the above figures suggest, higher education has become less expensive, not only for the lower income groups, but for the middle and upper middle as well. The fear that is so often expressed, that the middle class — too "rich" to qualify for financial aid and too "poor" to pay the rising tuition rates — is being squeezed out of higher education is based on myth. Even before passage of the Middle Income Student Assistance Act of 1978 the middle class was faring quite well in meeting its educational expenses, and since the passage of that bill, it is doing very well indeed.

There is no evidence that any significant number of middle class students have been unable to attend college because of financial reasons or have had to drop out because of money, and much evidence that, even before passage of the MISAA, they have been beneficiaries of much financial aid.[5] Students from families with income between $14,960 and $22,210 received 9 percent of the federal Supplemental Educational Opportunity Grants (SEOG), 16 percent of college work-study, 21 percent of the National Direct Student Loans (NDSL), and 36 percent of the Guaranteed Student Loans (GSL). Incomes of middle class families, moreover, have more than kept pace with rising college costs, better even than lower- or upper-income families: between 1967 and 1978, low-income families' income increased 101 percent; middle-income families' increased 116 percent, upper-middle families' increased 122 percent, and upper-income families' went up 104 percent. Even after taxes, upper-middle families' income went up 106 percent, while their educational expenses rose only 65 percent.[6]

Since the passage of the MISAA, middle-income families have had to spend even less on their children's college education. For families earning between $24,000 and $26,000, for example, under the new law the annual contribution has declined from $2,215 to $1,593, and the maximum amount expected of families to pay for higher education, no matter how high their income, has been limited to 10.5 percent of the family's adjusted gross income.[7]

The Bad News

As these figures suggest, the system of financial aid is making higher education more accessible to more people. But it is doing so at a tremendous cost, both in money and in values.

Educational subsidies do not make education cost less. They merely ensure that families of students *pay* less. On a national scale, the system of federal subsidies makes higher education cost more because it encourages colleges to raise tuition faster than they would otherwise be able to do and because it promotes inefficient proliferation of programs.

But real costs cannot be measured in money alone. Any program has its social and personal costs as well. What problems are we, as a society, inviting by relying so heavily on subsidized education? What risks are we, as individuals, running if we turn to these sources for financial aid?

As the national system of financial aid has grown, it has

become less consistent, less fair, and quite different from what it was intended to be. It was founded on a principle of educational justice: that lack of money should not prevent anyone from attending college. It was founded, that is, on the principle of need. As it evolved, however, this principle has been left behind. Many programs, such as the Veterans and Social Security benefits and the Guaranteed Student Loans, are not based on need at all, and the MISAA, which permits families earning $35,000 to qualify for financial aid, seems to have stretched the principle to the limit.

The financial aid system is becoming instead another pork barrel: a mechanism for disbursing bundles of special perquisites, not necessarily to the needy, but to those with the greatest political clout and, ultimately to the colleges and universities. In this way it corrupts. It corrupts not only the educational institutions, but also many students and their families as well.

Let us, for instance, see what is happening to the middle class. Why is it so widely believed that they are being squeezed out of higher education? Not because the middle class cannot pay their educational bills, but because they *won't* pay them. The Carnegie Council, for instance, notes "a growing reluctance of middle-income families to make the large sacrifices expected of them in the past."[8] Dr. James Bowman, Director of Financial Aid Programs at the College Scholarship Service, in a conversation with me, concurs. "There has been," he says, "a declining willingness of middle-income families to pay for their children's education."

Why is this? It could be that parents recognize a college education is not worth what it was, that both the quality of instruction and the economic value of a B.A. have declined. But surely it also reflects a change in values: that education is not perceived to have the intrinsic worth it was once thought to have, or that sacrifice for one's children is no longer worth it. In either case, this trend is disturbing. As Dr. Sidney Wertimer, Provost of Hamilton College, told me, "The first generation of immigrants to this country would make any sacrifice to see that their children got the best possible education. They wanted their children to lead better lives than they had been able to lead. Few people today — many grandchildren of these immigrants — feel the same way. Fewer are willing to spend more to send their children to a better college."

Here is another downward spiral, created by the decline of our educational institutions, affluence, and the growth of financial aid. The quality of instruction today is indeed poorer than it was. The spread of affluence during the sixties and seventies has made people more selfish; they are less willing to do without, whether forbearance is for their children, for future generations, or, as our national reluctance to conserve energy suggests, for their own benefit.

A few years ago a major fishing tackle manufacturer marketed a good bamboo fly rod that sold for $100. It did not sell. Market research showed that people thought bamboo rods were supposed to be very expensive and that, as this rod was relatively inexpensive, it could not be very good. Therefore, the company raised the price of the rod to $250 and it became a very good seller. This appears to be happening to higher education, but in reverse. Most people are being asked to spend less on education and, as a consequence, they value it less. Some of the reasons for this decline in value are justified and some are not. For although the quality of *instruction* at America's educational institutions may have declined over the past fifteen years, the value of *education* remains as high as ever. Clearly to encourage a recommitment to this value, we must return the system of financial aid, once again, to the principle of need. And this will be accomplished by spending less, not more.

Understanding Financial Aid

Values are subtle. As they do not submit easily to quantification, they can change without notice. The system of financial aid can have that effect on us. It has grown so large that it touches nearly all of us, and its effects are not restricted to encouraging us to take education for granted. Before one applies for financial aid, therefore, it is important that one understand it and its effects. Yet this is difficult to do. As we saw in the preceding chapter, it is hard to find information on financial aid. The system has become Byzantine: diffuse, inconsistent, and complicated. Consequently, many people, mostly the poor, to be sure, who would qualify for financial aid, either apply for the programs that are wrong for them or they do not apply at all. According to one study, 22 percent of all postsecondary institutions failed to tell students of aid for which they qualified. According to another survey conducted in New Jersey, more than 25 percent of all students whose family income was below $6,000 failed to apply for aid, and more than 40 percent of those whose families earned between $6,000 and $12,000 failed to apply.[9]

In short, among the failures of the system is the failure to be understood. Let us examine it, therefore, to see how it works and what, in part, are the pitfalls to be avoided.

Besides the parental contribution, there are four sources of financial support for college education: public grants, private scholarships, undergraduate employment, and student loans.

Public Grants. The list of public grants for which students are eligible is nearly endless, but there are six kinds that comprise the bulk of all aid actually received: the Basic Educational Opportunity Grant, the Supplemental Educa-

tional Opportunity Grant, state scholarships, veterans' benefits, Social Security, and food stamps.

1. BEOG. The BEOG is, next to the parental contribution, the single largest source of student support, providing aid for nearly a third of all entering freshmen. Although administered by the college, the money is awarded
to the student. The size of the grant is the difference
between $1,800 and the expected family contribution, or
one half of the estimated college expenses, whichever is
less. Since the MISAA revised the expected family contribution sharply downward, many middle-income families could qualify for this aid. This grant program, in fact,
may favor the middle class over the lower-income groups,
for poorer people tend to go to less expensive institutions
and therefore fail to qualify for the maximum amount of
scholarship.

2. SEOG. The SEOG is funds that the federal government gives to the college (not the student) and that the
college then gives to especially needy students according
to a formula established by the Department of Education.
The program provides up to $1,500 to any student who ex-
hibits "exceptional financial need."

3. State Scholarships. In 1972 the federal government
created the State Student Incentive Grant Program. This
provides matching ("incentive") grants to any state with a
scholarship program based on need. Individual states,
however, calculate need in a variety of ways, and according to the Carnegie Council, "It has been the exception,
rather than the rule, for states to adjust their eligibility
rules, award amounts, cost allowances or application dead-
lines to those of the federal program."[10] Five states (California, Illinois, New York, Pennsylvania, and New Jersey)
provide over 65 percent of all state-based financial aid.
Also, in a very few places (Connecticut, Delaware, Massa-

chusetts, Rhode Island, Vermont, Washington, D.C., and the Virgin Islands) the award is "portable": that is, can be used by the student at any accredited institution of his choice in any location in the country. The other states require the award to be used within the state.

4. Veterans' Benefits and Social Security. The former, of course, is the GI Bill, for which any veteran is eligible. Social Security provides aid for dependents of deceased, aged, or disabled participants in the Social Security system. Both are quite generous, but they do not particularly help the needy. Only 26 percent of Social Security benefits are distributed to the poorest 25 percent of students, and only 43 percent of the veterans' benefits are distributed to the most needy quartile.[11]

5. Food Stamps. This is one of a number of federal welfare programs that were not intended for the benefit of students but, in fact, an extraordinary number of students are taking advantage of food stamps. In one community, for instance, 30 percent of all "families" in the food stamp program were student households. Nationally, many of the students come from families who earn over $20,000 a year.[12]

6. Other Public Programs. The list could go on. For there are many special sources of support, including: Vocational Rehabilitation Benefits, Department of Interior Bureau of Indian Affairs Higher Education Program, Families with Dependent Children, and so on.

Private Sources of Aid. There are two kinds of private aid: campus-based and national.

1. Campus-based Aid. This, of course, is the old, familiar scholarship, with one exception. In the old days most colleges provided scholarships from the income of endowment set aside for that purpose. Today, a majority

of colleges and universities (62 percent) supplement this aid with funds diverted from general operating revenues.[13] This means that those colleges, in their attempts to attract students, are operating their own income redistribution schemes: the students who pay full tuition are subsidizing those who do not, and the net effect for the college is that it is receiving less real income than might appear. These programs are almost all based on need, as determined by the CSS/ACT schedules (see below).

2. Nationally Based Private Aid. The best known of these are the National Merit Scholarship Program and the National Achievement Scholarship Program for Negro Students. These are based largely on test scores (the Preliminary Scholastic Aptitude Test/National Merit Scholarship Qualifying Test) and application is done at the time when the student signs for the test. Although most National Merit Awards are for freshman year only (typically $1,000), there are some endowed four-year scholarships providing up to $2,000 per year for four years.[14]

Student Employment. The most neglected area of student financial aid is work by the student himself. This is overlooked not only by many college students and their parents, but also by the colleges themselves and the institutions that determine financial need. There are two categories of student employment: term-time work-study and summer employment.

1. Work-Study. This is a federally subsidized campus-based job program, for which students are eligible if they enroll at a college participating in this program. The government underwrites 80 percent of the cost of salaries to students who take part-time term-time jobs around campus. Approximately 16 percent of all entering freshmen participate in this program, averaging $500 a year each.[15]

2. Summer Earnings. Fewer than half of all undergraduates use revenues from summer employment to defray college expenses, yet it can be a significant amount. For those who did save summer earnings for college, the average earned was nearly $700. It could be more. The Carnegie Council estimates that a reasonable amount a student could be expected to contribute from earnings (term-time and summer) is $1,800. Yet typically financial aid officers expect much less from students.[16] The result of this oversight is that parents may be required to make significant sacrifices to meet their assigned contribution while their children — by earning more than expected — are able to have more for spending on luxuries than the financial aid office calculated.

Loans. There are two types of commonly used student loans, both supported by the federal government: the National Direct Student Loan and the Guaranteed Student Loan. The basic difference between the two is that the NDSL is a campus-based loan program, and the GSL is not. In the former program the college administers loan funds provided by the government. The student automatically applies for the NDSL when he applies to the college for financial aid. The GSL is a community-based loan. The student must apply through his home-town bank. The NDSL is much preferable to the GSL. The former provides up to $5,000 over a four-year undergraduate program, the borrower paying no interest so long as he is a student at least half time. After graduation or leaving college, the interest begins to accumulate at 3 percent. The GSL, which provides up to $7,500 over a four-year period, requires a lot of red tape to get. The loan must be approved by the bank, must be scrutinized by the college, the state (or federal) officials. Often the student must put up collateral. The amount the student may borrow is not limited by need, and the use of the loan is not restricted. It may, for instance, be simply a "loan of convenience." Because the NDSL is preferable and because a college's NDSL money may be limited, many colleges run out of such funds and then must ask the student to apply for a GSL.

It is well known by now that these loan programs are a national scandal. The default rate is grotesquely high: 19 percent of NDSL and 13 percent of GSL are in default (as compared with 1.7 percent default rate on auto loans). The rate of nonrepayment on high risk loans is 44 percent. Sixteen hundred GSL borrowers have declared bankruptcy to avoid repayment and 20,245 NDSL borrowers have done the same.[17]

How Financial Need Is Determined

The "means test" is the device by which colleges and the government agencies determine financial need and eligibility for assistance. There are three agencies that administer such tests: the Basic Educational Opportunity Grant System, the College Scholarship Service, and the American College Testing Service. The latter two are private, nonprofit corporations, and their systems are very similar. Until the passage of the MISAA all three were roughly identical; since then the Basic Grants test expects a greater contribution from lower-income families and less from upper-income families than do the private tests.[18] The Basic Grants test is used in determining eligibility for any federal program. CSS/ACT are used to determine eligibility for private funds. Either or neither may be used by the states. Some colleges, usually in the East, use CSS, and others, more often in the West, use ACT.

In any of its forms, the means test works just like the federal income tax. Parents fill out a financial statement and provide copies of their federal income tax form. A rate table is applied to the family's income after certain specified deductions are subtracted. The trend in recent years has been for the private tests to lower the family contribution by increasing the number of permissible deductions, while the public test has accomplished this by liberalizing the rate table. The deductions exclude portions of fixed assets (like equity in a house or retirement savings), but above some threshold a certain percentage of these assets is considered "liquid."

A friend of mine noted that his uncle had a farm that never made any money but that put his five children through college. This is very possible. The means test is not perfect, and I believe it tends to favor the self-employed, who have more deductions. In any case, here, as a rule of thumb, is what you can expect: if you are a family of four with one in college and standard deductions and your pre-tax income is:

$6,000 you pay no educational expense;
$12,000 you pay $270;
$18,000 you pay $1,150;
$24,000 you pay $2,420;
$30,000 you pay $4,130;
$36,000 you pay $5,680.[19]

The CSS and ACT send to the financial aid office their recommendations on the basis of information collected from parents on the Financial Aid Form (FAF) or Family Financial Statement (FFS). Meanwhile the student and his family will have applied for a BEOG using either the FAF or FFS or the Basic Grants application form. The Basic Grants office, after processing the application, sends the student a Student Eligibility Report, which, in turn, the student must forward to the college to which he has applied for aid. When all this information is collected, a financial aid package is put together. Suppose, for instance, that tuition, room and board, plus fees come to $5,000. To this will be added an estimate of the student's personal and incidental expenses (books, laundry, etcetera) plus travel (typically, the cost of two round trips home each year). Say the total package is $5,550. From this figure are subtracted the parental contribution and the student's own savings and earnings, as well as any private or state scholarships, Social Security, or veterans' benefits for which the student may be eligible. For instance, for a family of four earning $18,000, the family contribution might be $1,150 (parents) plus, say, $400 for the student's summer earnings, or a total of $1,550. Subtracting this from the total costs leaves $4,000, which is the estimate of financial need. To this figure is applied, first, any federal grants for which the student is eligible. In this case, the family might receive a BEOG grant of $650. Then the student is enrolled in student work-study ($500). Next he is asked to apply for an NDSL loan ($1,200). The sum of this aid is $2,350, leaving $1,650 as the outstanding need, which the college will supply in the form of scholarship aid.

As this process works in practice, there are a few important points to keep in mind.

First, many colleges have a "rolling" system of financial aid. That is, they do not make all the financial aid decisions at once, after all applications are in; rather, they make decisions as they receive them. This is a "first come, first served" system. Most applicants do not know this and as a result, many apply too late. To be safe, Dr. Bowman of CSS told me, "spring of junior year is not too early" to apply.

Second, in many cases, the college supplies scholarships only when loans and all other forms of aid are exhausted. This means, in effect, that they are demanding that the student incur up to $7,500 in debts by graduation. For many students this may be too much. They are put behind the eight ball before they graduate. The bankruptcies and other questionable practices associated with these loans, therefore, are actually being encouraged by the colleges.

Third, most colleges have limited amounts of NDSL loan money available and therefore they may ask the applicant to seek a GSL loan in his community. As these loans are not limited by need or use, they can encourage students to be irresponsible with money. This system not only discourages thrift but may be one reason why so many dormitories are overstuffed with hi-fi equipment. In most cases, a student will not need the parents' permission to take out a loan. How much experience have most college freshmen had with money?

Fourth, many financial aid officers assume parents intentionally underestimate income (even though CSS says few do). Therefore, if the estimate of parental contribution appears too high, one should give the financial aid office a ring to discuss the matter.

Fifth, as we have seen, most estimates of family contribution underestimate the earnings potential of the student.

Sixth, incidental and travel expenses are usually underestimated by the college financial aid office.

Seventh, financial need is figured on the previous year's earnings. If earnings this year are much less or much more, one should notify the financial aid office.

Eighth, as financial need is based on family income, many students are tempted to "emancipate" themselves — declare themselves independent of their parents so that they will qualify for more financial aid. This, too, is becoming a national problem, as we shall see. The number of independent students increased from 18 percent of all students in 1974–1975 to 24 percent in 1976–1977.[20]

Ninth, as with any other welfare program, this one is subject to abuses. Over 40 percent of the 1.4 billion in Veterans' Administration overpayments is due to failure of veterans or their schools to tell the Administration when they leave. Some enroll in college just to qualify for benefits. Fraud occurs also. At one college in Pennsylvania, according to the Carnegie Council, 106 students were arrested for fraud in connection with financial aid.[21]

Tenth, some colleges are tempted to indulge in dishonest practices. Riverside University in California, for example, was closed because, among other things, according to the Carnegie Council, it "failed to notify students that loans had been received or to refund loans when students withdrew prior to actual enrollment."[22]

The Social Costs

We can see now that there are considerable social costs attached to the national system of financial aid. The system does not help the poor as much as it should because it is not understood by them, and because some colleges take advantage of this ignorance. The system is probably helping the middle class too much. It has encouraged students to borrow more than they should and has discouraged thriftiness. It has promoted a rash of unethical behavior, including declaring bankruptcy to avoid repayment of debts, fraud on financial aid applications, and failure to report all income. It has rewarded irresponsible parenting and further weakened the family by tempting students to declare themselves independent so that their parents might escape any financial obligation for their education. It has not asked enough from students themselves, and it has become so complicated that many families have been defrauded by institutions.

These social costs can be translated into personal risks. One should apply for financial aid just the way one goes to the bank for a loan: after carefully considering all the alternatives and with full knowledge of the risks involved. These risks are not all pecuniary. At this state of a family's life, the college — in the form of the financial aid office — intrudes between student and parent, making sensitive relations even more difficult. Too many people become involved in important family decisions. The student on financial aid is in an ambiguous position to begin with, lying somewhere between childhood and adulthood. Being a beneficiary of financial aid adds to this ambiguity. The student is in a sense a quasi-independent (after all, he, not his parents, is responsible to pay any debts incurred). Parents may find themselves increasingly frustrated with the red tape necessary to obtain financial aid, and they may resent both the scholarship committee's recommendations and their child (because not enough is expected of him). Both sides may be tempted by these frustrations to decide the student should declare independence. The student may be further tempted to declare bankruptcy on graduation: hardly a good way to start adulthood.

For these reasons it is important to keep in mind that the scholarship committee's analysis of financial aid is an estimate only. The family need not follow it. It would probably be wise for most students, for example, to borrow less than the committee will recommend. No one should be forced by a college to borrow. In many cases, more contribution should be expected from the student's earnings, which should go to minimize the debt. Many middle-class families can contribute more than is asked of them and thereby further minimize their own debt, if not do away with the need for it altogether.

"Lead us not into temptation, but deliver us from evil." It is much easier for the poor to be good than for the rich, for they have fewer temptations. We are a rich country and therefore it is more difficult, today, to be a good person than it once was. College today is more accessible than ever, but the result is a decline in the value our country places on education, charity, incentive, thrift, honesty, and the family. Being affected by this decline is the principal risk the financial aid applicant runs. But this does not mean that he need succumb to it.

13

COLLEGE DAYS
Planning Studies and
Choosing Options

Sow a Thought, and you reap an Act;
Sow an Act, and you reap a Habit;
Sow a Habit, and you reap a Character;
Sow a Character, and you reap a Destiny.

— Anonymous

Study as if you were to live for ever; live as if you were to die
tomorrow.

— EDMUND OF ABINGDON

Freshman Orientation Week

It is one of my eccentricities that I dislike bingo, and that
is why, I think, I never liked freshman orientation week.
The two are very much the same.

Both my aversions have a long history. More than twenty
years ago, when I was a second lieutenant in the army, I
was ordered by my commander to "officiate" at a bingo
game being held for senior officers' wives at the officers'
club. This was, I thought, such a demeaning requirement
that I did something perhaps unprecedented in the annals
of army history: I resigned from the club. That was the
beginning of the end of my military career. My "automatic"
promotion to first lieutenant was denied (later granted

under protest), and my friends were told that being seen in my company would hurt their careers.

What I managed to avoid in the army, however, I met in academe. As a member of the faculty of Macalester College I was required to take part in freshman orientation week. This is, like bingo, essentially a lottery. The role of the faculty is not unlike calling numbers in bingo. The student, fresh on campus, is offered several hundred courses and asked to pick four (and plan, tentatively, twenty-eight more). He is given a schedule card on which, through course choice, he tries to trace a coherent pattern (bingo). Meanwhile, various faculty members are barking course numbers at him, suggesting that he pick one or drop another.

During the first few days of the week faculty members are asked to hold departmental orientation sessions, to which all freshmen are invited. The purpose of this is to encourage each department to sell its audience on the intrinsic and extrinsic value of its field. Then, later in the week, the whole college assembles in the gym for registration. The gym is lined with booths, each occupied with representatives from the departments. Little hand-drawn signs identify the booths.

Students mill around, course schedules in hand, giving the impression that a gigantic treasure hunt is in progress. They stop first at one booth, then another, like shoppers at a small-town bazaar. They seem to be in a daze, and no wonder. They don't know what they're doing.

A freshman approaches the philosophy booth. He peers at his card to see what time slots are still vacant. "What do you have between eleven and twelve?" he asks.

"Only Problems and Foundations. The others are filled," I answer.

"What are they about?" he asks, straining to read my sign-up sheet upside down.

"Foundations is an upper-level course," I reply; "you are

not eligible for it. Problems, however, is intended to be an introduction to philosophy."

"Sounds boring. Introductions always are, aren't they?"

Secretly agreeing with him — that Problems is boring since I know who will be teaching it — I answer with clenched teeth, "Not really, you will study some interesting things: the problems of free will and determinism, personal identity, the existence of the material world. . . ."

"The existence of *what?*"

"The material world."

"Is that a problem? Sounds crazy. But it fits my schedule. I'll take it."

Bingo.

In these circumstances, it is no wonder that students quickly become disillusioned. They come to college with high hopes that are all too soon dashed. In a 1970 poll, for example, 43 percent of all seniors said they were treated like "numbers in a book" and 45 percent said they "felt lost" when they got to college.[1] Yet this is worse today, as colleges leave so many important decisions to the student. More than ever, it is important for students to plan their undergraduate careers before they even set foot on campus and, once there, immediately know how to make their way through this anonymous environment, instantly understand how to make intelligent choices, how to avoid mistakes, and how, in the midst of the formless freedom of today's campuses, to give constructive shape and direction to their lives.

Hedging Bets

Whether you go to college for the intellectual stimulation, cultural enrichment, or money, it is important to keep in mind that, in planning your undergraduate career, you should hedge your bets. If you focus your studies too narrowly too soon, you may discover you have crawled out on a limb that, in your senior year, you must saw off, for few students enter, upon graduation, the careers that, in freshman year, they intended to enter. Of those who, as freshmen, intend to go to medical school, only 40 percent are still on this track four years later. Of the freshmen who plan to go for the Ph.D., only 19 percent will later apply to graduate school. Less than a third of those who, in freshman year, want to be engineers still want to be engineers upon graduation, and 50 percent more seniors are interested in a business career than are freshmen.[2] In short, between freshman and senior years a majority of students change their career plans; so it is wise to chart one's course of studies in a way that anticipates this. Doing this requires planning studies that are broad rather than narrow, of course, but it also requires planning your extracurricular activities and living arrangements as well, for everything a student does will have an effect on how much he learns, how much he grows, and how successful he will be later in life.

To make wise decisions about studies requires a good advisor. For a student needs to know something, not only about the characteristics of the various disciplines, but also about the relative strengths and weaknesses of the departments. He needs to know what likely effects will ensue from following a particular course of studies.

Advisors. As we know, however, a student today is unlikely to find a good advisor. Besides, the student has no way of knowing — until it is too late — whether his advisor is good or not. Therefore, in the absence of foreknowledge, it is best to arrange to have more than one advisor. That is, the student should, as soon as possible, simply strike up an informal acquaintance with one or more faculty members in addition to his regular advisor. These informal advisors should not be in the same department and, preferably, not in the same area. One should be chosen, say, in the social sciences, another in the humanities, and perhaps a third in the natural sciences. There is much evidence that the more contact students have with the faculty, the more they learn and grow.[3]

What Study Does to You. Different fields teach different things and have different effects. Dr. Whitla, for instance, found that what you major in determines what kind of "cognitive style" you develop.[4] Natural science majors tend to work out systematic strategies to problems; social science majors tend to solve problems by looking for facts, and humanities majors tend to solve problems by trying to categorize all new information. Humanities majors are likely to be interested in liberal education; students in the social sciences are likely to be politically liberal, altruistic, hedonistic, to lack interest in business, and to be less religious than average. Natural science and mathematics majors are likely to be conservative, not so altruistic, to have high self-esteem. Engineering majors are also less liberal and less altruistic, but more interested in business and have lower self-esteem. Premed students have high self-esteem, are relatively altruistic, and tend to have business interests.[5]

Choosing a Major: Caveat Emptor! Choosing a major at a liberal arts college should seldom be based on vocational concerns. A few fields, such as accounting and engineering, are directly helpful in obtaining postgraduate employment, and a few others, such as geology, psychology, and biology, are indirectly helpful, but by and large, as we have seen, the benefits of liberal arts study are long-term and indirect. No graduate school, for instance, has prerequisites as part of its admissions policy that specify the subject in which a student must major in order to gain admission (even though graduate schools usually do require that the student major in something and they do set certain course prerequisites for admission). The major, therefore, should be chosen because you like it, because you do it well, and because the department that offers it is a good one.

In the last regard, students are usually far more credulous of departmental claims than they should be. Many faculty members, through ignorance or desperation, make claims for their field that would put a snake oil salesman to shame. They are particularly prone to exaggerate the vocational opportunities afforded by their field, all the while clinging to their tenure like rats to a raft in the realization that, if they left teaching, they would be nearly unemployable in the "real world." But if possessing a Ph.D. wouldn't help them find a job, why should a B.A. in the same field help you?

The single most important thing for a student to know is the quality and composition of the department of his interest. Yet few students learn this until they are well along in their major, if at all. Until the 1960s, a role of the dean of faculty was to assure that each department was well balanced: that, for instance, the philosophy department had historians of philosophy as well as linguistic analysts; existentialists as well as philosophers of science; or that the economics department had some microeconomists as well as macroeconomists, some Keynesians as well as followers of Milton Friedman. Today, because of the growth of departmental power and the tendency of colleges to pick weak deans, few departments are well balanced. "Birds of a feather flock together" is the guiding principle of departmental assimilation today, as departments have become mutual-admiration societies populated by overlapping specialists.

So any student, before majoring in a subject, should investigate the department. First, he should if possible read some introductory survey work in order to acquaint himself with the major issues and schools of thought. If, for instance, he is contemplating majoring in sociology, he should find the biases of the sociologists at his college. Are they functionalists (structuralists), formalists, social behaviorists, methodological individualists? Do they follow Talcott Parsons, Lévi-Strauss, C. Wright Mills? If the subject is psychology, what kind of psychology is practiced? Experimental psychology? Social psychology? Cognitive psychology? What is the anthropology department like? Many, according to some reports, are dominated by Marxists.[6] What is the physics department like? Are they doing high-energy or low-energy physics? College physics may be much different from high school physics, and today many college physics departments are dying on the vine. What do the historians teach? Do they teach all the periods of history in which you are interested? What of the English department? Do they teach all the courses they list in the catalogue? (At one college with which I am familiar, a course on Chaucer was left in the catalogue for at least seven years without being taught. A senior member of the department insisted that, if it were to be taught, only he was qualified; yet he never wanted to teach it. Such a dog-in-the-manger attitude is not uncommon.)

Another important question to ask is whether it is possible to *progress* in the major. Many departments — particularly at smaller liberal arts colleges — in an attempt to attract *new* students, fail to serve the *old* ones. They do this by allowing the freshman to take upper-level courses. Upper-level courses always sound more interesting, more challenging. They have names like "metaphysics" while lower-level courses have names like "problems." But many teachers, by allowing freshmen to take upper-level courses, find they must scale down their expectations of the students in these courses. The result is that upper-level courses become disguised lower-level ones and fail to challenge the upperclassman. This way the upperclassman finds, by junior year, there are no more courses left to take; his department, he discovered too late, offers only introductory courses. This is why many students transfer.

Grading Options. There are three popular grading options and many colleges offer all of them. First, the traditional letter grades — A, B, C, D, F — second, Pass/Fail; and third, "written evaluations." The third may be combined with either of the others. The first, with all its imperfections, is the only one that will help the student. Remember, the function of the grade is to tell you how you're doing and to certify you. It is, after all, only the certificate that has much economic value. Studies have shown that students do not work as hard in courses where they take the pass/fail option, and your prospective employer will know this.[7] Everyone will read "pass" as "C." Written evaluations are either redundant or meaningless or both: redundant because any professor worth his tenure should give you verbal and written evaluations on your work anyway, and if he doesn't you have the right to visit him about it; meaningless because, as we saw in Chapter 3, the Buckley Law makes too many evaluators too cautious.

At most schools students have the option of choosing the method of grading. Watch for this. Many professors falsely tell students signing up for their courses that they *must* opt for a pass/fail grade. This is not only usually against college policy, it is also a sign the professors don't want to "waste a lot of their valuable time" reading your written work.

Individually Prescribed Majors, Interdepartmental Majors, Etcetera. I sympathize with students who want to take this route, but I advise against it, for several reasons. First, it will look like Mickey Mouse on your résumé. Second, every person should have the experience of mastering a discipline. In all likelihood, this will not happen in an idiosyncratic major. Third, no one will really take responsibility for your education. You will be in a disciplinary no-man's-land, and in all probability no one will understand what you are doing, or care. Fourth, cross-disciplinary work is most productive only after you have mastered the disciplines that you desire to bridge.

Honors Programs. Like other features of the curriculum, these have multiplied in recent years. Some honors today are just based on grades, some exempt students from courses or examinations, some require comprehensives with internal or external examiners, some require senior theses, and many combine these elements. Many are also gimmicks, requiring less of the honors student than of the nonhonors student. The guiding principle, in fact, should be: if the honors program does require more of the student, it is probably worth taking. If it requires less, it is probably best avoided.

Study Abroad. Once upon a time there was something called junior year abroad. Now a student can go almost anytime and stay away as long as he wishes. My niece, for instance, recently graduated from Princeton after being on campus only two years. The rest of the time she was overseas. The fact that students may study abroad as early as sophomore year and may do it without their parents' permission often takes parents by surprise. Not a few parents have had their children come home for their first summer vacation to learn they were already signed up for a term in Paris, under no supervision at all.

There are, however, two good reasons why a student should still wait until junior year to go abroad. First, most students will get more out of a year abroad when they are a year older and know the language better. Second, how are you going to keep them at Princeton, once they've seen Paris? For many students it is difficult to spend sophomore year abroad and then return to face two more years in college. Going abroad early does encourage students to drop out early.

Planning Extracurricular Activities

David was a National Merit Scholar and held a National Scholarship at Harvard. Much was expected of him, by his parents, by the admissions office, and by his teachers. His parents hoped he might become a Rhodes Scholar and eventually go to law school. The admissions office and faculty saw in him a potentially brilliant scholar. He disappointed all of them. His grades were terrible, so terrible he did not even qualify for honors. He did win the Bowdoin Prize senior year for the best undergraduate essay. The ease with which he tossed this off just showed, everyone thought, what he could have done if he had just applied himself. It seemed as though a lot of talent had been wasted. What happened?

In his sophomore year David founded a poetry magazine. For three years his life revolved around this project, absorbing almost all his energies, as he struggled to make the magazine grow. He had little time for studies.

As it turned out, this was probably the best path David could have followed during college. He did not waste his time at all; he used it very efficiently. He was doing what he wanted to do, and he was learning. At graduation he was immediately hired as assistant to the editor of a national magazine. He had got a good start in life.

David is our oldest son. It was we who pushed him wrongly toward grade-getting. It was not until I began to do research for this book that I realized how right he was. He was, according to studies, typical of the student who gets most from college.[8] From a purely vocational point of view, his time was better spent than it could have been any other way.

The challenge of college today is to avoid being a *Lumpenstudent*, to escape anonymity, to grow, and to develop wider interests. At one time, when curricula were better balanced, it might have been possible for the student to concentrate on his studies and still build the character and skills that would do him well in life, but this is unlikely today.

It is therefore more useful than ever for a student to engage a project outside the curriculum, a project in which he may become absorbed and that will challenge him. It matters less what the student does than that he does something. He may start a magazine, like David, or join an established one. He may work with a political society, or welfare organization, do research, join the dramatic society, become a painter. If the organization does not exist that suits his talents and interests, he can found his own.

It is a common complaint among educators today (including myself) that college life is too "unstructured." This is true, but it is more harmful than perhaps it should be because too many students do not know how to use the great freedom they find at college. Their lives, until they enter as freshmen, have been too structured, and in the wrong way. Their time has been occupied, but not their minds or creative energies. Few children today are allowed to be Huck Finns. Life as a young person in suburbia is likely to be plotted as full of appointments as any plastic surgeon's. Young people are managed in Little League and pee wee hockey; they are sent to summer camp; they are driven to school and home; they are sat in a classroom and talked to; they watch endless hours of television.[9]

It is no wonder, therefore, that at college many students express the need for freedom. But not knowing how to use this freedom they often go to seed: keeping messy rooms, sleeping late, missing classes. This has been confirmed by studies that show that college promotes the hedonistic lifestyle: drinking, smoking, using pot. Students engage in constructive extracurricular activities — attending concerts, playing a musical instrument, even checking a book out of a library — less frequently at college than they did before they came.[10]

The student's greatest challenge is to use his college time creatively. Some students, of course, will turn their back on this freedom, burying their heads in their specialties or tracking to medical school. This may be fine for some; but for most using this freedom, although requiring more effort and imagination, can be far more rewarding.

Food and Housing. Living in a dormitory accentuates, as we have seen, all the effects of living in college. It is, in short, more intense than living at home or off campus. Dorm living, therefore, like college, is both good and bad.

First, just as single-sex colleges are most conducive to higher learning and better living, so, we might assume, are single-sex dorms. This is especially apt to be true for women.

Second, how the dorm is governed is vitally important. Most people will be less happy in self-governing dorms.

Third, "entry" dorms are far preferable to "corridor" dorms.

Fourth, most students should *not* choose single rooms, even if they seem attractive. They will be more lonely in singles.

Many colleges have cooperatives, usually available for upperclassmen. These are simply houses, with or without a resident counselor. Usually students share a common kitchen and share the cost of food. Most students like this arrangement (it is, after all, much like a fraternity or sorority, although usually coeducational), but it may not be suitable for everyone. Taking care of meals takes time and these arrangements are awfully — what the English call matey. That is, they are *intimate*. If you don't get along with your housemates, or have an affair with one whom you then want to drop, you may find living too cramped. It is difficult to get away from anyone in a cooperative.

Should you opt for the ten-meal-a-week food plan, or the twenty-meal plan? The only reason for opting for the ten-meal plan is lack of money. But if you can't afford to eat three meals a day you can't afford college. Many students make the mistake of skipping college meals to save money (or to pocket money sent by their parents for food), only to find, often too late, that they made few friends in college. The dining commons may be one of the few places on campus where a student has the chance to make new friends.

Few in the faculty or administration like fraternities and sororities, partly because they are islands of conservatism in an otherwise liberal campus and partly because some fraternities are boozy, sexist, and prone to violence. But it is wrong to condemn the system because some are uncivilized. On a national average, according to studies, fraternities and sororities enhance a student's intellectual self-esteem. They encourage persistence in college and promote greater satisfaction with courses of instruction and social life.[11] For some, therefore, fraternities might be helpful.

The College Experience

When I was a student at University College, Oxford University, the Master of the college was a kindly, brilliant man named Arthur Goodhart. The first evening of our first term, all freshmen, dressed in the formal subfusc for the occasion, gathered in the Hall of the college to be greeted by the Master. This is what he said, as I remember it:

You are about to embark on what can be the most exciting, most rewarding, and most important years of your lives. The scholarly and intellectual resources of Oxford are nearly boundless, and I hope you take advantage of them. You are in the company of like minds, of people of honor dedicated to the truth. You should and will learn much from them. But do not, while you are here, make the mistake of assuming that it is only the treasures of the mind which Oxford can give you. What it offers is far richer than that. Do not, therefore, simply study. Look around you. Make friends, enjoy the beauty. Go punting, play sports, dance, debate. All this is Oxford and all this is meant for your benefit.

That was my freshman orientation, twenty years ago. Isn't that advice better than bingo?

14

PREPARING FOR THE REAL WORLD

There is a kind of education in which our sons should be trained not because it is useful or necessary for a specific purpose but because it is liberal and noble.

— ARISTOTLE

Education is what survives when what has been learnt has been forgotten.

— B. F. SKINNER

A Fable

Once upon a time there were triplets named Richard, Rebecca, and Rolf. When they turned eighteen, their father called them before him.

"Now that you are of age," he said, "you must decide what you want to do."

"I want to be a lawyer," said Richard; "I want to go to a good college, to law school, and then make a lot of money."

"I want to be an engineer," said Rebecca; "I want to build things people want and that way live a safe, secure life."

"I don't know what I want," said Rolf. "I am curious about many things. I think I'll just snoop around for a while."

Richard went to a famous college and graduated with distinction. He entered a famous law school and made the

Law Review. He became clerk to a Supreme Court Justice and later was hired by a prestigious law firm. He married a beautiful debutante and raised three pretty children. He made a lot of money.

Rebecca went to college and majored in engineering. At graduation she went to work for a large automobile company. "Transportation is a social necessity," she thought. "People will always need cars."

Rolf went to college to explore. He studied Gödel's proof and worried about the chromosome. He read Tolstoy and wrote about Gibbon. He also stayed up late and slept through classes. His parents worried about him.

After graduation, Rolf could not find a job. Since he had majored in social science, he first looked for a job with a welfare agency. "What can you do?" the personnel officer asked.

"I know all about Lévy-Bruhl and have mastered Piaget," Rolf replied.

"I did not ask you what you *knew;* I asked you what you could *do,*" the personnel officer answered. "Besides," he added, "I've never heard of those Mexicans you mentioned."

Rolf did not get the job.

Yet neither did all go well with his siblings. While Richard was making a lot of money he was not seeing much of his wife. She became unhappy and divorced him, taking their children and money with her. Richard was poor again, and unhappy. He found his job boring but could not afford to quit. He had an expensive cooperative apartment to pay for and child support checks to write.

"There must be more to life than this," he mused.

At the same time the world ran out of gas. The automobile company for which Rebecca worked stopped making cars and began to make solar collectors instead. Rebecca did not know how to make solar collectors. She was fired. That hardly mattered, for she had no gas to get to work, anyway.

Rebecca moved into the city and found a job with an electric company. "People will always need electricity," she thought. But the company for which she worked generated its power with fission reactors. One day a truck hauling waste away tipped over and fell into a reservoir. All the plants were closed. Rebecca was unemployed again.

"What can I do," she wondered, "that is secure? Where will the jobs of the future lie?"

Someone told her, "Wood. That's where our future lies. The world is running out of fossil fuels and we must live by renewable resources. Wood is a renewable resource."

So Rebecca went to work for a company that made wood heaters. They were pretty black and green things and she liked the work. She felt needed.

Then the country discovered that all its forests were being stripped bare. They were running out of wood. People stopped buying wood heaters. Rebecca was fired again.

Rolf still could not get a job. Everywhere he applied he was told the same thing: "We don't care what you know; it is what you can do that matters."

He finally landed a job with a plumbing contractor, but was quickly fired. He had been late to work three times because he overslept. His employer didn't like that, Rolf discovered. This had surprised him. At college no one had minded when he was late with his work, or whether he even showed up for class. Punctuality was new to him.

After being fired, Rolf found work even harder to get. People were always asking him what he had done previously and then asking him why he had been fired. Rolf was surprised his past mattered to these people. At college it mattered to no one. When he wrote a poor paper, the professor let him rewrite it; when he flunked a course, the grade did not go on his transcript; when he was caught cheating, he was given another chance. His previous grades were never held against him. Each year at college he was able to start afresh. Now his past was dogging him.

By the time Rolf was thirty-two, he was broke and still unemployed. He decided to pull himself together. If no one would have him, he had to make his own work, he decided. He wondered what he could do.

He had always liked to fiddle with electric circuitry, ever since he had discovered, in college, some interesting applications of symbolic logic to this. He began to fiddle. He worked hard and changed his habits. He got up early and went to bed early. He cut his hair, stopped smoking, and began to eat yogurt. One day he discovered something.

He discovered a marvelous way to convert sunlight to electricity. It was so simple he built it out of parts of an old Polaroid camera. He went to a patent attorney and got a patent. The patent attorney was a beautiful and brilliant woman. They married and became business partners. He became rich and solved America's energy problem. He was famous.

The triplets were united at their twenty-fifth college reunion. Richard, who spent his life making money, was now poor. Rebecca, who spent her life in search of security, was unemployed. And Rolf, who never knew what he wanted to do, was doing *just* what he wanted to do.

"Why should you succeed," Richard and Rebecca asked Rolf, "when it was we who had the superior training?"

"I don't know," replied Rolf. "I just couldn't find a job, so I decided to do some work instead."

Moral: College does not train, but sometimes it educates.

The Real World

It is significant that academics refer to society as "the real world," for campus life is different. It is sheltered; it deals with theory, not practice. Few people on any campus have had any experience outside of school. The faculty went from school to college to graduate school to teaching. They know how things are supposed to work, not how they work. It is no wonder, therefore, that colleges are poorly equipped to prepare students for "the real world."

In his essay, "Notes for a Dissenting Commencement Address," which appeared in a recent issue of the *Chronicle of Higher Education*, Carter A. Daniel, head of the writing program at Rutgers graduate school of business, makes the following notes to tell his mythical graduating seniors:

You've finished the easy part; anybody can get a college degree;

Era starting today is less interesting, less fun, much harder;

World is filled with people who couldn't make transition;

What you've done in past four years has little relation to what follows;

Colleges have failed to prepare you for next 50 years.[1]

This is not a surprising observation. Colleges seldom help students find their first jobs, seldom provide them the training they need to excel at them or give them the maturity to make the right decisions about life. In fact, the college experience may have a negative impact. The qualities that probably are most important in finding, holding, and succeeding in a job are emotional maturity, punctuality, thrift, ambition, honesty, energy, reliability and ability to get along with others. Yet these are things that, especially today, colleges do not teach. As Rolf discovered, college is more permissive than the real world. According to studies, as we have seen, those who get high grades in college may have more personal problems later in life; students, when they graduate, are less ambitious, less honest, less sociable, and less punctual than they were when they entered as freshmen. Further, because so many are required to put themselves into debt to get an education, and because borrowing money is so easy for undergraduates to do, the system of financial aid does not promote thrift. In short, students may be taught bad habits in college and, like Rolf, they must break these habits before they can accomplish anything.

Yet to criticize colleges because they do not train is unfair. They were never intended to do so. They educate, and that is something else. Training provides special skills necessary to do a specific job. The effects of education are long-term and indirect. Rolf benefited from his college education, but it took him ten years to derive this benefit. He discovered that education's greatest virtue is that it is portable and cannot, like money or security, be lost. The educated man always has the potential to change, to adapt, to survive.

Planning one's education, therefore, must be directed not to the next job, but to the entire life. It must be designed to have a lifetime of utility. That is why a narrow education is so ephemeral. Just as any living being loses its ability to adapt and risks extinction when it becomes too specialized, so becoming an expert increases the risk of economic extinction. A person too specialized can find himself with what economists call trained incapacity. That is when he is an expert in a field that is no longer in demand. Any dislocation in the job market can create trained incapacity, and sometimes this dislocation can be, as Rebecca discovered, impossible to predict. Ten years ago there was a shortage of teachers; few at that time foresaw that there would be an oversupply by the early seventies. Recently, also, we have seen job dislocations in high energy physics and architecture.[2] In the next decade they may be in law and medicine. But who can be sure?

During the last decade, in increasing numbers, people

have changed careers, partly because of rapid and unpredictable shifts in our economy and partly because we are living longer. As Gail Sheehy notes in *Passages*, "The single fact that people are living longer in better physical condition than ever makes commitment to a single, forty-year career almost predestinate stagnation."[3] Ms. Sheehy's comment seems supported by the facts. According to the 1977 *Quality of Employment Survey*, worker job satisfaction has been declining in recent years, and now over 50 percent of all workers feel "locked into" their jobs.[4] At the same time, a 1979 Bureau of Labor Statistics *Bulletin* reports, "Americans are changing occupations more frequently than they used to." The rate of job changes for professionals, for instance, is now 8½ percent a year.[5]

For the same reasons, job dislocations and career changes are likely to become more common in the eighties, for these will be times of flux, of energy shortages of long duration, which will require massive shifts in our economy as we search for alternative sources of energy. They will also be times when our lifestyles will change and with them our patterns of consumption. Our standard of living, as economists measure it, may decline. Whole industries will probably disappear and others will emerge. Cities may experience a renaissance and suburbs become ghosts towns, shopping centers atrophy and resorts die as energy scarcity affects every aspect of our lives.

None of this may happen, of course. No one knows. Neither do we know, if these things occur, how they will affect us. They may bring us closer together as a people, and they may divide us further. All we know is that they will be exciting times, and times of change, and for the student preparing for the days ahead, it means, first, resisting the negative effects colleges are inclined to have on the average student and second, preparing for the long haul.

Resisting the Negative

To say that college does not instill good work habits does not mean that a student cannot, while he is at college, train himself. It just means that to do this the student must be more self-disciplined than his parents had to be. The professor is not going to insist that papers be on time; only the student can see to this. The school is not going to provide the student's motivation; he must supply it himself. The financial aid office is not going to prevent the student from taking out a loan to buy a hi-fi; the student must stop himself.

Colleges today, as we have seen, teach consumption. They teach students to be consumers, not producers, by promoting a hedonistic lifestyle, debt, and a policy of options. But the philosophy of consumption is running out of gas. It will be an anachronism in the eighties. The student must, therefore, while using the resources of his college, teach himself to live on less and to be productive rather than consumptive.

The student will also find preparing for the long haul more difficult than it once was. Colleges are today, more than ever, forsaking the pursuit of knowledge for the pursuit of training. The sixties were supposed to be the time when campuses gave in to student demands for relevance; the seventies were supposedly the decade of quiet seriousness; and the eighties are anticipated, by many, as a decade of reform. It is ironic that most colleges have returned to relevance with a vengeance. While the prestigious liberal arts colleges capture the headlines with their core curricula, the bulk of the small liberal arts colleges and state institutions are working quietly but frantically to transform themselves into vocational schools. Made anxious by declining enrollments, student career anxiety, and declining job prospects, they are modifying traditional liberal arts courses by infusing them with a panoply of experiential learning, multidisciplinary perspectives, student internships, and faculty externships; and they are adding, at a feverish pace, new strictly vocational programs on such subjects as prenuclear medicine, criminal justice, secretarial science, recreation, and nursing. They are retraining faculties in the career relevance of their disciplines, so that these faculties, as advisors, may be better able to sell the student on the practicality of their field. Thus, Northwestern College in Orange City, Iowa, now has introduced a "career concentration"; Fort Wright College in Spokane, Washington, now allows students to earn academic credit for "past experiential learning"; the University of Dubuque, Iowa, has formed "marketing committees"; other colleges are developing "career clusters," "multifaceted processes for career/ life planning," "faculty-student cadres to facilitate the work/learning interface," and "individualized, self-paced, multimedia learning packages."

This bandwagon is gathering momentum as it is propelled by a business community increasingly skeptical of the competency of liberal arts graduates. Grinnell College in Iowa reports that use of their Career Services Office has increased 102 percent since 1973. Survey research has indicated that many employers have a neutral or somewhat negative attitude toward liberal arts graduates.[6]

At the reins of this bandwagon is a new breed of educators trained to the nuances of an obfuscating vocabulary. In a secret language that not even they can understand, they talk of "skills assessment materials," "delivery modes," "transitional services," "interagency teaching centers," "reality testing," "impact funds," "prioritizing," and "preplanning." It is these bureaucrats who, although they cannot write a plain English sentence, took over secondary edu cation some time ago and have rendered that virtually ineffective. Now they are turning their special skills for the teaching of illiteracy to the colleges.

There is, of course, nothing wrong with vocational training, and it is laudatory that colleges are paying more attention to career guidance. For too many years they have done almost nothing. But the danger is that many colleges are being propelled into career guidance for the wrong reasons and risk doing students more harm than good. Many colleges, to make the liberal arts more relevant, are simply taking the liberal arts out of the curriculum. Others are turning themselves into employment agencies. By emphasizing job getting, they overstimulate student anxieties about their personal future and force students to make career decisions before they are ready. Some colleges, for instance, *require* students to take courses on career placement. Thus they are contributing to the ethical decay on campus. By preoccupation with training students in special skills for the marketplace, they overlook the more fundamental and broader capabilities that will help the students most and that it has always been their mission to teach: the three R's and the development of character. For what most employers look for is literacy in natural and symbolic languages and those traits of personality that make students reliable and effective workers. By failing to teach these things, colleges are putting students at a disadvantage for which no specialized training can compensate.

If colleges do not prepare students for the next fifty years, students must prepare themselves. The short-term interests of most students is, legitimately, developing a specialty; but the long-term interest is in obtaining a general education. These are not incompatible. Indeed, as we saw in Chapter 4, they complement each other. In all fields, with the possible exception of medicine, colleges offer students the means both for entering a specialized field and for achieving a general education, for almost all graduate schools have minimal prerequisites for entry.

For graduate study in *architecture*, for instance, a student need take only one studio art course in college, one physics with laboratory, and one calculus.

To enter *business school*, the prerequisites are one year of economics, one semester of computer programming, one semester of statistics, and one of accounting. In addition, according to the *Journal of College Placement*, a student has a good chance of landing a job in business directly from college if: "(1) he completes two semesters of accounting, and an introduction to business principles and management; (2) completes one summer of business related work, (3) completes one course in economics; and (4) does not slant the remainder of an undergraduate program toward preparing for a job."[7]

To enter graduate school in *public policy and administration*, the student must have had one year of calculus, a semester of statistics, and a semester of computer programming.

There are no prerequisites for entry to any graduate schools of *journalism, education,* or *law*.[8]

Medicine is a special case. In theory, the premed student may major in anything he chooses, so long as he takes one year of biology with laboratory, one year of inorganic chemistry with laboratory, one year of organic chemistry with laboratory, and one year of physics with laboratory. In addition, fourteen medical schools in the country require calculus.

In fact, however, medical schools grossly favor the student who majors in a life science, and thus they put unfair pressures on premed undergraduates to specialize. As Dr. Lewis Thomas, author of the book *The Lives of the Cell* and president of the Memorial Sloan-Kettering Cancer Center, reported in the *New England Journal of Medicine:*

There is still some talk in medical deans' offices about the need for general culture, but nobody really means it, and certainly the pre-medical students don't believe it. They concentrate on science.

They concentrate on science with a fury, and they live for grades. . . . The atmosphere of the liberal-arts college is being poisoned by pre-medical students, who do not start out as a necessarily bad lot. They behave as they do in the firm belief that if they behave any otherwise they won't get into medical school.[9]

In these circumstances, what can the student do? Until medical school admissions offices are reformed, he must either major in a life science or forget medicine as a career.

For the student who does not know what he wants to do but who, like Rebecca, wants to go into a field that is not crowded, there is not much he can be told. No one knows where the jobs will be in the eighties. Predicting attractive employment opportunities is like announcing where there's gas during a shortage. If we knew today where the jobs would be tomorrow, the line would be long by morning.

So choosing any job, as Rebecca discovered, involves risk. To minimize this risk, however, you may want to ask the college to give you a vocational interest test, such as the Strong-Campbell Interest Inventory, but don't expect too much from it.[10] It will probably tell you what you already know: that, for instance, you'd be happier being a writer than a bricklayer. You may also want to know where the U.S. government *thinks* the jobs will be in the eighties. The Bureau of Labor Statistics publishes a number of helpful books. The most complete is entitled *Occupational Outlook Handbook*.[11] Besides providing projections on the labor market in every field, it also describes all conceivable occupations and tells you the earnings you can expect in each. Most libraries have this book. Otherwise, it may be purchased from the U.S. Government Printing Office, Washington, D.C. 20402.

In a 1978 issue of the *Chronicle of Higher Education,* Marvin Feldman, president of the Fashion Institute of Technology, noted that although our country is short of jobs, it is not short of work.[12] This is a profound distinction. A job is already there; it is not designed to fit any particular person's talents but to solve a problem or satisfy a need — one, perhaps, that no longer exists. It takes no imagination to apply for a job. By contrast, work is what needs to be done; it requires imagination to know what this is, what will succeed, and what won't. Jobs are already waiting for college graduates to take them; work must be created.

In the eighties, work may be far more important than jobs, for as our society's problems change, the jobs that exist now may become totally inappropriate for the times.

Students should be preparing for work, not jobs, but society expects colleges to prepare students for jobs. This is one reason why creativity in America is declining, as is reflected in the decline of our lead in technology over the rest of the world. In 1968, for instance, 300 high-technology small companies were founded; yet not one such company was founded in 1977.[13] We are facing a crisis of creativity, for the economic and social demands of the eighties will place a premium on imagination. To prepare to play a valuable role in our society during these times, students should plan, not so much for one specific job or career, but to use their imagination. This is what they should use the resources of the college to develop, for this is where our future lies.

15

SURVIVAL

Despite the manifold imperfections of the Ik study, the facts illustrate the extremes to which adaptation to deprivation can lead a human society, extremes at which sociality becomes extinct for all intents and purposes, but the people survive.

— COLIN TURNBULL

We would discover, in ourselves, the sources of wonderment and delight that we have discovered in all other manifestations of nature . . . We might even acknowledge the fragility and vulnerability that always accompanies high specialization in biology, and movements might start up for the protection of ourselves as a valuable, endangered species.

— LEWIS THOMAS

Whose Survival?

In 1953 Dr. Charles Houston, an American, led an expedition to attempt to climb K-2, the world's second highest mountain. K-2, in Pakistan's Karakoram range, at 28,250 feet, is much more formidable than Everest, and has been described as "the classic example of an inaccessible peak."[1]

After six weeks of climbing, all eight in the party had reached Camp VIII, at 25,500 feet. The weather had been good and their spirits were high as they prepared for the final assault on the summit the next day. That night, however, a fierce snowstorm, with hurricane-force winds, enveloped them. They would have to wait out the storm. They remained trapped in their tents, which were lashed to the near-vertical surface of the mountain, for six nights as the storm raged outside. On the seventh day, during a lull, one of the climbers, Arthur Gilkey, was discovered to have thrombophlebitis, a condition that would definitely be fatal unless he received immediate medical attention. Houston was in a dilemma: if he waited for the storm to pass, Gilkey would die. But if he tried to bring him down the mountain in the storm, he would risk the lives of everyone. "I knew," writes Houston,

we all knew, that no one could be carried, lowered, or dragged down the Black Pyramid, over the dreadful loose rock to camp V, down House's Chimney. My mind flew over the whole route. There was no hope, absolutely none. Art was crippled. He would not recover enough to walk down. We could not carry him down. . . . But we could try, and we must.[2]

After eight nights at Camp VIII, longer than any men had ever lived above 25,000 feet, they made a stretcher for Gilkey and started down the mountain. Their ordeal, as they descended, narrowly missing avalanches, suffering from frostbite, and, once, five falling from a cliff, to be saved by a single rope, was one of the most grueling in mountaineering history. Yet all save one made it down alive. The one who didn't was Gilkey, who, ironically, did not die of the thrombophlebitis. He was swept to death, in his stretcher, by an avalanche.

Despite Gilkey's death, this was a tale of survival, and it shows on what survival depends. It shows that the survival of the individual and the survival of the group are not always compatible, and it shows that survival is not simply a matter of expertise and strength of character, but is, primarily, a question of moral choice. It is sometimes possible for the group to survive, but not all individuals, as in the case of the Houston party; and it is often possible for the individuals to survive as the group disintegrates, as we shall see was the case with the Ik tribe. But in many cases one must choose between those two alternatives, as Houston did, and that is a moral problem.

Survival, then, is not just a matter of expertise, something to be learned in Outward Bound, the way we learn to drive a car. It is, more than anything else, an act of choice, an act of will.

This book has been about survival, survival of the student, the college, and, indirectly, the society. It has presented variations on the theme that it is the role of our institutions of higher education to promote the survival of us, as individuals and as society, and that it is only if the institutions play this role that they, too, will survive. In this way our colleges and universities are the keepers of our group memory: they should pass on the knowledge that is necessary for each succeeding generation to have if it is to survive. But, since the interests of individuals and society are not always compatible, since it is often necessary to choose, as Houston did, which of these goods to pursue, our institutions of higher education are inevitably put in the position of making moral choices. This they do, although they do not, as we have seen, often admit that they do. Most of the time they make these choices by omission.

Our society requires, as a minimum for its survival, that its members share a common set of beliefs, abide by a common set of rules, and, through a refined division of labor, recognize their mutual dependence. In addition, society must possess the means of adapting to changes in the environment and of living in equilibrium with its resources.

Without common beliefs, without rules, without cooperation, and without ability to live in equilibrium with its environment, a society will die, although not necessarily the individuals in it. The Ik are a society that disintegrated and was outlived by its members. The Ik now are a people who, through environmental degradation, are reduced to laughing at each other's misfortune, defecating on each other's doorsteps, and snatching food from each other's mouths.[3]

Individuals, to survive, must be able to adjust to change. They must be able to recognize what they must do, and they must be able to act on what they know. Both a broad range of intelligence and talents as well as strength of character are necessary ingredients for individual survival. Yet individuals living in society may find that society discourages development of these traits. Whereas the individual, to be adaptable, must be, to some extent, a generalist, society requires specialists to fill the slots in its divisions of labor. Whereas the individual must be able both to think and act, society may require some individuals — such as college professors — who think but don't act and others — such as soldiers — who act but don't think. Whereas society requires laws and common beliefs to hold itself together, individuals may find these common beliefs constricting and the laws inconsistent with their interests. And whereas society must not incur a deficit with nature, some individuals, whose profligacy may be compensated by others' frugality, may, at least temporarily, do so.

A healthy society balances these two kinds of interests. The exercise of its moral life lies in making the choices to maintain this balance. Yet today, in America, these interests are not in balance. For on one hand, that individual survival has been maintained at the expense of society is suggested by the way in which individuals are permitted to live in deficit with their environment, by the decline in the promotion of shared values and by increasing disregard for law. Yet, on the other hand, society's preeminence is suggested by the way individuals are pigeonholed, tracked, specialized, and placed in jobs that discourage their growth. So it would seem that *both* the individual and society are in trouble.

It is in relation to our environment that our vulnerabilities as both a society and as individuals are most evident. For we are, as a nation, living in imbalance with nature, and we are doing so simply because of our inability to change, to act. This is due, primarily, I think, to what I shall call the Jellyby gap.

Mrs. Jellyby, a character in Charles Dickens's *Bleak House,* devoted all her time and money to helping the starving children in the far off "settlement of Borrioboola-Gha," all the while neglecting her own children.[4] This form of unconscious hypocrisy was simply a sign of her inability to see the connection between what she thought — her abstract reasoning — and what she did in her daily life. There was a gap between the two, which her actions did not bridge.

The Jellyby gap is fast becoming a common phenomenon in America. We can all cite examples of it: the student who was arrested for stealing a book on ethics from a campus bookstore; the liberal who fights for integration of the local high schools and then sends his children to a private boarding school; the trucking executive who fights simultaneously for free enterprise in his industry and government regulation of highways; the member of the Wilderness Society who owns a (redwood) hot tub; the young people who fight air pollution but pollute their lungs with pot and their noses with coke; a Congress that passed the Civil Rights Act but specifically exempted itself from obeying portions of it. At the national level we have become a country that preaches conservation but practices profligacy. We elect politicians who promise to preserve the environment and to initiate sensible policies; then we refuse to accept any plans they offer. We are, in short, unable to change, to live in equilibrium with nature, because we are unable to cross the gap between thought and action, to translate what we know we should do — our abstract principles — into actions and habits that comprise our personal lives.

I have tried to show in this book that these trends that

affect our future — excessive specialization, the retreat from values, our inability as a people to translate thought into action, our unwillingness to live on less, the decline of shared beliefs and viable laws, and, in general, the imbalance between the interests of society and the interests of the individual — have been greatly and needlessly exacerbated by current policies at America's colleges and universities and that the same policies threaten the existence of these institutions themselves.

Our colleges and universities — the keepers of the group memory — have forgotten their role. They have promoted special knowledge, which makes individuals more vulnerable to the random eddies of economic and political currents. They have abandoned their responsibilities to interpret and preserve those rules and values that embody the group memory and hold society together. They have failed to teach students what obligation means and what value rules have for society. They have driven a wedge between learning and living and failed to teach how one must be made consistent with the other. They have been teaching consumption, not conservation, all the while they are spending, growing by accretions, rather than saving and consolidating. They have worshipped relevance, rather than teaching students to have a deeper sense of history and a broader concern for society's future. They have been handmaidens of technology rather than the servants of truth. Finally, they have failed to teach that the problems before us are, at bottom, ones of moral choice.

Our colleges and universities have pretended to be value-neutral whereas in fact they have been making fundamental decisions about values. They have, moreover, made it even more difficult for us, as a people, to see that our problems are not technical ones, but ones of choice.

For by emphasizing the relativity of all values, our colleges and universities are teaching, implicitly, that no idea is worth struggling for. It is no wonder, in this context, that so many people feel that what they do as individuals is inconsequential. This feeling, moreover, deepens as we become a nation of specialists with no understanding of, nor control over, the whole. In this way we, as individuals, lose sight of the connection between our actions and social policy and we, as a group, become a nation wedded to the idea that technology will save us. For as we believe that what we do does not matter, we come to believe that our future depends less on our moral choices and are tempted to take refuge in our faith in science; we come to believe that, for instance, our energy problem can be solved through the development of alternative sources of energy, rather than through changing our habits of living.

In World War II, until the very end, Hitler promised the German people that a "wonder weapon" would save them. They believed him, with tragic results. Today we are susceptible to the same specious claim. We are today, as the Germans were then, inclined to believe that our problems could be solved, not by choice, but by invention. Yet unless and until we understand that our problems are ones of choice, and that solving them requires the will to act on this understanding, neither we as a society nor as individuals will fare well.

For the individual, this message — that the problem of survival is a problem of values, of choice, of reestablishing the balance between our needs as individuals and our needs as a society — should come as a source of hope, not despair, for it means our future is within our control. What we have seen is that our colleges and universities, whose traditional role has been to guide us through the rite of passage to adulthood, no longer serve as a guide. The average student, going away to college, is more on his own today than ever before, even though the dangers, and possible mistakes he can make, have multiplied greatly. He must have his guard up, and, having few landmarks to follow, must rely on his own sense of direction and a hand-drawn map. He must, at the same time, as he tries to find his way, also work to restore the fabric of society and to rebuild the guideposts for the benefit of those who follow. Part II of this book, I hope, by noting the dangers and opportunities of college — economic, emotional as well as moral — might help the student draw his own map and begin the task of rebuilding.

My purpose in offering this advice, however, is not just to help the student survive college and later life. That would be a grim and meager goal indeed. For survival is a minimal and temporary condition; it should never, and can never, be the end of life. One can and should expect more: to accomplish something, to be good, as a child, parent, citizen, and human being. This is far more difficult to accomplish. But if we try to lead the good life, survival will take care of itself.

NOTES AND SOURCES

For complete publishing information consult the Bibliography.

Preface

1. The total national education budget was over 130 billion dollars in 1976–1977. See Paul Copperman, *The Literacy Hoax*, p. 54.
2. There were 3,075 institutions of higher education in 1977. See National Center for Education Statistics, *The Condition of Education*, p. 124.

Prologue: Group Memory

1. I first heard the term *group memory* from Patrick Hemingway, although he used it in a more restricted sense than I do. He, in turn, claims that the idea for group memory occurred to him in reading *Mountain Sheep: A Study in Behavior and Evolution*, by Valerius Geist.
2. Plato, *The Meno*, translated by W. K. C. Guthrie. In *The Collected Dialogues of Plato*, edited by Hamilton and Cairns, p. 354.
3. Plato, *The Meno*, p. 378.
4. Plato, *The Meno*, p. 380.
5. Solzhenitsyn, "The Exhausted West," p. 22.
6. Solzhenitsyn, "The Exhausted West," pp. 22–24.
7. Solzhenitsyn, "The Exhausted West," p. 26.

1. Introduction: Surviving the 1980s

1. Orwell, *1984*.
2. The National Association of Independent Colleges and Universities, "Openings, Closing, Mergers and Accreditation Status of Independent Colleges and Universities," reported in *The Chronicle of Higher Education*, November 21, 1977, p. 10. Also cited by Baker, "Kirkland and Hamilton: Does Father Know Best?" See also Magarrell, "Financial Woes Worsen at Some Private Colleges," and "Antioch Given until Monday to Raise $1 Million for Debts," *The Washington Post*, June 2, 1979.
3. *Comptroller General's Report to Congress*, p. 24.
4. National Center for Education Statistics, *Fall Enrollment in Higher Education*, 1976, p. 2; NCES *Bulletin*, "Fall Enrollment in Colleges and Universities, 1978," Table C, and Magarrell, "State Colleges Confronting Politics of Frugality."
5. Yale, for instance, had a $6 million deficit in 1976–1977. See *The Chronicle of Higher Education*, September 26, 1977.
6. Typical of this interpretation was the article entitled "Small is Perilous," *Newsweek*, July 16, 1979. See also *The Chronicle of Higher Education*, "Government and Higher Education: The Relationship Remains

Troubled," April 26, 1979; "Beset with Inflation, Many Colleges Plan Hefty Increases in Tuition," March 26, 1979, and Magarrell, "The Enrollment Roller Coaster: Colleges Fear the Big Dip."

7. The Carnegie Foundation for the Advancement of Teaching, reported in *The Chronicle of Higher Education*, December 19, 1977, p. 7.

8. Carnegie Council on Policy Studies in Higher Education, *Fair Practices*, pp. 3 and 5; Firkes, "The Marketing of Colleges," and Omang and Bonner, "Colleges Struggle with the Baby Bust."

9. Magarrell, "The Enrollment Roller Coaster." Also in Hecker, "The Jam at the Bottom of the Funnel."

10. National Assessment of Educational Progress, *First National Assessment of Careers and Occupational Development: An Overview*.

11. National Center for Education Statistics, *The Condition of Education*, pp. 132–133.

12. Barron's Educational Services, *Barron's Profiles of American Colleges*. See also Lovejoy, *Lovejoy's College Guide*; Zuker and Hegener, *Peterson's Guide to College Admissions*; and Cass and Birnbaum, *Comparative Guide To American Colleges*.

2. Colleges and Students in Crisis: The Funny-Money Sheepskin

1. National Center for Education Statistics, *Digest of Education Statistics, 1977–78*, p. 102.

2. The Latin root is *universitas*. This was the concept of the "fictitious person" that emerged in the Middle Ages as the forerunner of the modern corporation. See Gierke, *Political Theories of the Middle Age*, pp. xvii–xliii.

3. See, particularly, Immanuel Kant's doctrine of "inner sense," which is developed in the first-edition version of the transcendental deduction (*The Critique of Pure Reason*), specifically A 133. See also the First Analogy: "We require an underlying ground which exists *at all times*, that is, something abiding and permanent, of which change and coexistence are only so many ways . . . in which the permanent exists," p. 213.

4. The first government was formed by the Massachusetts Bay Colony charter obtained in 1629 by John Winthrop. It was annulled in 1684. The second, short-lived, "royal" government was inaugurated in 1686 and ended in 1691. The third government lasted from 1692 until the Revolution. See Bryant, Gay, and Brooks, *Scribners' Popular History of the U.S.*, vol. II, chap. 16.

5. Morris, *The Oxford Book of Oxford*, p. 78.

6. Rudolph, *Curriculum*, p. 30.

7. Smith College *Bulletin*, 1978–1979; Harvard University *Courses of Instruction*, 1978–1979, and Wesleyan University *Bulletin*, 1978–1979. The Smith figure includes colloquia. The Wesleyan Classics Department offering is entitled "American Culture and Its Background."

8. The figure on course changes was given to me by the Yale registrar,

Richard R. Shank. For the list of major departments, see Yale University, *Yale College Programs of Study, 1978–9.*

9. National Center for Education Statistics, *Education Directory,* pp. xxxii–xxxlv. The annual rate of turnover for chief academic officers at private colleges is 18.6 percent. The turnover rate for deans of students is 18.3 percent. The tenure of college presidents is much shorter than it was two decades ago while the tenure of undergraduates — since more are experiencing interruptions in their college careers — is increasing. Among 1,582 private colleges, 214 had new presidents in 1977–1978.

10. Durkheim, *Suicide,* pp. 30–38.

11. Most college health departments I contacted suggested that the incidence of suicide had increased at their institutions. National tables show that the suicide rate for white males aged 14 to 24 (the college age) increased from 9.6 per 100,000 population to 19.6 between 1965 and 1975. For females in that age group, the increase was not so dramatic, but was still considerable. See Wattenberg, *U.S. Fact Book.* For more on the epidemic of suicides and emotional problems on campus, see Lamont, *Campus Shock,* especially chap. 9.

12. *Comptroller General's Report to Congress,* p. 60.

13. From an unpublished study conducted in 1978 by Dr. Dean K. Whitla of Harvard University's Office of Instructional Research and Evaluation.

14. Loughlin, "The Agency Nobody Loves"; *The Chronicle of Higher Education,* "$200 per Student for Energy," December 5, 1977; and "College Investments Outperform Market, but Still Lose Ground to Inflation," December 11, 1978. See also Chapter 1, n. 6.

15. A compilation of these suggestions, as made by college administrators, appears in the *Comptroller General's Report to Congress,* chap. 4. See also Roark, "40 Science and Education Groups Lobby for More Basic Research."

16. The impression that a reform bandwagon is beginning has been created largely by the publicity that the Harvard Core Curriculum proposal has received. A few other colleges have recently changed their curricula, but whether these changes constitute reforms remains to be seen. For a full discussion, see Chapter 5.

3. Government: The Green Eminence

1. Harvard University Register, *Information About Harvard and Radcliffe,* pp. 13–14. For a discussion of the Santa Cruz "cluster colleges" see Grant and Riesman, *The Perpetual Dream,* chap. 8.

2. Alden Dunham supplied me with this information in an interview.

3. *The Washington Post,* "Shielding Sociologists' Targets," February 20, 1979, and U.S. Department of HEW, "Protection of Human Subjects."

4. Loughlin, "The Agency Nobody Loves."

5. The National Center for Education Statistics, *The Condition of Education,* p. 214; The Carnegie Council, *Next Steps,* p. 67; The National Endowment for the Humanities, *13th Report,* p. 112; and Kilpatrick, "Where to Begin an Austerity Program," *The Washington Post,* January 4, 1979.

6. *The Chronicle of Higher Education,* "U.S. Commitment to Scientific Research Deteriorating Rapidly, MIT President Warns," November 13, 1978, and Silber, "The Tuition Dilemma."
7. Magarrell, "The Enrollment Roller Coaster."
8. See Chapter 1, note 6, and Chapter 2, note 14.
9. This, of course, was the argument used to press for passage of the Middle Income Student Assistance Act.
10. *Comptroller General's Report to Congress* (1978), p. 17.
11. The National Center for Education Statistics, *The Condition of Education,* p. 234, and *Projections of Educational Statistics to 1986–87,* pp. 158–159.
12. Minter and Bowen, *Private Education,* p. 40.
13. Minter and Bowen, *Private Education,* pp. 7–16, 28, 34. The faculty salary index rose, between 1971 and 1977, from 127.2 to 168.7, while the consumer price index rose from 119.0 to 175.8 during that period (see the National Center for Education Statistics, *The Condition of Education,* p. 224). According to Bowen, faculty salaries rose 6 percent a year since 1969, while the average of all other workers' salaries rose 8 percent per year during that time period (see *The Chronicle of Higher Education,* "Professors' Salaries Not Keeping Pace," March 27, 1978).
14. According to the Carnegie Council, the Congressional Budget Office showed that median family income for families with dependents aged 18 to 24 increased about 79 percent between 1967 and 1976, while costs of attending a private college increased around 77 percent during this time period. See The Carnegie Council, *Next Steps for the 1980's in Student Financial Aid,* p. 144.
15. Staple, "Financial Need Analysis," pp. 13–14.
16. *Comptroller General's Report,* p. 18.
17. *Comptroller General's Report,* pp. 28–29.
18. *Comptroller General's Report.*
19. Minter and Bowen, *Private Education,* pp. 28–30 and table 9.
20. United States Department of Health, Education and Welfare, National Center for Education Statistics, *The Condition of Education,* p. 184.
21. The American Association of University Professors, "The Disclaimer Affidavit: A Valediction."

4. Advising: The Pedagogical Cop-Out

1. Williams, *Report of the Task Force on College Life,* Appendix B, p. 8.
2. Amherst College, *Education at Amherst,* p. ix.
3. For an account of the development of this curriculum, see Rudolph, *Curriculum,* p. 131.
4. At the national level, between 1967 and 1974, general education requirements dropped from 43 percent of a student's course load to 33 percent. See Grant and Riesman, *The Perpetual Dream,* p. 363. President Bok of Harvard reports that on a national level "the portion of the college curriculum devoted to concentrations has risen from 30 to 35 percent since 1969 while electives have increased their share from 29 to 35 percent." See "The President's Report."

5. The Yale offering is made by its Film Studies Department; the Harvard offerings are made by its Biology Department.
6. *Yale College Programs of Study*, 1978–1979, pp. 14–15.
7. Smith College, *Catalogue*, 1978–1979, p. 45.
8. Montana State University, for instance, has this policy.
9. Ladd and Lipset, "The Faculty Mood: Pessimism is Predominant."
10. Goldman, "Just Don't Get Any Students Angry."
11. *Ibid.*
12. Lynn, "Son of Gen Ed," p. 65.
13. Copperman, *The Literacy Hoax*, p. 42.
14. Weeks, "Fewer Jobs for Humanities Ph.D.s: Should Market Be Left Alone?"
15. Harvard University, *The Freshman Year at Harvard and Radcliffe Colleges*, prepared for the members of the class of 1983 and their parents by the Office of the Dean of Freshmen, p. 2. See also *The Handbook for Harvard/Radcliffe Freshmen*, 1978–1979, pp. 10–11.
16. Moses, *Handbook for Freshman Advisers*, 1978–1979, p. 45.
17. Wesleyan University Bulletin, 1978–1979. *Announcement of Courses and Academic Regulations* (Wesleyan University, 1978), pp. 142–150.
18. Amherst College, *Education at Amherst*, p. 70.
19. Williams, *Report of the Task Force on College Life*, p. 12; Whitla and Pinck, *Perspectives on the Houses at Harvard and Radcliffe*, p. 47. The latter report also notes that the tenure of house tutors, once five years, is now two (p. 71).
20. Raskin, *Course Evaluation Guide*, p. xiii.
21. Yale College, *Report on the Effectiveness of the Guidelines System*, p. 2. See also Taft, "New Distributional Requirements for Yale College."
22. Kehoe, *Yale Course Critique*, p. 7.
23. Katz, "Collaboration of Academic Faculty and Student Affairs Professionals towards Student Development."

5. Curriculum: The Patina of Reform

1. On a national average, enrollment in German has fallen 11 percent since 1974, while enrollment in all foreign languages has fallen 9 percent since 1970. See *The Chronicle of Higher Education*, "An End to the Decline in Language Study?" December 12, 1977. According to the Modern Language Association, foreign language enrollment had already declined from 17 percent of total undergraduate enrollment in 1960 to 12.6 percent in 1970. See Modern Language Association, *Summary Table A*.
2. According to the National Assessment for Educational Progress, 13 percent of all seventeen-year-olds, and a distressing 42 percent of black seventeen-year-olds, are functionally illiterate. See National Assessment of Educational Progress *Reading: Report of the Second Functional Literacy Assessment*. See also Copperman, *The Literacy Hoax*, pp. 37–42, and McGovern, "The Miseducation of Millions: The Alarming Rise of Functional Illiteracy in America."
3. Scully, "General Education: 'A Disaster Area.'"

4. Martin Griffin, memorandum to Yale College Executive Committee (mimeographed). Subject: "Marks of Temporary Incomplete." Yale College, January 26, 1978.

5. Ladd and Lipset, "The Faculty Mood: Pessimism Is Predominant," and Paul Copperman, *The Literacy Hoax*, pp. 112–117.

6. The Carnegie Council, *Fair Practices*, p. 5.

7. In 1957, 421 out of a class of 1,048 graduated from Harvard with honors. In 1977, 908 out of a class of 1,095 graduated with honors. For trends at Yale, see "Grading In Yale College."

8. Connecticut College *Catalogue*, 1978–9, p. 17. At Yale, as we have seen, there were 50,000 course changes one year.

9. Unity College *Catalogue* for the years 1978–80, p. 3.

10. Harvard University Registrar, *Tentative Final Examination Schedule*, April 9, 1979.

11. The Rockefeller Foundation held these colloquia during the fall of 1978. For a report of one, see the Rockefeller Foundation, *Working Papers*. The Reverend Ernest Bartell, Executive Director of the Fund for the Improvement of Post-Secondary Education, told me in February, 1979, that the feasibility of a White House Conference is being discussed, something about which many educators are less than enthusiastic. For examples of articles by college presidents decrying the present decline of the liberal arts, see entries for Sawhill and Simmons in the Bibliography. For the "crisis" in humanities and what is being done about it, see Scully, "The Plight of the Humanities to Receive National Attention"; Sterne, "Dream of Humanities Center About to Come True"; and *The Chronicle of Higher Education*, "New Organization Aims to Advance Humanities."

12. Taft, "New Distributional Requirement for Yale College"; Yale College, "Report on the Effectiveness of the Guideline System"; and Hamilton College *Catalogue*, 1978–1979, pp. 10–11 and 13–14.

13. From a draft of the catalogue copy of the 1979–1980 College of Arts and Sciences *Catalogue*. According to Assistant Dean Mark A. Brown, the final version will not differ substantially from this.

14. Connecticut College is a special case. Their faculty passed, by a narrow margin, a new program for general education which appears in the 1978–1979 *Catalogue*. After the *Catalogue* went to press, however, the faculty changed its mind and the college printed a special set of new guidelines in a booklet entitled *A Manual of General Education for the Class of Eighty-one.*

15. Bok, "The President's Report," p. 19.

16. Simmons, "Harvard Flunks a Test."

17. Amherst College, *Education at Amherst*, pp. 47–52, 57–65.

18. Harvard University Faculty of Arts and Sciences, "Report on the Core Curriculum," p. 3.

19. Lynn, "Son of Gen Ed," p. 65.

20. Bok, "The President's Report," pp. 22–23.

21. Amherst College, *Education at Amherst*, pp. 47–49.

22. Ryle, *The Concept of Mind*, pp. 27ff. For a similar distinction, see Oakeshott, *Rationalism in Politics*, p. 8.

23. Copperman, *The Literacy Hoax*, p. 62.

24. Council for Basic Education, *Bulletin*, June, 1978, p. 6.

25. The National Assessment for Educational Progress, *Bicentennial Citizenship Survey*; *Second Citizenship/Social Studies Assessment* and *Third Science Assessment*.
26. Mullis, Oldefendt, and Phillips, *What Students Know and Can Do*.
27. Rudolph, *Curriculum*, pp. 250–251.
28. *Ibid.*, pp. 76–77.
29. McKeon, editor, *The Basic Works of Aristotle*, pp. 752–753.
30. Pythagoras thought the universe was made up of numbers. The sixteenth-century natural philosophers thought things in the universe were numerable. For an interesting introduction to Pythagoras, see Stace, *A Critical History of Greek Philosophy*. For a good account of Kepler's rejection of Aristotle, see E. A. Burtt, *The Metaphysical Foundations of Modern Physical Science*, especially pp. 52–56 and 63–71.
31. Locke, *An Essay Concerning Human Understanding*, pp. 63–73.
32. Kohlberg, "Stage and Sequence: The Cognitive Developmental Approach to Socialization"; Perry, *Forms of Intellectual and Ethical Development in the College Years: A Scheme*, and "Growth in the Making of Meaning: Youth into Adulthood," in Arthur Chickering (ed.), *Future American College*, San Francisco: Jossey-Bass, 1980.
33. Rosenblatt, "Scholars and/or Teachers."
34. Richardson quotation taken from Etzioni, "Social Science vs. Government: Standoff at Policy Gap."
35. Loughlin, "Arts, Humanities Endowments Reject Criticism from House Panel."
36. Quotation from the report of the National Academy of Science taken from Etzioni, "Social Science vs. Government: Standoff at Policy Gap."
37. *Newsweek*, for instance, reports that physical science "is feeling the impact of sheer size. . . . Experts find it difficult enough to keep up with their own specialties, let alone others'. 'We have no idea what the fellow next door is doing,' laments Princeton University physicist Eugene Wigner" (March 12, 1979). See also Scully, "The Condition of Scholarly Communication: Serious but Not Fatal, National Study Finds."
38. Kicklefs, "Publish or Perish: Professors Discover Perishing Is Simpler."
39. Kicklefs, "Publish or Perish: Professors Discover Perishing Is Simpler."
40. *Newsweek*, March 12, 1979.

6. Student Living: Whatever Happened to In Loco Parentis?

1. Sennett, *The Fall of Public Man*, p. 311.
2. Baker, *I'm Radcliffe, Fly Me!* chapter 3, especially p. 67, and Levine, *Handbook on Undergraduate Curriculum*, p. 526.
3. From 1945 to 1965, the number of American institutions of higher education restricted to men fell from 13.1 percent of all institutions to 10.7 percent, while women's institutions fell from 16.4 percent to 12.8 percent. From 1965 to 1975, men's institutions shrank to 4.3 percent and women's to 4.7 percent. The National Center for Education Statistics, *Digest of Education Statistics, 1977–1978*, p. 102.
4. Humphrey Doermann, director of Harvard's Office of Admissions during

this period, is often credited with making this discovery. See Baker, *I'm Radcliffe, Fly Me!* pp. 17–18. See also Doermann, "The Market for College Education" and "Future Market for College Education."

5. *Comptroller General's Report to Congress,* p. 29.

6. Wolfe, *The Kandy-Kolored Tangerine-Flake Streamlined Baby,* introduction.

7. Burtt, *The Metaphysical Foundations of Modern Physical Science,* chapter 4. Psychophysical parallelism, of course, has been the principal philosophical problem since Descartes, the one to which almost all major philosophies since have been addressed.

8. This is not to say that this distinction has not gone unchallenged, but rather it is to say it remains a problem. For an account of some reactions to dualism, see Lovejoy, *The Revolt against Dualism.*

9. Lamont, *Campus Shock,* p. 6.

10. Yale College, *The Size of Yale College,* p. 5.

11. *The Chronicle of Higher Education,* "Coeducation May Place Women at Disadvantage, Study Finds," January 8, 1979, p. 20. This was a comparative study of seven colleges and universities, financed by grants from the Ford Foundation and Rockefeller Family Fund. See also Astin, *Four Critical Years,* pp. 232–233 and 246: "Single sex colleges show a pattern of effects on *both* sexes that is almost uniformly positive" (Astin, p. 246).

12. Letter from Professor Katz to author, May 7, 1979.

13. Princeton University, Committee on Undergraduate Residential Life, *Second Interim Report,* pp. 1–2.

14. Letter from Professor Katz to author, May 7, 1979.

15. Goldberger statement quoted with permission from letter to author, dated October 15, 1979.

16. Carnegie Council, *Fair Practices,* pp. 3–17.

17. Carnegie Council, *Fair Practices,* p. 11.

18. Lamont, *Campus Shock,* p. 80.

19. Carnegie Council, *Fair Practices,* pp. 4, 10.

20. Lamont, *Campus Shock,* p. 53.

21. Lamont, *Campus Shock,* p. 17.

22. For an interesting treatment of this problem, see Ryle, *The Concept of Mind.*

23. One of the earliest theories basing personal identity on memory was developed by John Locke. See *An Essay Concerning Human Understanding,* pp. 188–200.

24. The self in this sense is what Kant sometimes called the "transcendental unity of apperception" and at other times called the "noumenal self," and to think it could be known is to be guilty, he thought, of a kind of logical error known as a "paralogism." See Kant, *The Critique of Pure Reason,* pp. 328–383.

25. Sennett, *The Fall of Public Man,* pp. 333–336, and Lasch, *The Culture of Narcissism.*

26. Sennett, *The Fall of Public Man,* pp. 316–323.

27. *The Chronicle of Higher Education,* "Yale will Cut Enrollment of Undergraduates," February 13, 1979, and Princeton University Committee on Undergraduate Residential Life, *Second Interim Report.*

28. Sennett, *The Fall of Public Man,* pp. 327–333.

7. Campus Indecision-Making: The Slippery Slope

1. Rudolph, *Curriculum*, pp. 257–259.
2. Levine, *Handbook*, pp. 510–513.
3. Stace, *A Critical History of Greek Philosophy*, especially pp. 106–126.
4. This is the argument of Plato's *Republic*.
5. Arguments against the Sophists crop up throughout Plato's work. The arguments summarized here come principally from the *Theaetetus*.
6. Jencks and Riesman, *The Academic Revolution*.
7. Radical empiricism is the view that all meaningful or scientific statements are either about immediate sense experience or are sentences that can be translated into statements about immediate sense experience. On the basic doctrine, see Ayer (editor), *Logical Positivism*.
8. Urmson, *Philosophical Analysis*, chapters 7 and 8.
9. Ayer, *Language, Truth and Logic*, chapter 6, and Stevenson, *Ethics and Language*.
10. Urmson, *Philosophical Analysis*, part III; Pap, *An Introduction to the Philosophy of Science*, chapter 3, and Hempel, *Aspects of Scientific Explanation*, chapters 5 and 8.

8. The One Room University: Higher Education in an Age of Limits

1. Fitzgerald, *Tender Is the Night*, p. 232.
2. For more on diversity in admissions, see Chapter 11.
3. Clark, *Academic Power in Italy*, pp. 123–133; Altbach, "A System in Stalemate"; Scully, "Conservative Scholars Fear '60's Reforms Have Perverted Universities' Mission," and Lurie, "Terror on Italy's Campuses."

9. Going to College: What It Does for the Student and What It Does to Him

1. Bowen, *Investment in Learning*, p. 84.
2. That is, among male freshmen at four-year institutions. Lutz, *Do They Do What They Say They Do?* p. 13 and table 4.
3. Gordon K. Douglas, "Economic Returns on Investments in Higher Education," in Bowen, *Investment in Learning*, pp. 359–387.
4. Whitla, *Value Added*, p. 1.
5. Bird, *The Case against College*, pp. 62, 64–65.
6. Douglas, "Economic Returns on Investment in Higher Education," p. 375.
7. *The Chronicle of Higher Education*, "Youth Unemployment Stirs In-

ternational Concern," May 22, 1978; "25 Percent of College Graduates to Be Under-Employed," July 31, 1978; "Jobless Rate Increases among Young Graduates," January 30, 1978; and Hecker, "The Jam at the Bottom of the Funnel."

8. The effect of family background on education and earnings is a hotly debated topic. See Bowen, *Investment in Learning*, pp. 186 and 369–370, and Jencks, *Inequality*, pp. 158–159 and 226–232. As this manuscript was being completed, Jencks's new book, *Who Gets Ahead? The Determinants of Economic Success in America*, just appeared. In the new book he continues to give great weight to the significance of family background in determining economic success, but gives greater weight than before to the college degree as such a determinant.

9. Whitla, *Value Added*, p. 36.

10. Bowen, *Investment in Learning*.

11. Whitla, *Value Added*, p. 9.

12. Bowen, *Investment in Learning*, pp. 71, 74; and Trent and Medsker, *Beyond High School: A Psychosociological Study of 10,000 High School Graduates*, p. 176.

13. Whitla, *Value Added*, p. 11.

14. Bowen, *Investment in Learning*, pp. 85–86.

15. *Ibid.*, pp. 33 and 349. Quotation of Woodrow Wilson taken from Martin Trow (ed.), *Teachers and Students*, p. 270; Bowen, *Investment in Learning*, pp. 33, 349.

16. Wing and Wallach, *College Admissions and the Psychology of Talent*, p. 150.

17. Bowen, *Investment in Learning*, p. 179; Quinn and Baldi de Mandilovitch, *Education and Job Satisfaction: A Questionable Payoff*, p. 23; and Quinn and Staines, *The 1977 Quality of Employment Survey*, pp. 287ff.

18. Carnegie Council, *Fair Practices*, pp. 3–17.

19. Whitla, *Value Added*, p. 23.

20. Bowen, *Investment in Learning*, pp. 119–120; Feldman and Newcomb, *The Impact of College on Students*, vol. II, pp. 71–74.

21. Whitla, *Value Added*, p. 21.

22. *The Chronicle of Higher Education*, "Coeducation May Place Women at Disadvantage, Study Finds," January 8, 1979. See also Chapter 6, note 11.

23. Bowen, *Investment in Learning*, pp. 124–125.

24. *Ibid.*, p. 125. See also Feldman and Newcomb, *The Impact of College on Students*, vol. II, pp. 25–36, and Sanford (ed.), *The American College*, p. 826.

25. Lannholm, "Educational Growth During the Second Two Years of College," p. 647. See also Bowen, *Investment in Learning*, pp. 66–67.

26. Lannholm and Pitcher, "Mean Score Changes on the Graduate Record Examinations Area Test for College Students Tested Three Times in a Four-Year Period," p. 4. See also Bowen, *Investment in Learning*, p. 69.

27. Hyman, Wright, and Reed, *The Enduring Effects of Education*, pp. 164–183; and Powers, *An Inquiry into the Effects of a College Education on the Attitudes, Competencies and Behavior of Individuals*, pp. 63–66.

28. Feldman and Newcomb, *The Impact of College on Students*, vol. II, pp. 47–48; Trent and Medsker, *Beyond High School: A Psychosociological Study of 10,000 High School Graduates*, pp. 144–145; and Clark and

others, *Students and Colleges: Interaction and Change*, pp. 219–223. See also Bowen, *Investment in Learning*, p. 86.

29. Hyman, Wright, and Reed, *The Enduring Effects of Education*, pp. 132–146; Yankelovich, *The New Morality: A Profile of American Youth in the 70's*, pp. 120–121.

30. Gallup, *Attitudes of College Students on Political, Social and Economic Issues*, p. 16.

31. Morgan, Sirageldin, and Baerwaldt, *Productive Americans: A Study of How Individuals Contribute to Economic Progress*, pp. 344–351. See also Bowen, *Investment in Learning*, p. 140, and Spaeth and Greeley, *Recent Alumni and Higher Education*.

32. Bowen, *Investment in Learning*, p. 195; Juster, *Education, Income and Human Behavior*, pp. 187–194; Gurin, Veroff, and Feld, *Americans View Their Mental Health*, p. 135.

33. Bowen, *Investment in Learning*, p. 197; Jencks, *Inequality*, p. 227; Fetters, *National Longitudinal Study of the High School Class of 1972: Student Questionnaire and Test Results by Sex, High School Program, Ethnic Category, and Father's Education*; and Cobern, Salem, and Mushkin, *Indicators of Educational Outcome*, Fall, 1973. What this correlation means, however, is a hotly debated topic. Some, such as James Fallows (in "The Tests and the 'Brightest'") and, reportedly, Ralph Nader and Alan Nairn (in a report on the Educational Testing Service due to be published shortly after this book goes to press), suggest that, as measured intelligence also is correlated with family income, intelligence tests may be biased in favor of the more privileged classes.

34. Hinkle and others, "Occupation, Education and Coronary Heart Disease," p. 245; U.S. Bureau of Labor Statistics, *Survey of Consumer Expenditures*; and Kitagawa and Hauser, *Differential Mortality in the United States: A Study in Socioeconomic Epidemiology*, pp. 11–33.

35. Astin, *Four Critical Years*, pp. 110–115. In 1976, 925,746 people graduated with B.A. degrees; 62,649 earned first professional degrees, 311,771 earned masters' degrees, and 34,064 doctorates. See The National Center for Education Statistics, *The Condition of Education*, p. 138.

36. Whitla, *Value Added*, p. 28, and Bowen, *Investment in Learning*, p. 109.

10. Choosing a College: Why It Matters

1. Carnegie Council, *Fair Practices*, pp. 49–50.
2. *Ibid.*, pp. 3, 33. See also Fiske, "The Marketing of the Colleges."
3. Carnegie Council, *Fair Practices*, Chapter 3.
4. *Ibid.*, p. 34.
5. Whitla, *Value Added*, p. 28, and Bowen, *Investment in Learning*, p. 109.
6. At a typical college, a few fields — and the courses in those fields — are overcrowded, while other courses are underenrolled. At Harvard, for example, in 1976–1977, while 35 percent of all courses offered had enrollment of fewer than ten students, nearly 50 percent of all student registrations were in courses with enrollment greater than fifty. From an unpublished study conducted by Dean K. Whitla of the Harvard University Office of Institutional Research and Evaluation.
7. For the declining significance of financial reasons in explaining attrition,

see the Carnegie Council, *Next Steps for the 1980's in Student Financial Aid*, p. 124.

8. Carnegie Council, *Fair Practices*, p. 34.
9. Bowen, *Investment in Learning*, p. 257.
10. *Newsweek*, "Vintage Harvard," Januray 18, 1979, p. 76.
11. Astin, *Four Critical Years*, see esp. p. 229.
12. *Ibid.*, Bowen, *Investment in Learning*, p. 240.
13. Astin, *Four Critical Years*, p. 229.
14. Campbell, "The Vocational Interests of Dartmouth College Freshmen: 1947–67," and "Admissions Policies: Side Effects and Their Implications."
15. Astin, *Four Critical Years*, p. 89.
16. *Ibid.*, p. 231.
17. *Ibid.*, p. 232.
18. *Ibid.*, pp. 235–236.
19. *Ibid.*, p. 232.
20. *Ibid.*, pp. 220–221. See also Bowen, *Investment in Learning*, pp. 248–249; Chickering, *Commuting versus Resident Students: Overcoming Educational Inequities of Living off Campus*, pp. 84–85; Feldman and Newcomb, *The Impact of College on Students*; and Harrington, "The Literature on the Commuter Student."
21. *Ibid.*, pp. 237–239.
22. Merton, "Hanging on (by a Jockstrap) to Tradition at Dartmouth." Closely resembling the quarter system is the trimester. See Levine, *Handbook*, p. 236.
23. See Chapter 5, note 4. The semester is still the most popular calendar, being used by 58 percent of all four-year colleges. See Levine, *Handbook*, p. 236.
24. This calendar was first proposed in 1958 as part of the Hampshire College Plan. In 1960 Eckerd College adopted it. See Levine, *Handbook*, p. 511.
25. Colorado College introduced this calendar in 1970. For a discussion of its advantages and disadvantages, see Levine, *Handbook*, pp. 239–240. The Colorado College *Catalog* notes that an advantage of this plan is that it permits great flexibility in scheduling. "A Southwestern Studies course, for instance, can meet in Santa Fe for three and a half weeks; an astronomy course at midnight." The Colorado College *Catalog*, 1976–1977, p. 9.
26. See Bibliography and Chapter 1, note 11.
27. Raskin, ed., *Course Evaluation Guide*, 1978, and Kehoe, et al., *Yale Course Critique*, also Harvard *Crimson, Confidential Guide*.

11. Admissions: Unnatural Selection

1. To correct this glaring oversight, the College Board and the Educational Testing Service initiated, in 1978, the first phase of a long range longitudinal study of this kind. But of course the results of this study will not be known for some time. The colleges participating in this are· Bucknell University, Colgate University, Hartwick College, Kalamazoo College, Kenyon College, Occidental College, Ohio Wesleyan University, University of Richmond, and Williams College.

2. Campbell, "Admissions Policies: Side Effects and Their Implications."

3. Wing and Wallach, *College Admissions and the Psychology of Talent*, pp. 17ff.

4. Campbell, "Admissions Policies: Side Effects and Their Implications."

5. As there is a paucity of information on this subject, there is a paucity of information to suggest that admissions policies are less narrow than they were. During my visits to colleges throughout the country, I saw little reason to believe that things had changed since *College Admissions and the Psychology of Talent* was published.

6. Wing and Wallach, *College Admissions*, p. 32.

7. Wing and Wallach, *College Admissions*, pp. 45–57.

8. Although far from perfect, the Harvard College admissions policy is a case in point. In the early sixties Harvard began to make a systematic effort to recruit students with a wider range of interests (although they, too, to my knowledge, never conducted long-range longitudinal studies of their decisions). As a result of the shift in policy, for instance, the number of applicants who scored between 700 and 800 on the SAT (verbal) test who were admitted dropped from 55.8 percent (for the class of 1964) to 42.7 percent (for the class of 1967). See Glimp and Whitla, "Admissions and Performance in College: An Examination of Current Policy."

9. Wing and Wallach, *College Admissions*, pp. 80–86.

10. Campbell, "The Vocational Interests of Dartmouth Freshmen: 1947–67."

11. Richards, Holland, and Lutz, *The Prediction of Student Accomplishment in College*; Munday, *Comparative Predictive Validities of the American College Tests and Two Other Scholastic Aptitude Tests*, and Wing and Wallach, *College Admissions*, pp. 7–10.

12. Astin, *Four Critical Years*, p. 252.

13. *Ibid.*

14. Holland and Richards, *Academic and Non-Academic Accomplishment: Correlated or Uncorrelated?* p. 22.

15. Wing and Wallach, *College Admissions*, p. 22.

16. Bowen, *Investment in Learning*, p. 84.

17. Jacobson, "Does High Academic Accomplishment Create Problems Later On?"

18. Holland and Richards, *Academic and Non-Academic Accomplishment: Correlated or Uncorrelated?*; Richards, Holland, and Lutz, *The Prediction of Student Accomplishment in College*; and Wing and Wallach, *College Admissions*, p. 23.

12. Financial Aid: Good News and Bad News

1. The National Center for Education Statistics reports, "College enrollment rates have declined among males and increased among females since 1967, and they are now higher for females than males." At the same time the absolute number of women attending college has not yet quite surpassed that of men. In 1978 total national enrollment was 5,693,948 men and 5,660,579 women. The enrollment of minorities has increased from 8 percent of all enrollment in 1969 to 13 percent in 1977.

See the National Center for Education Statistics, *The Condition of Education*, p. 117, and *The Chronicle of Higher Education*, "Minorities Share of College Enrollment Only 8 Pct. in 1969, Was 13 Pct. in 1977," October 16, 1978.

2. Carnegie Council, *Next Steps*, pp. 140, 67.
3. *Ibid.*, p. 83, and Staple et al., "Financial Need Analysis, Some Policy Questions," pp. 13–14.
4. Carnegie Council, *Next Steps*, p. 124.
5. *Ibid.*, pp. 143–146.
6. *Ibid.*, pp. 15, 37, 106.
7. *Ibid.*, pp. 38–41.
8. *Ibid.*, p. 81.
9. Carnegie Council, *Fair Practices*, pp. 42–43.
10. Carnegie Council, *Next Steps*, p. 92.
11. *Ibid.*, p. 104.
12. *Ibid.*, pp. 99, 102. Nationally, 1.4 percent of those students whose parents earn more than $20,000 receive food stamps.
13. Carnegie Council, *Next Steps*, p. 73.
14. The National Merit Scholarship Corporation, *Annual Report*, 1977–1978.
15. Carnegie Council, *Next Steps*, pp. 8, 94–95, 101, 150.
16. *Ibid.*, pp. 7, 158–159.
17. *Ibid.*, pp. 50, 173, 174; and Carnegie Council, *Fair Practices*, p. 18.
18. The crossover point is $18,000. Below that level of earnings, the CSS/ACT test is more generous; above that level, the Basic Grants test is more generous. Carnegie Council, *Next Steps*, pp. 38–40.
19. The Carnegie Council, *Next Steps*, p. 83.
20. *Ibid.*, p. 108.
21. Carnegie Council, *Fair Practices*, p. 19.
22. *Ibid.*, p. 44.

13. College Days: Planning Studies and Choosing Options

1. Astin, *Four Critical Years*, p. 175.
2. *Ibid.*, p. 137.
3. *Ibid.*, p. 223, and Bowen, *Investment in Learning*, pp. 250–251.
4. Whitla, *Value Added*, pp. 12–14.
5. Astin, *Four Critical Years*, pp. 226–227.
6. This has been reported to me by many sociologists and anthropologists.
7. Levine, *Handbook*, p. 96.
8. Astin, *Four Critical Years*, pp. 115–122, and Wing and Wallach, *College Admissions*, p. 23.
9. During the seven years in which my wife and I have run our environmental program for teenagers, passivity has been the most consistent and disturbing trait we have observed among these youngsters.
10. Astin, *Four Critical Years*, pp. 74–75.
11. *Ibid.*, p. 222.

14. Preparing for the Real World

1. Daniel, "Notes for a Dissenting Commencement Address."
2. U.S. Department of Labor, *Occupational Outlook Handbook.*
3. Sheehy, *Passages,* p. 282.
4. Quinn and Staines, the 1977 *Quality of Employment Survey,* p. 169.
5. U.S. Department of Labor, news release, February 5, 1979.
6. College Placement Council and the Western College Placement Association, "Survey on Liberal Arts Recruitment," 1974.
7. *Journal of College Placement,* Fall, 1975.
8. Raskin, *Course Evaluation Guide,* p. xvi.
9. Thomas, *The Medusa and the Snail,* p. 138.
10. Campbell, *Manual for the SVIB-SCII Strong Campbell Interest Inventory.*
11. U.S. Department of Labor, *Occupational Outlook Handbook.*
12. Feldman, "We Must Prepare Students for Work, Not Jobs."
13. *Ibid.*

15. Survival

1. Styles, *The Top of the World,* p. 216.
2. Charles Houston, *K-2, The Savage Mountain.* Quoted from Styles, *The Top of the World,* p. 223.
3. Colin M. Turnbull, "Rethinking the Ik: A Functional Non-Social Study of Deprivation," in Loughlin and Brady, *Extinction and Survival in Human Populations,* pp. 126–129.
4. Dickens, *Bleak House,* p. 168.

BIBLIOGRAPHY

Altbach, Phillip G. "A System in Stalemate," *The Chronicle of Higher Education*, January 16, 1978.

American Association of University Professors. "The Disclaimer Affidavit: A Valediction," *American Association of University Professors Bulletin*, Winter, 1962.

American College Testing Program. *Applying for Financial Aid: A Guide for Students and Parents, for the 1979–80 Family Financial Statement*. Iowa City: American College Testing Program, 1979.

———. *College Planning/Search Book*. Iowa City: American College Testing Program, 1978.

———. *Nonintellective Correlates of Grades, Persistence and Academic Learning in College: The Published Literature through the Decade of the Sixties*. Monograph 14. Iowa City: American College Testing Program, 1974.

———. *Trends in the Source of Student Support for Postsecondary Education*, Joseph Froomkin, editor. ACT Special Report, Number 16. Iowa City: American College Testing Program, 1976.

Amherst College. *Amherst Reports: The Curriculum, 1976*. Amherst: The Amherst College Press, 1976.

———. Select Committee on the Curriculum. *Education at Amherst Reconsidered: The Liberal Studies Program*. Amherst: The Amherst College Press, 1978.

———. *Introduction to Liberal Studies, Courses, 1978–9*. Amherst: The Amherst College Press, 1978.

Andrewartha, H. G. *Introduction to the Study of Animal Populations*. Chicago: University of Chicago Press, 1961.

Armytage, W. G. G. *Four Hundred Years of English Education*. 2nd ed. Cambridge: Cambridge University Press, 1970.

Astin, Alexander W. *Four Critical Years*. San Francisco: Jossey-Bass, 1978.

Averill, Lloyd J., and Jellema, William W., editors. *Colleges and Commitments*. Philadelphia: The Westminster Press, 1971.

Ayer, A. J. *Language, Truth and Logic*. London: Victor Gollancz, 1960.

Ayer, A. J., editor. *Logical Positivism*. Glencoe: The Free Press, 1960.

Baird, Leonard L., and Holland, John L. *The Flow of High School Students to Schools, Colleges and Jobs*. ACT Research Report Number 26. Iowa City: The American College Testing Program, June, 1978.

Baker, Liva. *I'm Radcliffe, Fly Me!* New York: Macmillan, 1976.

———. "Kirkland and Hamilton: Does Father Know Best?" *Change* Magazine, May, 1978.

Barron's Educational Services. *Barron's Profiles of American Colleges*. 11th ed. Woodbury, N.Y.: Barron's Educational Services, 1978.

Becher, Ernest, *The Structure of Evil*. New York: The Free Press, 1968.

Bird, Caroline. *The Case against College*. New York: David McKay, 1975.

Bok, Derek, "The President's Report," Harvard University, 1976–1977. Reprinted in *Harvard Magazine*, May–June, 1978.

Bowen, Howard R. *Investment in Learning: The Individual and Social Value of American Higher Education.* San Francisco: Jossey-Bass, 1978.

Brechner, Irv. *The College Survival Kit.* New York: Bantam Books, 1979.

Bryant, William Cullen; Gay, Sidney Howard; and Brooks, Noah. *Scribners' Popular History of the United States,* volume 2. New York: Charles Scribners' Sons, 1897.

Buckley, William F., Jr. "Giving Yale to Connecticut," *Harpers,* November, 1977.

Burnett, Donald H. Letter to Princeton University Trustees, February 26, 1979.

————. *Report on Comparative Academic Course Requirements, 1950–1 vs. 1976–7.* April, 1978 (mimeographed). Reprinted in abridged form, in the *Princeton Alumni Weekly,* October 9, 1978.

Burtt, E. A. *The Metaphysical Foundations of Modern Physical Science.* New York: Doubleday, 1954.

Cahn, Steven M. *Education and the Democratic Ideal.* Chicago: Nelson Hall, 1979.

————. *The Eclipse of Excellence.* Washington, D.C.: Public Affairs Press, 1973.

————. *Scholars Who Teach.* Chicago: Nelson Hall, 1978.

Campbell, David P. "Admissions Policies: Side Effects and Their Implications." Address to the American Association of Collegiate Registrars and Admissions Officer, New Orleans, April, 1970. Reprinted in the *American Psychologist.*

————. *Manual for the SVIB-SCII Strong-Campbell Interest Inventory.* Stanford University Press, 1977.

————. "The Vocational Interests of Dartmouth Freshmen: 1947–67," *Personnel and Guidance Journal,* February, 1969.

Cantor, Norman E., and Claster, Jill N. "Position Paper on the Undergraduate Core Curriculum for New York University." Mimeographed.

Carnegie Council on Policy Studies in Higher Education. *Fair Practices in Higher Education.* San Francisco: Jossey-Bass, 1979.

————. *Next Steps for the 1980s in Student Financial Aid.* San Francisco: Jossey-Bass, 1979.

Carnegie Foundation for the Advancement of Teaching. *Missions of the College Curriculum.* San Francisco: Jossey-Bass, 1978.

Cass, James, and Birnbaum, Max. *Comparative Guide to American Colleges.* 8th ed. New York: Harper and Row, 1977.

Chase, Alston. "Skipping through College: Reflections on the Decline of Liberal Arts Education," *The Atlantic Monthly,* September, 1978.

Chickering, Arthur W. *Commuting Versus Resident Students: Overcoming Educational Inequities of Living Off Campus.* San Francisco: Jossey-Bass, 1974.

Clark, Burton R. *Academic Power in Italy: Bureaucracy and Oligarchy in a National University System.* Chicago: The University of Chicago Press, 1977.

Clark, Burton R., and others. *Students and Colleges: Interaction and Change.* Berkeley: Center for Research and Development in Higher Education, University of California, 1962.

Cobern, M., Salem, C., and Mushkin, S. *Indicators of Educational Outcome,*

Fall 1973. (Publication No. (OE) 73–11110, Department of Health, Education and Welfare) Washington, D.C.: U.S. Government Printing Office, 1973.

College Entrance Examination Board. *The College Handbook, Index of Majors.* New York: College Entrance Examination Board, 1977.

————. *On Further Examination: Report of the Advisory Panel on the Scholastic Aptitude Test Decline.* New York: College Entrance Examination Board, 1977.

Commoner, Barry. *The Closing Circle.* New York: Bantam, 1972.

Connecticut College, Dean of Faculty. "Report on a Summer Study of General Education Requirements." October 10, 1978, Mimeographed.

Copperman, Paul. *The Literacy Hoax.* New York: William Morrow and Co., 1978.

Cornford, Francis MacDonald. *Plato's Theory of Knowledge.* New York: Humanities Press, 1951.

Cottle, Thomas J. *College: Reward and Betrayal.* Chicago: University of Chicago Press, 1977.

Daniel, Carter A. "Notes for a Dissenting Commencement Address," *The Chronicle of Higher Education,* May 7, 1979.

Dewey, John. *Philosophy of Education.* Totowa, N.J.: Littlefield, Adams and Co., 1958.

Dickens, Charles. *Bleak House.* New York: Dutton, 1954.

Dobie, J. Frank. *The Voice of the Coyote.* Lincoln, Neb.: Bison Books, 1949.

Doermann, Humphrey. "The Future Market for College Education." College Board Colloquium on College Admissions, May 16–18, 1976.

————. "The Market for College Education," *Educational Record,* Winter, 1968.

Dunham, E. Alden, "Crosscurrents in the College Curriculum." 1978, Mimeographed.

Durkheim, Emile. *Essays on Sociology and Philosophy.* Edited by Kurt H. Wolff. New York: Harper and Row, 1964.

————. *Suicide, A Study in Sociology.* Translated by John H. Spaulding and George Simpson. Edited by George Simpson. London: Routledge and Kegan Paul, Ltd., 1963.

Educational Testing Service. *The Graduates: A Report on the Characteristics and Plans of College Seniors.* Leonard L. Baird, Principal Investigator. Princeton: Educational Testing Service, 1973.

Elkind, David. *Child Development and Education: A Piagetian Perspective.* New York: Oxford University Press, 1976.

Engstrand, Gary. *A Longitudinal Study of Grades Awarded at the University of Minnesota.* Part I: *Summary and Analysis.* Minneapolis: Twin Cities Student Assembly, 1975.

Etzioni, Amitai. "Social Science vs. Government: Standoff at Policy Gap," *Psychology Today,* November, 1978.

Fallows, James. "The Tests and the 'Brightest': How Fair Are the College Boards?" *The Atlantic Monthly,* February, 1980.

Feldman, K. A., and Newcomb, T. M. *The Impact of College on Students.* 2 vols. San Francisco: Jossey-Bass, 1969.

Feldman, Marvin. "We Must Prepare Students for Work, Not Jobs," *The Chronicle of Higher Education,* September 5, 1978.

Fetters, W. B. *National Longitudinal Study of the High School Class of 1972: Student Questionnaire and Test Results by Sex, High School Program, Ethnic Category, and Father's Education.* U.S. Department of Health, Education and Welfare, National Center for Education Statistics, publication number NCES75–208. Washington, D.C.: U.S. Government Printing Office, 1975.

Fields, Cheryl M. "Why the Big Dip in S.A.T. Scores?" *The Chronicle of Higher Education,* September 6, 1977.

Fiske, Edward B. "The Marketing of the Colleges," *The Atlantic Monthly,* September, 1979.

Fitzgerald, F. Scott. *Tender Is the Night.* New York: Charles Scribners' Sons, 1961.

Friedenberg, Edgar Z. *Coming of Age in America: Growth and Acquiescence.* New York: Random House, 1963.

Frost, Robert. *Poems.* New York: Modern Library, 1946.

Furth, Hans G., and Wachs, Harry. *Thinking Goes to School: Piaget's Theory in Practice.* New York: Oxford University Press, 1974.

Gallup, George. *Attitudes of College Students on Political, Social and Economic Issues.* Princeton, The Gallup Poll, 1975.

Geist, Valerius. *Mountain Sheep: A Study in Behavior and Evolution.* Chicago: The University of Chicago Press, 1971.

Gierke, Otto von. *Political Theories of the Middle Age.* Translated by F. W. Maitland. Cambridge University Press, 1958.

Glimp, Fred L., and Whitla, Dean K. "Admissions and Performance in College: An Examination of Current Policy," *Harvard Alumni Bulletin,* June 11, 1964.

Goldberger, Nancy. "Breaking the Educational Lockstep: The Simon's Rock Experience." In *The Early College in Theory and Practice.* Great Barrington: Simon's Rock Press, 1977.

———. "Developmental Assumptions Underlying Models of General Education." Read at the Third Annual Conference on General Education and Entering Learners, at William Paterson College (New Jersey) on April 27, 1979.

Goldman, Ivan. "Just Don't Get Any Students Angry," *The Washington Post,* April 3, 1979.

Goodman, Ellen. "All that Yelling About Regulation," *The Washington Post,* December 16, 1978.

———. "The Anxiety Syndrome," *The Washington Post,* March 14, 1978.

Grant, Gerald. "The Overoptioned Curriculum." In *Towards the Restoration of the Liberal Arts Curriculum, Working Papers, The Rockefeller Foundation.* New York: The Rockefeller Foundation, June, 1979.

Grant, Gerald, and Riesman, David. *The Perpetual Dream: Reform and Experiment in the American College.* Chicago: University of Chicago Press, 1978.

Greenberg, Daniel S. "Academe's Desperate Money Chase," *The Washington Post*, October 3, 1978.

————. "The Stalingrad of the Science Establishment," *The Washington Post*, April 24, 1979.

Gurin, G., Veroff, J., and Feld, S. *Americans View Their Mental Health.* New York: Basic Books, 1960.

Hall, Edward T. *The Hidden Dimension.* New York: Doubleday, 1969.

Hamilton College, Office of the Dean. "Grade Distribution Surveys," 1976 and 1979. Mimeographed.

Harrington, T. F., Jr. "The Literature on the Commuter Student," *Journal of College Student Personnel*, November 1972, pp. 546–550.

Harvard University. Report to the Dean of the Faculty of Arts and Sciences from the Chairman of the Committee on Admissions and Scholarships for the academic years *1975–6 and 1976–7*.

————. "Dean's Conference on the Freshman Experience, the First Three Weeks. Conference Record." Harvard University, April 13 and 14, 1978. Mimeographed.

————. Faculty of Arts and Sciences. "Dean's Report, 1977–8." Mimeographed.

————. Faculty of Arts and Sciences. "Report on the Core Curriculum." April 3, 1978. Mimeographed.

————. Office of the Registrar. *Information about Harvard and Radcliffe.* Braintree, Mass.: Semline Press, 1978.

————. Office of the Registrar. *Candidates for Degrees According to Fields of Concentration*, March and June, 1957.

————. Office of the Registrar. *Candidates for Degrees According to Fields of Concentration*, March and June, 1977.

————. Office of the Registrar. *Tentative Final Examination Schedule*, April 9, 1979.

Haven, Elizabeth W., and Horch, Dwight H. *How College Students Finance Their Education: A National Survey of the Educational Interests, Aspirations and Finances of College Sophomores in 1969–70.* Princeton: College Scholarship Service of The College Entrance Examination Board, June, 1972.

Hecker, Daniel E. "The Jam at the Bottom of the Funnel: The Outlook for College Students," *Occupational Outlook Quarterly*, U.S. Department of Labor, Bureau of Labor Statistics, Spring, 1978.

Hempel, Carl. *Aspects of Scientific Explanation.* New York: Free Press, 1965.

Hinkle, L. E., Jr., and others. "Occupation, Education and Coronary Heart Disease," *Science*, July 19, 1968, pp. 238–246.

Holland, John L., and Richards, James M., Jr. *Academic and Non-Academic Accomplishment: Correlated or Uncorrelated?* ACT Research Report. Iowa City: American College Testing Program, 1965.

Hoyt, Donald P. *The Relationship Between College Grades and Adult Achievement: A Review of the Literature.* ACT Research Report Number 7. Iowa City: American College Testing Program, September, 1965.

Hume, David. *Enquiries.* Edited by L. A. Selby-Bigge. Second ed. Oxford: Oxford University Press, 1902.

312 / BIBLIOGRAPHY

——. *A Treatise of Human Nature.* Edited by L. A. Selby-Bigge. Oxford: Oxford University Press, 1958.
Hyman, H. H., Wright, C. R., and Reed, J. S. *The Enduring Effects of Education.* Chicago: The University of Chicago Press, 1975.

Jacobson, Robert L. "Does High Academic Accomplishment Create Problems Later On?" *The Chronicle of Higher Education,* May 23, 1977.
Jencks, Christopher. *Inequality: A Reassessment of the Effect of Family and Schooling in America.* New York: Basic Books, 1972.
Jencks, Christopher, and Riesman, David. *The Academic Revolution.* New York: Doubleday and Co., 1969.
Jolna, Stacy. "Faculty Claims Victory as Strike Ends at Boston University," *The Washington Post,* April 14, 1979.
Juster, F. T. (ed.). *Education, Income, and Human Behavior.* New York: McGraw-Hill, 1975.

Kant, Immanuel. *The Critique of Pure Reason.* Translated by Norman Kemp Smith. New York: St. Martin's Press, 1956.
Katz, Joseph. "Collaboration of Academic Faculty and Student Affairs Professionals towards Student Development." State University of New York at Stony Brook. Mimeographed, 1978.
Kaysen, Carl. "Government and Higher Education: The Significant Policy Issues in their Context." Draft prepared for the Sloan Commission on Government and Higher Education, August, 1978. Revised, September 20, 1978.
Kehoe, David S., et al. *Yale Course Critique.* New Haven: *Yale Daily News,* 1978.
Kett, Joseph F. *Rites of Passage: Adolescence in America 1790 to the Present.* New York: Basic Books, 1977.
Kicklefs, Roger. "Publish or Perish: Professors Discover Perishing Is Simpler," *The Wall Street Journal,* May 25, 1979.
Kilpatrick, James. "Where to Begin an Austerity Program," *The Washington Post,* January 4, 1979.
Kirk, Russell. *Decadence and Renewal in Higher Learning.* South Bend: Gateway, 1958.
Kitagawa, E. M., and Hauser, P. M. *Differential Mortality in the United States: A Study in Socioeconomic Epidemiology.* Cambridge: Harvard University Press, 1973.
Knight, Michael. "Boston University Threatened by Strike as Teachers' Talks Deteriorate," *The New York Times,* January 30, 1979.
Koenig, Lilli. *Studies in Animal Behavior.* New York: Thomas Y. Crowell, 1958.
Kohlberg, Lawrence. "Stage and Sequence: The Cognitive Developmental Approach to Socialization." In D. A. Goslin, editor, *Handbook of Socialization Theory and Research.* New York: Rand McNally, 1969.

Ladd, Carl Everett, Jr., and Lipset, Seymour Martin. "The Faculty Mood: Pessimism is Predominant," *The Chronicle of Higher Education,* October 3, 1977.
Lamont, Lansing. *Campus Shock.* New York: Dutton, 1979.
Lannholm, G. V. "Educational Growth During the Second Two Years of

College," *Educational and Psychological Measurement*, Winter, 1952, pp. 645–653.

Lannholm, G. V., and Pitcher, B. "Mean Score Changes on the Graduate Record Examinations Area Tests for College Students Tested Three Times in a Four-Year Period." Mimeograph. Princeton: Educational Testing Service, 1959.

Lasch, Christopher. *The Culture of Narcissism: American Life in An Age of Diminishing Expectations*. New York: Norton, 1978.

Laughlin, Charles D., Jr., and Brady, Ivan A. *Extinction and Survival in Human Populations*. New York: Columbia University Press, 1978.

Leonard, George B. *Education and Ecstasy*. New York: Delta Books, 1968.

Levine, Arthur. *Handbook on Undergraduate Curriculum*. San Francisco: Jossey-Bass, 1978.

Locke, John. *An Essay Concerning Human Understanding*. Edited by A. S. Pringle-Pattison. Oxford: Clarendon Press, 1950.

Lopez, Barry Holstun. *Of Wolves and Men*. New York: Charles Scribners' Sons, 1978.

Loughlin, Ellen K. "The Agency Nobody Loves," *The Chronicle of Higher Education*. September 19, 1977.

————. "Arts, Humanities Endowments Reject Criticism of House Panel," *The Chronicle of Higher Education*, May 14, 1979.

Lovejoy, Arthur O. *The Revolt against Dualism*. Lasalle: Open Court, 1960.

Lovejoy, Clarence E. *Lovejoy's College Guide*. 13th ed. New York: Simon and Schuster, 1976.

Lucretius. *On the Nature of Things*. Translated by Cyril Bailey. Oxford: Oxford University Press, 1950.

Lurie, Theodore. "Terror on Italy's Campuses," *The Chronicle of Higher Education*, March 27, 1978.

Lutz, Sandra W. *Do They Do What They Say They Do?* ACT Research Report Number 24. Iowa City: The American College Testing Program, 1968.

Lynn, Kenneth. "Son of Gen Ed," *Commentary Magazine*, September, 1978.

Maeroff, Gene I. "Honors Programs Spreading," *The New York Times*, January 30, 1979.

Magarrell, Jack. "Beset with Inflation, Many Colleges Plan Hefty Increases in Tuition," *The Chronicle of Higher Education*, March 26, 1979.

————. "The Enrollment Roller Coaster: Colleges Fear the Big Dip," *The Chronicle of Higher Education*, September 5, 1978.

————. "Financial Woes Worsen at Some Private Colleges," *The Chronicle of Higher Education*, July 31, 1978.

————. "State Colleges Confronting Politics of Frugality," *The Chronicle of Higher Education*, February 20, 1979.

McGovern, George. "The Miseducation of Millions: The Alarming Rise of Functional Illiteracy in America," *The Congressional Record*, September 8, 1978.

McKeon, Richard, ed. *The Basic Works of Aristotle*. New York: Random House, 1941.

McMahon, W. W., and Wagner, A. P. *A Study of the College Investment Decision*. ACT Research Report Number 59. Iowa City: The American College Testing Program, July, 1973.

Meadows, Donella H. and Dennis L., Randers, Jørgen, and Behrens, William W., III. *The Limits to Growth*. New York: Signet Books, 1972.

Merton, Andy. "Hanging on (by a Jockstrap) to Tradition at Dartmouth," *Esquire*, June 19, 1979.

Miller, Gordon P. *After High School*. New York: Cornerstone Library, 1978.

Minter, W. John, and Bowen, Howard R. *Private Education: Third Annual Report on Finances and Educational Trends in the Private Sector of American Higher Education*. Washington, D.C.: Association of American Colleges, 1977.

Modern Language Association of America. "Fall, 1977 Survey of Foreign Language Registrations in United States Institutions of Higher Education." Mimeographed.

———. "Report of the Task Force on Institutional Language Policy." Mimeographed 1977–1978.

———. "Summary Tables, Table A: Enrollments in Higher Education Compared with Registrations in Modern Foreign Languages, 1960–70." Mimeographed.

———. "Summary Tables: Table B. Fall, 1970 Survey of Foreign Language Registrations in United States Institutions of Higher Education." Mimeographed.

Montaigne, Michel E. de. *The Complete Works*. Translated by Donald M. Frame. Stanford: Stanford University Press, 1958.

Moore, Donald R. *Money for College! How to Get It*. Woodbury, N.Y.: Barron's Educational Series. 1979.

Morgan, J. N., Sirageldin, I. A., and Baerwaldt, N. *Productive Americans: A Study of How Individuals Contribute to Economic Progress*. Ann Arbor: Institute for Social Research, University of Michigan, 1966.

Morris, Jan. *The Oxford Book of Oxford*. Oxford: Oxford University Press, 1978.

Moses, Henry C. *Handbook for Freshman Advisers*. Cambridge, Mass.: Harvard University, 1978.

Mowat, Farley. *Never Cry Wolf*. Boston: Atlantic Monthly Press, 1963.

Moynihan, Daniel Patrick. "Government and the Ruin of Private Education," *Harpers*, April, 1978.

Mullis, V. S., Oldefendt, Susan J., and Phillips, Donald L. *What Students Know and Can Do. Profiles of Three Age Groups*. Denver: The National Assessment for Educational Progress, 1977.

Munday, Leo. *Comparative Predictive Validities of the American College Tests and Two Other Scholastic Aptitude Tests*. ACT Research Report. Iowa City: American College Testing Program, 1965.

Nash, Roderick. *Wilderness and the American Mind*. Revised edition. New Haven: Yale University Press, 1973.

National Merit Scholarship Corporation. *Annual Report, 1977–78*. Evanston: National Merit Scholarship Corporation, 1978.

National Assessment of Educational Progress. *Bicentennial Citizenship Survey*. Denver: Education Commission of the States, 1976.

———. *Career Development*. Denver: Education Commission of the States, 1978.

———. *Citizenship/Social Studies: Report of the Second Citizenship/Social Studies Assessment*. Denver: Education Commission of the States, 1976.

————. *First National Assessment of Careers and Occupational Development: An Overview.* Denver: Education Commission of the States, 1976.

————. *Reading: Report of the Second Functional Literacy Assessment.* Denver, Education Commission of the States, 1975.

————. *Science: Third Science Assessment.* Denver: Education Commission of the States, 1977.

————. *Update on Education, A Digest of the National Assessment of Educational Progress.* Denver: Education Commission of the States, 1975.

New York University, Ad Hoc Subcommittee. "An Integrated Core Curriculum for New York University." December 5, 1978. Mimeographed.

New York University, Ad Hoc Subcommittee on Ethical Studies and Moral Concerns. "Curricular Goals in the Area of Ethical Studies and Moral Concerns." December 5, 1978. Mimeographed.

Oakeshott, Michael. *Rationalism in Politics and Other Essays.* London: Methuen, 1962.

Olsen, Larry Dean. *Outdoor Survival Skills.* 4th ed. New York: Pocket Books, 1976.

Omang, Joanne. "Shielding Sociologists' Targets," *The Washington Post,* February 20, 1979.

Omang, Joanne, and Bonner, Alice. "Colleges Struggle with the Baby Bust, Fast-Buck Recruiting Snares Student Applications from Unwary Aliens," *The Washington Post,* April 23, 1979.

Orwell, George. *1984.* New York: Harcourt Brace Jovanovich, 1949.

Pap, Arthur. *An Introduction to the Philosophy of Science.* Glencoe: The Free Press, 1962.

Patterson, Colin. *Evolution.* Ithaca: Cornell University Press, 1978.

Perry, William, Jr. *Forms of Intellectual and Ethical Development in the College Years: A Scheme.* New York: Holt, Rinehart and Winston, 1970.

Phillips, Donald L., and Ward, Barbara. "What Do Students Know about Jobs?" *Industrial Education,* December, 1977.

Piaget, Jean. *The Moral Judgment of the Child.* New York: The Free Press, 1969.

Plato. *The Collected Dialogues.* Edited by Edith Hamilton and Huntington Cairns. New York: Pantheon Books, 1963.

Powers, J. *An Inquiry into the Effects of a College Education on the Attitudes, Competencies, and Behavior of Individuals.* Claremont, California: Claremont Graduate School, 1976.

Princeton University, Committee on Undergraduate Residential Life. "Second Interim Report." Mimeographed.

————. "Special Report on Undergraduate Residential Life," *Princeton Weekly Bulletin,* May 28, 1979.

Project on Institutional Renewal through the Improvement of Teaching, Project on General Education Models, Jerry Goff, Project Director. *Idea Papers:* 1 (January 2, 1978); 2 (January 11, 1979), and 4 (December 27, 1978). Mimeographed.

Quinn, R. P., and Baldi de Mandilovitch, M. S. *Education and Job Satisfaction: A Questionable Payoff.* Ann Arbor: Survey Research Center, University of Michigan, 1975.

Quinn, R. P., and Staines, Graham L. *The 1977 Quality of Employment Survey*. Ann Arbor: Institute for Social Research, University of Michigan, 1979.

Ramirez, Anthony. "Elite Colleges Consider Many Factors in Search for a Mix of Students," *The Wall Street Journal*, April 6, 1979.

Raskin, Thomas R., editor. *Course Evaluation Guide*. Cambridge, Mass.: Committee on Undergraduate Education, Harvard University, 1978.

Richards, James M., Jr. *Can Computers Write College Admissions Tests?* ACT Research Report Number 15, Iowa City: American College Testing Program, October, 1966.

Richards, James M., Jr., Holland, John L., and Lutz, Sandra W. *The Assessment of Student Accomplishment in College*. ACT Research Report Number 11. Iowa City: The American College Testing Program, March, 1966.

————. *The Prediction of Student Accomplishment in College*. ACT Research Report. Iowa City, American College Testing Program, 1966.

Riesman, David, Gusfield, Joseph, and Gamson, Zelda. *Academic Values and Mass Education*. New York: McGraw-Hill, 1975.

Roark, Anne C. "40 Science and Educational Groups Lobby for More Basic Research," *The Chronicle of Higher Education*, April 23, 1979.

The Rockefeller Foundation. *Working Papers, Toward the Restoration of the Liberal Arts Curriculum*. New York: The Rockefeller Foundation, June, 1979.

Rosenblatt, Roger. "A Campus Rumpus over Writing," *The Washington Post*, October 3, 1977.

————. "Scholars and/or Teachers," *The Washington Post*, December 12, 1978.

Rudolph, Frederick. *Curriculum: A History of the American Undergraduate Course of Study, since 1636*. Prepared for the Carnegie Council on Policy Studies in Higher Education. San Francisco: Jossey-Bass, 1977.

Ryle, Gilbert. *The Concept of Mind*. London: Hutchinson, 1949.

Sanford, N. (ed.). *The American College*. New York: Wiley, 1962.

Sawhill, John C. "The Unlettered University," *Harpers*, February, 1979.

Schumacher, E. F. *Small is Beautiful: Economics as if People Mattered*. New York: Harper and Row, 1975.

Scully, Malcolm G. "The Condition of Scholarly Communication: Serious but Not Fatal, National Study Finds," *The Chronicle of Higher Education*, May 7, 1979.

————. "Conservative Scholars Fear 60s Reforms Have Perverted Universities' Mission," *The Chronicle of Higher Education*, September 19, 1977.

————. "General Education: A 'Disaster Area.'" *The Chronicle of Higher Education*, December 19, 1977, p. 7.

————. "The Plight of Humanities to Receive National Attention," *The Chronicle of Higher Education*, July 10, 1978.

————. "Youth Unemployment Stirs International Concern," *The Chronicle of Higher Education*, May 22, 1978.

Sennett, Richard. *The Fall of Public Man*. New York: Alfred A. Knopf, 1977.

Seton, Ernest Thompson. *Lives of the Hunted*. New York: Charles Scribners' Sons, 1901.

Sheehy, Gail. *Passages: Predictable Crises of Adult Life.* New York: Dutton, 1976.

Silber, John R. "The Tuition Dilemma: A New Way to Pay the Bills," *The Atlantic Monthly,* July, 1978.

Simmons, Adele. "Harvard Flunks a Test," *Harpers,* March, 1979.

Slater, Philip. *The Pursuit of Loneliness: American Culture at the Breaking Point.* Boston: Beacon Press, 1976.

Smith, Virginia B., and Bernstein, Alison R. *The Impersonal Campus.* San Francisco: Jossey-Bass, 1979.

Snyder, Benson R. *The Hidden Curriculum.* Cambridge: MIT Press, 1973.

Solzhenitsyn, Alexander. "The Exhausted West," *Harvard Magazine,* July/August, 1978.

Spaeth, J. L., and Greeley, A. M. *Recent Alumni and Higher Education.* New York: McGraw-Hill, 1970.

Stace, Walter T. *A Critical History of Greek Philosophy.* New York: St. Martin's Press, 1960.

Staple, Alan, et al. "Financial Need Analysis, Some Policy Questions." Harvard University Office of Analytic Studies, 1979. Mimeographed.

Sterne, Michael. "Dream of Humanities Center About to Come True," *The New York Times,* July 2, 1978.

Stevenson, Charles L. *Ethics and Language.* New Haven: Yale University Press, 1944.

Styles, Showell. *The Top of the World, An Illustrated History of Mountain Climbing.* New York: Macmillan, 1967.

Taft, Horace D. "New Distributional Requirements for Yale College," *Yale Alumni Magazine,* November, 1978.

Thomas, Lewis. *The Lives of a Cell.* New York: Bantam Books, 1974.

――――. *The Medusa and the Snail.* New York: The Viking Press, 1979.

Trent, J. W., and Medsker, L. *Beyond High School: A Psychosociological Study of 10,000 High School Graduates.* San Francisco: Jossey-Bass, 1968.

Trow, Martin. (ed.). *Teachers and Students.* New York: McGraw-Hill, 1975.

United States General Accounting Office. *Comptroller General's Report to Congress: Problems and Outlook of Small Private Liberal Arts Colleges,* HRD–78–91. Washington, D.C.: U.S. Government Printing Office, 1978.

United States Congressional Budget Office. "College Costs." Correspondence Control No. 1436. Mimeographed, 1977.

United States Department of Health, Education and Welfare, Fund for the Improvement of Post-Secondary Education. "Current Fund Projects Aimed at Liberal Education Outcomes." Mimeographed, 1978.

United States Department of Health, Education and Welfare, National Center for Education Statistics. *Bulletin: Fall Enrollment in Colleges and Universities, 1978.* Washington, D.C.: United States Department of HEW/Education Division, December, 1978.

――――. *The Condition of Education: Statistical Report.* Edited by Mary A. Golladay and Jay Noel. Washington, D.C.: U.S. Government Printing Office, 1978.

――――. *Digest of Education Statistics, 1977–78.* Prepared by W. Vance Grant

318 / BIBLIOGRAPHY

and C. George Lind. Washington, D.C.: U.S. Government Printing Office, 1978.
———. *Education Directory, Colleges and Universities, 1977–78.* Washington, D.C.: U.S. Government Printing Office, 1978.
———. *Fall Enrollment in Higher Education, 1976.* Washington, D.C.: U.S. Government Printing Office, 1978.
———. *Financial Statistics of Institutions of Higher Education, Fiscal Year, 1976, State Data.* Edited by Paul F. Martins and Norman J. Brandt. Washington, D.C.: U.S. Government Printing Office, 1978.
———. *Inventory of Physical Facilities in Institutions of Higher Education, Fall, 1974.* Washington, D.C.: U.S. Government Printing Office, 1977.
———. *Migration of College Students, Preliminary Analysis of Trends in College Student Migration.* Washington, D.C.: U.S. Government Printing Office, 1976.
———. *Higher Education Prices and Price Indexes, 1978 Supplement.* Washington, D.C.: U.S. Government Printing Office, 1978.
United States Department of Health, Education and Welfare, Office of the Secretary. "Protection of Human Subjects." Washington, D.C.: *Federal Register,* Volume 43, number 231. November 30, 1978.
United States Department of Labor, Bureau of Labor Statistics. "New Labor Force Projections to 1990." *Special Labor Force Report 197.* Reprinted from *Monthly Labor Review,* December, 1976.
———. *Occupational Outlook Handbook, 1978–9 Edition.* Washington, D.C.: U.S. Government Printing Office, 1978.
———. *Occupational Projections and Training Data,* Bulletin 2020, 1979.
———. Survey of Consumer Expenditures, 1960–61. Supplement 2 to BLS Report No. 237–93. Washington, D.C.: U.S. Government Printing Office, 1966.
———. *United States Government, National Endowment for the Humanities. 13th Report, 1978.* Washington, D.C.: National Endowment for the Humanities, 1979.
———. *Projections of Education Statistics to 1986–7.* Edited by Martin M. Frankel. Washington, D.C.: U.S. Government Printing Office, 1978.
Urmson, J. O. *Philosophical Analysis: Its Development between the Wars.* Oxford: Oxford University Press, 1956.
Useem, Elizabeth L. and Michael. *The Education Establishment.* Englewood Cliffs, N.J.: Prentice-Hall, 1974.

Watson, Cathy. "Matching Personal and Job Characteristics," *Occupational Outlook Quarterly,* Fall 1978.
Wattenberg, Ben J. *U.S. Fact Book/The American Almanac.* New York: Grosset and Dunlap, 1978.
Weeks, Margaret L. "Few Jobs for Humanities Ph.D.s: Should Market Be Left Alone?" *The Chronicle of Higher Education,* April 25, 1977.
Weinstein, Marc. "The Free Employment Service for College Students," *Occupational Outlook Quarterly,* Summer, 1979.
Wells, H. G. *The Outline of History.* Garden City, N.Y.: Garden City Publishing Co., 1940.
Wheeler, John A. "The Outsider," *Newsweek,* March 12, 1979.
Whitla, Dean K. *Value Added: Measuring the Outcomes of Undergraduate*

Education. Cambridge, Mass.: Harvard University Office of Institutional Research and Evaluation, 1975.

Whitla, Dean K., and Pinck, Dan C. *Perspectives on the Houses at Harvard and Radcliffe.* Cambridge, Mass.: Harvard University Press, 1974.

Williams, Stephen, *et al. The Report of the Task Force on College Life.* Cambridge, Mass.: Harvard University, 1976.

Wilson, Edward O. *Sociobiology, the New Synthesis.* Cambridge, Mass.: Harvard University Press, 1975.

Wing, Cliff W., and Wallach, Michael A. *College Admissions and the Psychology of Talent.* New York: Holt, Rinehart and Winston, 1971.

Wolfe, Tom. *The Kandy-Kolored Tangerine-Flake Streamlined Baby.* New York: Farrar, Straus and Giroux, 1965.

Wolff, Robert Paul, Moore, Barrington, Jr., and Marcuse, Herbert. *A Critique of Pure Tolerance.* Boston: Beacon Press, 1969.

Yale College. "Grading in Yale College, A Report by the Course of Study Committee." December 4, 1978. Mimeographed.

————. "Joint Proposal of the Course of Study Committee and the Committee on Teaching and Learning for the Augmentation of the Distributional Requirements." Mimeographed, 1978.

————. "Report on the Effectiveness of the Guideline System." Mimeographed, 1976.

————. *The Size of Yale College: Report of the Committee on the Size of Yale College.* January, 1979.

Yale Daily News. *Course Critique.* New Haven: Yale Daily News, 1978.

Yankelovich, D. *The New Morality: A Profile of American Youth in the 70's.* New York: McGraw-Hill, 1974.

Zuker, F. Fred, and Hegener, Karen Collier. *Peterson's Guide to College Admissions.* New York: Monarch Press, 1976.

INDEX